MW01013794

north

NORTH

THE NEW NORDIC CUISINE OF ICELAND

Gunnar Karl Gíslason and Jody Eddy

FOREWORD BY RENÉ REDZEPI

Photography by Evan Sung

TEN SPEED PRESS
Berkeley

CONTENTS

FOREWORD

René Redzepi

The first time I went to Iceland was in 2002. It was late autumn. We swam in the hot springs, visited the beautiful waterfalls, and saw wild thyme growing all over the volcanic plains—and that was just on the ride from the airport into Reykjavík. I thought I had landed in a fairytale. I was blown away, and I remember that my first desire was to eat, to experience all the things I'd seen so far, distilled on a plate. I thought to myself, *This is going to be good; maybe the meal of a lifetime.* As I glanced up at the crystal clear blue sky, I dreamed about all the impossibly good fish and shellfish that would be part of the dinner.

I had virtually no experience with Iceland before that trip. I had heard of Björk and the crazy nightlife, of course, and if I remember right, we read the *Sagas of Icelanders* in school. (But that was in school, so there's a one hundred percent chance I didn't do much listening.) Prior to that first trip, I made the deliberate choice *not* to investigate the country's culinary traditions. So when I finally reached the outskirts of the capital, ready for some food, I was filled with a childlike sense of wonder and excitement.

On the ride from the airport, I wasn't shy about telling my host how hungry I was. "I need to eat," I reminded him again. "Don't you worry," he replied swiftly, in that distinct Icelandic-English accent that can at times seem a bit robotic and stern. "I have the right place for you."

We drove for a couple more minutes until we pulled over at Reykjavík's premier sushi restaurant. I gave him a skeptical look. "You're feeding me sushi? I've come here for inspiration," I said. "Yes, but this is Icelandic fish they serve here," he told me. My host apparently thought that even though it was sushi, the fact that the restaurant used local fish made it Icelandic. That was the first of several memorable moments for me. Just a few years later, during the early days of Noma, I found myself dissatisfied with making well-known, practically universal recipes with local ingredients. It didn't feel right. I remembered that disconnected feeling I experienced at the "Icelandic" sushi parlor—simple substitution doesn't make something of a place.

During that first visit, I spent a good week eating around town. There was a tapas place, an Argentinean steakhouse, and, I must admit, a few traditional restaurants. But those seemed more like caricatures than genuine, proud interpretations of tradition. I left Iceland blown away by the people and their spirit, and I was so taken by the wonderfully untouched natural landscape. I remember being on the plane, thinking that "untouched" was the word that defined the experience. It's a word, and an idea, that would become a major influence on our cooking in Copenhagen: *untouched.*

When I left Iceland, I didn't think I'd be returning for the food.

Years passed. I traveled back and forth a few times, to spend time with the Icelandic people and to seek out that "untouched" element. The food was always secondary, or even tertiary. Then one day I received a phone call. "René, something is happening in Iceland," said my friend from the region. "It's our friend Gunni," he murmured after a pause, using the nickname we've always had for Gunnar. "He wants to open a restaurant that works with the traditions and the history of our place."

I'll be honest: I was skeptical. "Sounds good," was my rather curt reply. We started talking about something else.

Not too long after that, I got a package in the post from Gunni. The letter read something like, "Hey chef, here are some presents for you." I opened up the box, and it was filled with food—food that I had seen before, but always in a mass-produced, industrial state. Suddenly I was tasting raw skyr and artisan bread that's baked in hot earth. I tasted dried seaweed with an umami richness that's matched only by certain Japanese varieties. As a chef, it was as if someone had gone to the bottom of the ocean, found a box full of treasures, and handed it over to me for free.

I was in the clouds. I wanted everything. To this day, we use that seaweed throughout our menu—to add a little depth to a vegetable stock or to give that little extra bit of flavor to almost anything.

That's why I think chefs like Gunni and his restaurant Dill are immensely important: they rediscover lost traditions, breathe life into old techniques, and support the good people out there producing food with quality and deliciousness as their only guiding principles.

I haven't been back to Iceland for years. I've actually never eaten at Dill, although I've met Gunni many times in Copenhagen. But after more than a decade, I feel differently about how my next trip is going to shape up.

I want to go back to Iceland for the food.

IN GRATITUDE

Many people helped to produce this book. Without their generosity, assistance, and encouragement, it would have never materialized. First and foremost, we wish to thank our families, including Freyja Ros Oskarsdóttir and our children, Hildur Gunnarsdóttir, Gísli Sigurgeirsson, Eric Schatzman, Mary Eddy, and Peter and Evelyn Bragelman.

We must thank the producers who met with us during the course of our research. Without them and their tireless efforts to preserve the culinary traditions of Iceland, we would not have been able to write the book. We will be forever grateful for their generosity and inspiration.

We also wish to thank Ölafur Agustsson, Mark Anderson, Carrie Bachman, Fredrik Berselius, Ali Bouzari, Cindy and Mark Bragelman, Browns Valley Market (Napa, California), Kristin Casemore, Amy Collins, Paul Duffy, Stephen Dufree, Clancy Drake, Sally Ekus, Inga Elin, Janine Ersfeld, Colleen Foster, Benjamin Freemole, Joe Frillman, Kjartan Gíslason, Lynn Grewing, Liz Grossman, Kristbjörg Gudmundsdóttir, Claire Handleman, Kate Heddings, Peter Jacobsen, Arnar Jakob, Mary and Lee Jones, Erin Jurek, Kim Kaechele, Gudbjörg Káradóttir, David Katz, Agust Kristjansson, Alex Lovick, Richard Martin, Gudfinna Mjoll Magnusdottir, Anne McBride, Bridget McGinty, Ölafur Örn Ölafsson, Chris Pandel, Sandeep Patwal, Sheila Pearson, Jim Poris, Chandra Ram, Cliff Redeker, Nanna Rognvaldardóttir, Peter Rosene, Ken Schumann, Sharon Silva, Toni Tajima, Aaron Wehner, Katie Wilson, and Dina Zobkova.

Finally, we must thank Jenny Wapner, our amazing editor at Ten Speed Press, for her belief in this book and encouragement throughout the writing process; and Emily Timberlake, who guided the book through production.

INTRODUCTION

In 2009, Iceland was in the middle of what would prove to be, relative to its size, the largest universal banking collapse experienced by any country in economic history. The ongoing financial implosion sent the nation's restaurants into a tailspin, as the cost of food skyrocketed and people could no longer afford the luxury of eating out. It is hard to imagine a more dismal time to open a restaurant, but Gunnar Karl Gíslason had no alternative.

Just prior to the crisis, Gunnar, who had introduced contemporary Nordic cuisine to his country, had left his position as executive chef of Vox, Iceland's most esteemed restaurant, determined to realize his lifelong dream of opening his own place. Despite the financial maelstrom engulfing his nation, he decided to move forward on this idea. He chose the name Dill for the restaurant, to honor one of the nation's most abundant herbs and to highlight the foraging principle integral to his cooking philosophy.

As the economy blazed a downward trajectory fierce enough to disrupt financial markets around the world, every one of Gunnar's investors pulled out of the plan to open Dill in Reykjavík's landmark Nordic House, designed by the famed Finnish architect Alvar Aalto. The building, the city's primary meeting place for cultural exchanges among the Nordic countries, seemed an ideal location for a restaurant celebrating the foods and cooking techniques of the region.

When the funding disappeared, Gunnar was forced to forge ahead with his plan with nothing but a resolute commitment to realize his dream and credit cards that "burned red" by the time he was finished. Since those dark days, Dill has become Iceland's most celebrated restaurant. But there is more to the story of its success than indefatigable work and enormous credit card debt. There is a promise made. And a promise kept.

The purveyors promised to supply the Dill kitchen with either free or heavily discounted products until Gunnar found his footing and could afford to pay them back. In most parts of the world, this arrangement would be unprecedented. In Iceland, it is a way of life. Icelanders know a thing or two about transcending struggle. This innate knowledge, born of an ancient and perpetual negotiation with the environment for survival, inspires an invincible kinship among the citizenry. That affinity expresses itself in a fidelity resolute enough not only to withstand the near collapse of an economy but also to open a restaurant with little more than a dream and a promise.

After months of working twenty hours a day, seven days a week, Gunnar's vision was realized, and his restaurant honoring Iceland's culinary heritage by showcasing its pristine products on a contemporary canvas quickly earned unparalleled success. It garnered acclaim around the world, becoming the must-visit restaurant for Icelandic tourists, a destination restaurant for culinary adventure seekers, and, most important for Icelanders, an establishment that finally put their nation on the international gastronomic map.

As successful as Dill became, Gunnar never forgot the debt he owed to his purveyors. He expressed his gratitude first through the repayment of his monetary obligations and then through a renewed commitment to protect the venerable culinary traditions of Iceland by showcasing local products on his restaurant menu in fresh, innovative ways. His approach is never to mask the integrity of the ingredients but rather to allow them to tell their own story. In doing so, they link diners to the past while simultaneously propelling them into the future—the essence of contemporary Nordic cooking.

This cooking model has been embraced not only in kitchens in Iceland and its neighboring countries but also by chefs around the world who want to fortify their cooking with something more elusive than flavor. They are striving to stake a claim to important roles in society as architects, ambassadors, and educators of a revolutionized food system, one that values sustainability over industrialization, products with an historical pedigree over factory-produced foods without lineage. For Gunnar, a chef who has always been ardently committed to his producers, the *terroir* of his nation, and the traditions of the past, this role is nothing new. It is as instinctive to him as plucking sea urchins from a cold, frothy sea; harvesting seaweed the color of iron from a black stone beach in the shadow of a glacier; or gathering sorrel and angelica from craggy volcanic crevasses to supplement a restaurant menu that celebrates the local resources of a place that has been dubbed the world's only sustainable nation.

Striking a covenant with the environment that you will never take more than you need and that you will fight to protect it as long as it provides you with the seafood, game, livestock, and produce necessary to survive is a way of life in Iceland. It was practiced long before the words *foraging*, *terroir*, and *sustainability* became commonplace. This simple cooking philosophy was employed by Gunnar years before new Nordic cuisine and The Manifesto for the New Nordic Kitchen (see page 259) came to be among the culinary world's hottest buzzwords.

This book celebrates the cuisine and nation of a forward-thinking chef and the producers who supply his restaurant. The alchemy of the relationship between chef and producers, and between that pairing and the environment, is revealed in Gunnar's contemporary recipes, which are approachable enough for the home cook, yet sufficiently challenging to entice the professional chef. Each recipe tells a story, contextualizing and integrating the tenets of the contemporary Nordic kitchen into the ongoing larger conversation in the culinary community, and by extension the world.

The principles of this modern Nordic culinary philosophy can be put to work anywhere on the planet. That fact prompts some questions: If any professional or home cook can celebrate regionality in his or her cooking repertoire, why is there such an intense focus on the Nordic countries leading the way? Why have the nations that hover so close to the Arctic Circle garnered such prodigious praise in recent years? Why are expectations running so high for the Nordic pioneers of the culinary world? It is because they are at the forefront of a revolution in our food system constructed on an ideology that embraces a respect for place as the foundation of their cooking style. It is a revolution that is not defined by innovation as much as it is by centuries-old principles.

This cookbook adds a unique voice to this conversation by examining the culinary narrative of Iceland, a fascinating nation with a compelling gastronomic heritage that until now has gone virtually unexplored. It opens the doors to an extraordinary country whose identity is shaped in equal measure by a rich, harrowing past and a bright future. Iceland's citizens have endured a perpetual struggle to survive ever since their Viking ancestors settled the country in the ninth century, yet have now arrived at a moment when they are always ranked near or at the top of a United Nations–compiled Gini index measuring such factors as life expectancy, educational attainment, literacy, and general standard of living. Iceland is one of the most egalitarian countries on the planet, and modern Icelanders are content despite the sometimes difficult circumstances they endure. This cookbook illuminates the continuity of past, present, and future, through Gunnar's contemporary recipes and through conversations with some of Iceland's traditional food purveyors. Together, they are preserving their nation's culture through the enduring language of food.

When I first visited Iceland in 2009—before most cooks in the United States had heard of the new Nordic cuisine—I returned extolling its virtues to my friends in the culinary industry. I declared that this new philosophy, with its focus on sustainable cooking practices, foraging, and *terroir*, would soon be embraced by chefs around the world. My enthusiasm was met with skepticism.

I returned to Iceland several times over the next few years to examine further what I knew was an extraordinary region on the verge of claiming the spotlight in the culinary world. I was fortunate to meet Gunnar Karl Gíslason during my first visit, and he became my culinary mentor on subsequent visits to the country. Walking with Gunnar through the country's breathtaking terrain proved to be part history lesson and part culinary tourism, and always a feast. To join him as he forages—not because it is trendy, but because it is inextricably woven into who he is as a chef and as an Icelander—is to become privy to wisdom acquired throughout a lifetime of living close to the land.

Several years ago, only one airline flew nonstop from the United States to Iceland. Then, in 2011 alone, four new airlines established routes between cities in the United States and Reykjavík. As travelers discover that Iceland is not only an incredible place to visit for the adventure seeker but also a top-notch culinary destination (not to mention that it is only a five-hour plane ride from New York City), it will grow into a travel and culinary hot spot.

Today, no one chastises me for my obsession with Iceland and its exceptional cuisine. Now I frequently hear from people asking for help planning a trip there. I always send them to Dill, where they are treated to the extraordinary cuisine and uncompromising hospitality of Gunnar and his staff. The reports on their return are unequivocally positive.

They are usually followed by a request for a recipe or two from Gunnar and an outline of additional places to visit on their return trip, for it seems once you've visited Iceland, you can never get enough.

∞

From his earliest days working with farmers in the distant corners of Iceland until now, in his role as the country's best-known contemporary chef, Gunnar has listened closely to the landscape of his country and the stories of its producers. These voices have found their way into his refined cuisine, celebrated in a restaurant that is more than a dining establishment. Dill is a reflection of Gunnar's philosophy of an allegiance to the artisans, food purveyors, and citizens of Iceland.

The restaurant's service ware is designed by local artisans, its furniture is by Alvar Aalto, and the artwork on the walls is a regularly rotating display of local talent. The refined space of muted colors, clean lines, and an absence of clutter reflects the Nordic aesthetic of less is more. Spanning one entire wall is a floor-to-ceiling window overlooking a bird sanctuary, abundant with the herb bushes and raised gardens from which Gunnar forages daily. A greenhouse glistens for the part of the year in which the sun never sets and sparkles in starlight during the months of long, cold nights. Iceland is situated on the Gulf Stream, making its climate more temperate than most would imagine. Even on an afternoon in the middle of winter, Dill's guests wander along the edge of the lake outside the restaurant, past the vast garden beds awaiting spring planting.

As idyllic as Gunnar's visits to his producers are, an underlying urgency accompanies these encounters—an urgency born of the need to preserve the traditional foodways of the country. The ingredients Gunnar serves at Dill reflect his devotion to ancient Icelandic traditions disappearing at a speed so alarming that he fears many of them will be gone within a generation. Because this urgency grows more acute with each passing day, this cookbook is both a recipe collection and a documentation of a way of life that is fast losing ground to the contemporary world.

If the next generation continues to eschew these traditional food craft jobs in favor of urban living, there may be nothing left to document in a decade or two. To combat that trend, this book is intended not only to remind Icelanders of their fascinating past but also to provide them with a road map for how to integrate tradition into their modern lives. And it is a powerful source of inspiration for others seeking to preserve the legacies established by generations of cooks, producers, and farmers in their corner of the world.

A NOTE ON THE RECIPES

More than anything else, Gunnar's cooking is about a sense of place. It follows that depending on where you live in the world, the ingredients available to you and the conditions in which you are cooking will vary (sometimes widely) from those of Iceland. This is something to embrace, since contemporary Nordic cooking is about celebrating the region in which you live and sourcing from it all that it has to offer. Gunnar is always saying to "cook it until it tastes good and use what you have," a philosophy to take with you into the kitchen and use as you re-create Gunnar's recipes in your surroundings.

Substitutions based on your resources will make each recipe your own. Examples of ingredients that might be difficult to find outside of Iceland and suggested replacements are noted throughout the book. But before you begin cooking, here are four recommended substitutions for common ingredients: bay leaf for birch; wood chips or dried tree leaves for hay for smoking; salting and rehydrating cod or another firm white fish yourself in place of bacalao; and catfish or another white fish in place of wolf fish. We can also suggest some herb substitutions for items that might be hard to source, such as tender celery leaves for lovage, tarragon for angelica, regular thyme for arctic thyme, and spinach or arugula sprinkled with a little lemon juice for sorrel.

Beer vinegar is called for in a number of recipes, and a recipe for it appears on page 30. Gunnar almost never uses pepper to season his dishes, as he feels it overwhelms most other ingredients. He replaces the typical seasoning combination of salt and pepper with salt and beer vinegar. But if you have neither the time nor the inclination to make beer vinegar, malt vinegar is a good substitute, or you can use whatever vinegar appeals to you. Vinegar brightens a recipe, and this vibrancy is a benchmark of Gunnar's cooking.

A few ingredients are especially difficult—or even impossible—to source outside of Iceland or other Nordic countries, and these have been replaced in the recipes and discussed in accompanying notes. Calf's liver in place of reindeer liver is one prominent example, since no matter how resourceful your local butcher is, tracking down reindeer liver is likely beyond his or her talents. Other examples include substituting a readily available herbal tea for Witch's Brew tea, which is made from a blend of Icelandic herbs, and using a local microbrew in place of an Icelandic-made one.

You can always source dairy products, but the cow's milk produced in Iceland typically has a high fat content, which sets it apart from what you find in many parts of the world. For example, the local cow's milk tastes sweeter and richer than nearly any milk on the planet, and depending on the fat content of the butter or milk you use, you may find you need to adjust the baking times for some recipes.

Environmental differences must also be considered when using these recipes. Iceland has extremely low humidity levels, which affect the timing of such techniques as proofing, fermenting, and aging. For example, depending on the everyday humidity level where you live, yeast activation may work faster or slower during fermentation. The best advice on how to deal with differences in environmental conditions is to keep an eye on what you're making, tasting it every so often if possible, and then give it the go-ahead once it is, in Gunnar's words, "to your liking."

The recipes include U.S. units of measurement along with standard metric units for ingredients, temperatures, and length equivalencies. In general, teaspoons and tablespoons are used for all ingredient measurements of $3^{1}/_{2}$ tablespoons or less, with the exception of some of the more finicky ingredients, such as soy lecithin and xanthan gum, which must be weighed precisely; in those cases, only grams are used. Readers are also advised to purchase a digital scale for measurement accuracy. It might seem like a pricey investment, but the confidence it instills when measuring easily transforms this gadget into a welcome kitchen companion.

Kitchen tools are another area where you may need to adapt. Whenever possible, alternative techniques are given for tools that may not be in the kitchen of most home cooks. These include a dehydrator, siphon, pressure cooker, and immersion circulator. One frequently used technique is smoking, which is used for everything from cheese to meat to oil to fish. Most of the time, there is no getting around smoking if you want to prepare authentic contemporary Icelandic recipes. But the good news is that smokers are extremely easy to construct using everyday kitchen equipment, such as a tiered steamer or hotel-pan setup. Instructions on how to assemble a simple smoker are on page 191.

Finally, the recipes were tested in America in the hope that they would be user-friendly to the home cook in most parts of the world. This means that most of the recipes have been tweaked from their original version to make them kitchen ready, no matter where you live. If despite those tweaks and the information provided in this section you still encounter a stumbling block, write to icelandcookbook@gmail.com. Your questions and your feedback are both welcome. Most important, remember that embracing the principles of contemporary Nordic cuisine means looking around at the resources available in your region and celebrating them in the same way that Gunnar celebrates the natural resources of Iceland.

THE BACALAO PRODUCER

Hauganes, Northern Iceland

∞

Salted Cod Tartar, Dill Mayonnaise, and Dulse Powder 14

Salted Cod Chips with Pickled Angelica Cream 19

Bacalao Potatoes with Fennel Ribbons and Sorrel Ash 20

Cod, Rutabaga Puree, and Dill Powder 22

Poached Cod Cheeks, Roasted Cod Soup, Potatoes,
and Charred Onions 26

Cod Cheeks, Onion Cream, and Pickled Root Vegetables 28

Beer Vinegar 30

Milk Ice Cream, Rutabaga and Apple Cider Granita,
and Sweet-and-Sour Dill Oil 32

Rhubarb and Herb Sugar 35

Elvar Reykjalín wears pristine white waders with black suspenders and a stoic expression as he strides past enormous white bags of salt. He is entering Ektafiskur, his factory, which stands at the edge of a picturesque harbor embraced by snow-capped mountains and is where he produces Iceland's most celebrated bacalao. Elvar spent a quarter century at sea plucking cod from its icy depths and has the souvenir ruddy cheeks to prove it. His factory gleams with order and a hint of bleach. A furious wind rattles its windows, as the July sun that never leaves this remote corner of northwestern Iceland beams brightly onto a massive table at the center of the room. Tubs of cod packed on ice surround the table; Elvar grabs a fish by the tail from one of them and slaps it down in front of him.

A furrowed line of purpose emerges between his eyes as he sharpens his filleting knife on a steel, moving with the precision of a man who has spent a lifetime wielding blades so sharp that they are capable of separating the flesh of a fish from its silver skin in one smooth, seamless motion. Elvar sets the knife down and reaches for his orange rubber gloves. As he pulls the first one on with a sharp tug, his stern expression is shattered by a grin so wide that it forces his sea-blue eyes into a mirthful squint. He pulls from the glove balls of crushed paper stuffed snugly into each finger. Two of his employees hovering nearby break into uncontrollable laughter. Elvar joins in as he says, "You see what I must put up with? My employees are always playing practical jokes on me. It's a wonder we ever get any work done at all."

Keeping a balance between purpose and joy is a specialty of Elvar's, a fifth-generation bacalao producer whose company sustains the village of Hauganes. The pressure of this responsibility, not to mention the backbreaking physical labor required to maintain one of the nation's last surviving factories producing bacalao in the traditional way, would defeat even the most stalwart man. But not Elvar, whose indomitable spirit is buoyed by his determination to preserve the ancient traditions of a resource so valuable to his nation that wars have been fought over it. With a steadfast resolve undeterred by the temptation to resort to cheaper, less time-consuming contemporary production methods, or by the crushing blow of an unprecedented economic crisis, Elvar's commitment to bacalao and to his village never wanes.

Gunnar stands beside Elvar as he breaks down the massive cod at breakneck speed, so cleanly that not a morsel of flesh remains on its bones. The men share a mutual reverence for tradition and for each other. Showcasing Elvar's bacalao on his menu at Dill has not only forged a bond between the chef and the fisherman but also between the present and the past. Elvar has visited Dill many times in recent years to enjoy his bacalao in ways he "could never have dreamed of." His smile disappears in a moment of contemplation. "Gunnar has realized the true potential of my bacalao and my gratitude is immeasurable," he says. With his grin firmly in place once more, the man of indefatigable enthusiasm adds, "Of course, it doesn't hurt that he's the kind of friend I would go to the ends of the earth for." Here, in this traditional bacalao factory just shy of the Arctic Circle, it seems he already has.

A Conversation with Bacalao Producer Elvar Reykjalín

Q **Did you always know you were going to take over your family's bacalao business?**

When I was growing up, there was really no other way. The men went to sea. I took my first job on a fishing boat with my father when I was ten years old, and I was at sea for over twenty-five years. The women had more choices. They could move away and marry men who had other careers and forge a different kind of life. But for the men in this region, fishing on your father's boat was the only life available. Cod is a part of my blood. It's who I am, and I can't really think of myself without my connection to fishing and producing bacalao. Without it, I'm not sure who I would be.

Q **Deep-sea fishing is such a dangerous profession. Have you experienced a close encounter with death?**

The conditions on the ship were always hard, but especially so in winter, with the freezing temperatures and the constant threat of the boat becoming stuck in the ice. We were generally out for a few days at a time, but once when we were out for around a week in the dead of winter, our boat was overtaken by a massive wave. It completely submerged the boat, and I was underwater clinging to the mast for what seemed like ages. I'm sure it was for only a minute, but when you think your life is going to end during that minute, it might as well be forever. I survived, but in my lifetime, around fifteen men from our village have perished at sea. It seems like a small amount, but we are a very tiny village.

Q **How do you produce your bacalao?**

Since I'm not fishing any longer, I purchase fresh cod from local fish markets or directly from the boats at the marina. I then remove the bones and break the cod down into fillets. I try to get as close to the bone as possible, in order not to let a single thing go to waste. One of my favorite things to do in the world is to break down a cod. I just smile and smile. My wife thinks I'm nuts, but like I said, it's in my blood.

I salt it in the traditional way for up to one year but never less than four months. It takes a lot of time, but there is really no other way to do it. True bacalao only develops its flavor after several months of salting. It requires a lot of salt. And even more patience. We use every single part of the fish. I sell the trimmings and skin to a company in France that turns them into cod fish balls. I sell the bones and heads to a company in Nigeria that uses them in soup. The cheeks and tongues I keep for my family and my employees' families. Or I give them to very important people in my life, like Gunnar.

Q **How have the production methods for bacalao changed in recent years?**

Today in Iceland, only two or three companies are still producing bacalao in the traditional way. Now they inject it with a saltwater brine, in the same way that industrialized chicken breasts are plumped up to make them heavier. I consider what I do slow food, and I would never change my methods; they are a part of who we are as Icelanders. I prepare it in exactly the same way my grandfather taught me. No chemicals. No injections. It's much more expensive and time-consuming to produce it this way, but it's worth it. I don't think you can call what is produced from this modern injection method bacalao. It's salted fish. But it's not bacalao. It tastes nothing like it. Today everything has to go so fast, and it is causing us to forget who we are.

Q **How has the economic crisis affected you?**

I've been having a very difficult time. I used to employ people seven days a week. Since the collapse, I employ far fewer people and for only a few days a week, plus the price of cod has risen drastically. Just like everyone else in Iceland, I am really struggling. I have had to eliminate most of my packaged-foods business because the high ingredient costs make it impossible to sell my products at a reasonable price to customers whose budgets are now stretched so thin. Many families in my village are on the verge of bankruptcy. It upsets me deeply, because I used to be the one to employ everyone and now I just don't have the resources to do that. But I am an optimist, and Iceland has endured hard times before. We will survive this too.

Q **How do you and Gunnar collaborate?**

From a cooking standpoint, I used to just eat my bacalao boiled in water, but Gunnar has shown me that bacalao has endless possibilities. I am always amazed by what he does with my bacalao, and it's very inspiring for me to eat it at Dill. His dedication to our traditional production methods gets me through the rough patches, and believe me, since the collapse, there have been many. When people taste my bacalao prepared by Gunnar in such creative ways, it creates an interest in it from his customers. Gunnar plays an important role in keeping this tradition alive.

Q **Is the next generation in your family interested in taking over Ektafiskur?**

I have three girls, and although they worked at Ektafiskur in their younger years, they are not interested in taking over the company. Fortunately, my grandson, who is thirteen, is interested in taking over the business. I will make sure he has pride in what he does and understands how important it is. Preserving this tradition for the generations to come is priceless. Not just for our village but for the Icelandic people.

SALTED COD TARTAR, DILL MAYONNAISE, *and* DULSE POWDER

SERVES 4 | PREPARATION TIME: ABOUT 2¹/₂ HOURS (PLUS 12 HOURS TO FREEZE THE COD)

This tartar recipe showcases cod in its purest, most pristine incarnation. It illustrates the shortcut to making salted cod by soaking fresh cod in salted water for thirty minutes. This method imparts the same briny flavor to cod as the salting and drying method does, and although it will not have the firm texture of traditional bacalao, it's a process that can be employed if bacalao proves difficult to source. Spiffed up with a blaze of color from dill mayonnaise and with brininess from powdered dulse (seaweed), it's a wonderfully refreshing way to begin a meal. Dill grows in abundance in the bird sanctuary that surrounds the restaurant, but if you lack a flourishing dill stand just outside your door, you can substitute any herb you like. The terms *bacalao* and *salted cod* are interchangeable, each meaning cod preserved by salting and drying.

DILL MAYONNAISE

1 egg yolk

2 teaspoons Angelica Mustard (page 139)

¹/₃ cup (80 ml) sweet-and-sour dill oil (page 32)

Distilled white vinegar, for seasoning

Salt

PICKLED DILL STALKS

Stalks from ¹/₂ bunch dill

¹/₄ cup (60 ml) distilled white vinegar

¹/₄ cup (60 ml) water

¹/₄ cup (50 g) sugar

CRISPY COD SKIN

(*see* NOTES, page 16)

Rapeseed oil, for frying

Skin from the cod (see notes, page 16), if available

Salt

SALTED COD TARTAR

Salt

7 ounces (200 g) cod, skin and bones reserved if intact

2 tablespoons rapeseed oil

1 sprig dill, finely chopped

TO SERVE

Powdered seaweed (see note, page 310)

To make the dill mayonnaise, in a bowl, whisk together the egg yolk and mustard until blended. Whisking constantly, slowly add the oil, drop by drop, until the mixture begins to thicken. Add the remaining oil in a slow, steady stream while whisking vigorously to form a mayonnaise. Season with vinegar and salt. Alternatively, to make the mayonnaise in a blender, process the egg yolk and mustard on medium speed just until blended, then, with the blender on high speed, add the oil in a slow, steady stream until the mayonnaise takes shape. Whisk in the vinegar and salt by hand.

To make the pickled dill stalks, put the dill stalks in a small, heatproof glass jar. Combine the vinegar, water, and sugar in a small saucepan and bring to a simmer over medium heat, stirring until the sugar has dissolved. Pour the hot liquid over the dill stalks, immersing them. Let cool to room temperature, then cover and refrigerate for at least 2 hours before using. The stalks will keep in the refrigerator for up to 2 weeks.

| *continued*

| Salted Cod Tartar, Dill Mayonnaise, and Dulse Powder, *continued*

NOTES

1. The crispy cod skin is optional. If the cod you have purchased came with skin or you have skin left over from filleting a fish, this is a good way to use it. If no skin is available, substitute another crispy item, such as salted cod chips (page 19) or crispy rye bread (page 72).

2. At Dill, the bacalao is processed through a ricer before it is thawed and served. It is a nice aesthetic touch, but the cod will taste just as good if it is finely chopped without freezing and ricing it. If you do employ the ricing method, the cod must be frozen in order to prevent it from turning into a fishy mess when passed through the ricer.

3. Much of the cod sold in the United States is skinned and filleted. But if you purchase cod with the bones intact, reserve them for making the consommé on page 94.

To make the crispy cod skin, pour oil to a depth of 4 inches (10 cm) into a deep, heavy pot and heat to 350°F (180°C). While the oil is heating, scrape the skin with a knife to remove any scales, rinse well under cold running water, and pat dry with paper towels.

When the oil is ready, immerse the skin in the hot oil and fry for 1 to 2 minutes, until golden brown, slightly puffed, and crispy. Transfer to paper towels to drain, then season with salt. Let cool before using.

To make the tartar, in a bowl, combine salt and water in a ratio of 2 to 1, using enough water to cover the cod by 2 inches. Add the cod and refrigerate for 30 minutes. Drain and rinse the cod under cold water for a few minutes. Pat dry using paper towels, wrap in two layers of plastic wrap, and freeze until solid, about 12 hours. Remove from the plastic wrap and pass through a ricer while still frozen (see notes). Allow to thaw at room temperature before serving, about 30 minutes. Drizzle with oil and stir gently until well coated.

To serve, place a generous spoonful of the tartar on a plate, dot with the mayonnaise, sprinkle with powdered seaweed, and garnish with crispy skin.

TRAVEL TO NORTHERN ICELAND

Elvar Reykjalín is always pleased to receive visitors at
Ektafiskur, in the speck of a village known as Hauganes.
You will be treated like a cherished friend as he demon-
strates how to make bacalao. During fillet sessions, where
Elvar works with deft hands to break down a monstrous
cod at the speed of light, he will regale you with stories of
his fishing life at sea and show you how to pick up a krona
using the tines of a forklift (by putting pressure on the top
of the coin, which flips it over, much to your disbelief and
utter awe). He will offer you his homemade moonshine to
wash down the *hákarl* (fermented shark, see page 274) that
he produces for a side income.

A man of mirth and boundless hospitality, Elvar will send
you home with a homemade birch box filled with his famed
bacalao and a grin wide as the village's picturesque harbor.
Hauganes is located about eighteen miles (twenty-nine kilometers) from Akureyri, the gateway to northwest Iceland,
a region affording unique dining, outdoor, and cultural
opportunities.

SALTED COD CHIPS *with* PICKLED ANGELICA CREAM

SERVES 4 | PREPARATION TIME: ABOUT 1 HOUR (PLUS 24 HOURS TO REHYDRATE
THE COD, 12 HOURS TO FREEZE THE COD, AND 12 HOURS TO DEHYDRATE THE CHIPS)

These snappy but pliant chips are an ideal way to showcase the naturally firm texture of salted cod. Sourcing salted cod in the United States can be a challenge. If you cannot find it where you live, cover a fresh cod fillet completely with kosher salt and refrigerate it for 24 to 48 hours. The cod will absorb enough salt to firm up its flesh. Rinse the cod well under cold running water for a few minutes to wash away any residual salt, then proceed with the recipe, beginning with the freezing step. The angelica cream here tempers the brininess of the cod, brightening it up with its pickling juice and adding a pop of mossy green color.

COD CHIPS

3½ ounces (100 g) skinned salted cod fillet

½ teaspoon ground fennel

PICKLED ANGELICA CREAM
(*see* NOTES)

1 egg

¼ cup (80 g) pickled angelica stalks (page 137; see notes)

Salt

1 cup (240 ml) rapeseed oil

TO SERVE

Fresh angelica leaves, for garnish

Pickled Angelica (page 137), for garnish

NOTES

1. Angelica is plentiful in Iceland, but it can be difficult to source in the United States and the rest of Europe. Pickled dill stalks (page 14) are a good substitute, though any herb will work in a pinch.

2. The cod must be rehydrated before it is frozen or it will not slice properly.

3. To make the cod easier to slice, try to purchase a square piece of fillet or trim a piece of cod into a neat square. A meat slicer is essential for slicing the chips thinly enough. A mandoline will not work.

To make the chips, immerse the cod in cold water to cover and refrigerate for 24 hours (see notes), changing the water several times to remove as much salt as possible. Drain, pat dry with paper towels, wrap in plastic wrap, and freeze overnight.

The next day, preheat a dehydrator to 147°F (64°C). Unwrap the frozen cod and, using a meat slicer, cut it into paper-thin slices (see notes). You will need 12 slices total. Arrange the slices on a dehydrator tray, sprinkle them lightly with the fennel, and dehydrate for 12 hours, until completely crisp and not at all pliable. Place the chips between sheets of parchment paper in an airtight container in the refrigerator until ready to use. They will keep for up to 1 week.

To make the angelica cream, prepare an ice bath. Bring a small saucepan of water to a lively simmer over medium-high heat. Using a slotted spoon, lower the egg into the water and cook it in the gently rolling water for 4 minutes. Transfer the egg to the ice bath and leave until well chilled. Remove the egg from the ice bath and immediately crack it lightly on all sides on a flat surface. Peel the egg, put it in a blender, and add the angelica stalks and a pinch of salt. (You do not need to dry the stalks before they go in the blender, as the pickling juice adds a nice touch of acidity to the finished cream.) Process on medium-high speed until fully blended, then add the oil in a slow, steady stream and process until the consistency of a thick mayonnaise. Taste and adjust with salt and pickling juice if needed.

To serve, place 3 chips on each plate and dot with the angelica cream. Garnish with angelica leaves and pickled angelica.

BACALAO POTATOES
with FENNEL RIBBONS
and SORREL ASH

SERVES 4 | PREPARATION TIME: ABOUT 1 HOUR (PLUS 24 HOURS TO REHYDRATE THE COD)

On a visit to northern Iceland, Gunnar and I stayed in an inviting apartment on the outskirts of Akureyri, the second largest town in the country (at a whopping eighteen thousand inhabitants) and Gunnar's birthplace. The only thing our cozy abode lacked was blackout curtains. Not surprisingly, the blinding July sun that drenches the country in light twenty-four hours a day results in severe sleep deprivation for anyone not accustomed to it. Gunnar, of course, is accustomed to his nation's days of perpetual light and slept soundly each night. Perhaps because he was not bleary-eyed by dinnertime (and because he is a naturally hospitable fellow), he took charge of the evening meal.

One of the first things he made was this creamy potato recipe incorporating Elvar's bacalao. It was not his intention to prepare it every night, but we couldn't seem to get enough of its comforting virtue. The bacalao infused it with just the right amount of brininess, and the pungent horseradish perked up any sleepy brains. It's hearty enough to work as a main dish and also makes a fantastic side. One night, Gunnar served it on toast; on another, he substituted smoked haddock, an ideal replacement for the cod. The profusion of herbs he added was dictated by whatever we foraged that day. This dish, which is inspired by a popular lunch item at Dill, is festively attired with fennel ribbons, a soft-boiled egg, and sorrel ash—the latter a mainstay of the Nordic kitchen.

POTATOES

1 pound (450 g) salted cod

1 pound (450 g) waxy potatoes

1/4 cup (60 ml) heavy cream, warmed

SORREL ASH

Leaves from 1 bunch sorrel

TO SERVE

4 carrots, peeled, cut into bite-size pieces, and roasted

2 fennel stalks, cut into long ribbons using a vegetable peeler (see note)

4 eggs, soft boiled

Freshly grated horseradish, for finishing

NOTE

To prevent browning, immerse the fennel ribbons in acidulated water until ready to use.

To make the potatoes, immerse the salted cod in cold water to cover and refrigerate for 24 hours, changing the water several times to remove as much salt as possible. Remove from the water and, if skin and bones are present, remove them. Preheat the oven to 400°F (200°C) and roast the cod until warmed through, about 8 minutes. Once it is cool enough to handle, break into flakes, and keep warm.

To make the sorrel ash, preheat the oven to 400°F (200°C). Line a baking sheet with parchment paper. Arrange the sorrel leaves in a single layer on the prepared pan and toast in the oven for about 8 minutes, until blackened. Let cool to room temperature, then pulverize the leaves in a spice grinder, transfer to an airtight container, and store at room temperature until serving. The ash will keep at room temperature for up to 2 weeks.

Boil the potatoes in salted water to cover for 18 to 20 minutes, until tender. Drain the potatoes, let cool just until they can be handled, then peel them, keeping the peel intact if possible.

In a saucepan, mash the warm potatoes and cream together until smooth. Add the warm cod and stir gently to incorporate. Keep warm.

To serve, spoon the potatoes into a bowl. Top with the carrots, a generous handful of fennel ribbons, a soft-boiled egg, and a spoonful of horseradish. Dust with sorrel ash.

COD, RUTABAGA PUREE, and DILL POWDER

SERVES 4 | PREPARATION TIME: 45 MINUTES (PLUS 24 HOURS TO REHYDRATE THE COD) | PICTURED ON PAGE 24

Unlike many other vegetables that are traditionally imported to Iceland, rutabagas have been grown in the nation for centuries. Here, rutabaga is pureed with caramelized sugar, which adds a toasted nuttiness to this mixture. At Dill, raw vegetables are often used in dishes to add texture and fresh flavor that is lost during cooking, and the rutabaga strings in this recipe are a good example of this technique. The bacalao in this recipe is rehydrated in order to release some of its salt and so that it is firm but pliant. This dish is a lovely celebration of the winter months, when foods such as root vegetables and salted cod brighten Iceland's dark season, and when little grows save for the beards on the men trying to stay warm.

BACALAO

14 ounces (400 g) salted cod, skinned after it is rehydrated and rinsed (see page 21)

1¹/₂ tablespoons rapeseed oil

RUTABAGA PUREE

1¹/₂ cups (200 g) peeled and coarsely chopped rutabaga

¹/₂ cup (120 ml) water

¹/₄ cup (60 ml) milk

¹/₄ cup (60 ml) heavy cream

¹/₂ teaspoon sugar

2 tablespoons unsalted butter, at room temperature

Beer Vinegar (page 30), for seasoning

Salt

RUTABAGA STRINGS

1 small rutabaga, peeled

Salt

DILL POWDER

1 ounce (30 g) fresh dill leaves

2 tablespoons rapeseed oil

¹/₂ cup (10 g) powdered tapioca maltodextrin (see notes)

Salt

Fresh dill leaves and other herbs of choice, for garnish

NOTES

1. Tapioca maltodextrin, which is naturally derived from tapioca, encapsulates fats such as butter and oils, turning them into a powder and increasing the volume of a small amount of fat dramatically. It's fun to transform ingredients such as peanut butter and olive oil into powders that will turn back into their original form once they come into contact with saliva. Although it is not necessary to transform the oil into a powder in this recipe, it is a nice way to add something unexpected to the dish.

To make the bacalao, preheat an immersion circulator to 133°F (56°C) (see notes). Place the cod and oil in a vacuum bag and seal on the lowest setting. Cook in the circulator for 11 to 12 minutes. To test if the cod is done in the circulator bag, pinch the fish through the bag. If it gives easily and flakes, it is ready. Remove the bag from the circulator and let cool until the cod can be handled, then remove the cod from the bag and break it into flakes, discarding any errant bones. Keep warm.

To make the rutabaga puree, put the rutabaga in a pressure cooker (see notes), add the water, lock the lid in place, and cook at medium pressure for 8 minutes, until the rutabaga is tender. Let the pressure release naturally, then remove the lid and drain the rutabaga, reserving the cooking liquid and rutabaga separately. Transfer the rutabaga to a blender and process at high speed, adding the reserved cooking liquid as needed to form a smooth puree. Leave the puree in the blender.

NOTES, continued

2. As an alternative to the immersion circulator method, add enough oil to a saucepan to cover the cod by 1 inch (2¹/₂ cm) and bring to a gentle simmer over medium-high heat. Do not let the oil boil. Reduce the heat to low and add the cod. Poach until cooked through (the cod should flake when broken apart with a fork). Remove using a slotted spoon and drain on paper towels. Keep warm.

3. If you do not have a pressure cooker (see page 50), you can boil the rutabaga in water to cover until tender, drain, and then proceed as directed.

4. A turning slicer is a rare find in the home kitchen, but if you want to treat yourself to a new kitchen gadget, this might be the perfect one. It transforms a vegetable into long ribbons that add a festive touch to nearly any plate and are a clever way to convince finicky children to eat their vegetables.

In a small bowl, stir together the milk and cream. Put the sugar in a small, heavy saucepan, place over medium-high heat, and heat without stirring until the sugar melts and turns a light golden brown. Once the color is right, carefully add the milk mixture to the sugar. The sugar will immediately seize but will then settle. Turn down the heat to medium and swirl the pan over medium heat until the sugar is fully incorporated into the liquid.

Pour the sugar-milk mixture into the blender with the rutabaga and begin processing on low speed to prevent the hot mixture from splattering. Once the elements are incorporated, increase the speed to high and continue to process until smooth. Season with the butter, vinegar, and salt. Keep warm.

To make the rutabaga strings, slice the rutabaga with a turning slicer (see notes) into strings. Alternatively, thinly slice the rutabaga into disks and, using a mandoline (see notes, page 73), cut the disks into strings. Season the strings with salt.

To make the dill powder, combine the dill and oil in the blender and process on high speed for 7 to 9 minutes, until steaming hot. Strain through a fine-mesh sieve into a small pitcher. Place the maltodextrin in a food processor. With the machine running, drizzle in the oil in a slow, steady stream. Continue to process for 4 to 5 minutes, until a powder forms. Season with salt and blend for a few seconds more.

To serve, spoon the rutabaga puree onto a plate, top with the cod and a handful of rutabaga strings, and sprinkle with the dill powder. Garnish with dill leaves and other herbs.

OPPOSITE: Cod, Rutabaga Puree, and Dill Powder (page 22)

ABOVE: Poached Cod Cheeks, Roasted Cod Soup, Potatoes, and Charred Onions (page 26)

POACHED COD CHEEKS, ROASTED COD SOUP, POTATOES, and CHARRED ONIONS

SERVES 4 | PREPARATION TIME: ABOUT 1½ HOURS | PICTURED ON PAGE 25

It's common to use meat bones, such as veal, chicken, and lamb, as the base for stocks, broths, and stews, but fish bones are not as familiar to many home cooks. The good news is that most fishmongers will sell them at a rock-bottom price if you make a special request for them. It's a great way to forge a lasting connection with your fishmonger, and once you do, he or she will often give you bones for free. Fish bones speak to Gunnar's never-throw-away-any-part-of-the-animal philosophy, and after tasting them roasted in this recipe, you will likely appreciate them as much as he does. One word of warning: chopping through fish bones can make quite a mess. Rinse them thoroughly to remove any residual blood and guts, then rely on the quick, deft chop of a cleaver to cut them cleanly.

COD CHEEKS

14 ounces (400 g) cod cheeks (see page 28)

Salt

1 tablespoon distilled white vinegar

ROASTED COD SOUP

Rapeseed oil, for sautéing

14 ounces (400 g) cod bones, coarsely chopped

2 tablespoons peeled and finely chopped carrot

2 tablespoons peeled and finely chopped celery root

2 tablespoons finely chopped white onion

3 tablespoons fennel fronds

Leaves from 1 bunch thyme

3 tablespoons finely chopped dill leaves

1 star anise pod

3 whole cloves

ROASTED COD SOUP, continued

2 cups (480 ml) water

⅓ cup (80 ml) heavy cream

⅓ cup (80 ml) milk

Salt

Cider vinegar, for seasoning

1 g soy lecithin (see notes)

CHARRED ONIONS

3 red pearl onions, halved lengthwise with root stem intact

3 white or yellow pearl onions, halved lengthwise with root stem intact

3 small shallots, halved lengthwise with root stem intact

Salt

POTATOES

2 teaspoons smoked oil (page 98)

3½ ounces (100 g) small potatoes, unpeeled and sliced into ¼-inch (6-mm) coins

1 tablespoon Beer Mustard (page 292), or store-bought stone-ground mustard

Salt

Garden cress, for garnish (see notes)

To make the cod cheeks, trim the cheeks of any sinew and cut into 2-inch (5-cm) cylinders using a ½-inch (12-mm) round cutter. Fill a saucepan with water to a depth of 3 inches (7.5 cm), season with a little salt, and bring to a gentle simmer. Add the vinegar and then the cheeks and poach gently for 5 minutes. Using a slotted spoon, transfer the cheeks to paper towels to drain. Keep warm.

To make the soup, place a cast-iron frying pan over medium heat and coat the bottom with a thin layer of oil. Add the bones and sauté, turning often with tongs to prevent scorching, for about 10 minutes, until caramelized. Use caution during this step, as the bones will splatter as they cook. Remove from the heat. Keep warm.

NOTES

1. Soy lecithin is a natural emulsifier derived from the fatty tissues of soybeans. Since it has low water solubility, it is capable of bringing elements together, such as water and oil, that are difficult to blend naturally. It is also added to dishes that are aerated, such as mousses and foams, since it has the ability to create a stable environment and support the structure for much longer than it would hold otherwise.

2. Any peppery green, such as arugula or mizuna, can be substituted for the garden cress.

3. Skimming off any fat and impurities from the surface of the soup is important because the fat will fight the soy lecithin, inhibiting bubbles from forming when the soup is frothed. Removing as much fat residue as possible enables additional bubbles to form.

Place a pressure cooker (see page 50) over medium heat and coat the bottom with a thin layer of oil. Add the carrot, celery root, onion, fennel, thyme, dill, star anise, and cloves and sauté for about 7 minutes, until the vegetables are tender and the spices are aromatic. Add the bones and sauté for 1 minute longer. Add the water, lock the lid in place, and cook at high pressure for 35 minutes. Let the pressure subside naturally. Remove the lid and strain the contents through a fine-mesh sieve into a clean, clear container. Let sit for a few minutes, then skim off any fat and residue that settles on the surface (see notes). Transfer the strained broth to a saucepan, place over medium-high heat, bring to a boil, and reduce by three-fourths, skimming the surface of residue as it cooks. Add the cream and milk, bring to a simmer, and season with salt and cider vinegar. Just before serving, reheat until warm, add the soy lecithin, and process with an immersion blender until foamy.

To make the charred onions, heat a dry frying pan over medium-low heat. Place the onions and shallots, cut side down, in the pan and caramelize them to the point of charring. Flip the onions and shallots over and caramelize the second side the same way. Remove from the heat and season with salt. Keep warm.

To make the potatoes, heat the oil in a frying pan over medium-low heat. Add the potatoes and sauté, being careful not to let them turn golden brown, for 6 to 8 minutes, until tender. Stir in the mustard and season with salt. Keep warm.

To serve, foam the soup once more just before service and pour it into bowls with a large lip. Place the cod cheeks on the lip on one side of the bowl and arrange the potatoes and charred onions alongside the cod. Garnish with cress.

COD CHEEKS, ONION CREAM, *and* PICKLED ROOT VEGETABLES

SERVES 4 | PREPARATION TIME: ABOUT 1 HOUR (PLUS 4 HOURS TO PICKLE
THE VEGETABLES)

Cheeks are one of the tastiest parts a fish has to offer, yet they are often relegated to a
fishmonger's offcut pile—a pile that interests few people. This is a good thing for the consumer in the know, because it often means they can be had for a song. As bacalao producer
Elvar Reykjalín butchers his cod for salting, he pops hundreds of cheeks out of his fish and
saves them for chefs like Gunnar, who know the value of a good cut. They can be hard to
source, but any fishmonger would be happy to supply them for you on special request, and
the extra effort to track them down is well worth it. Should cod cheeks be difficult to find,
halibut cheeks or halibut or cod fillet make a fine substitute.

Unlike the pickles in some of the recipes in this book that require a day, a week, or
sometimes a month to cure, these pickles are fairly quick to produce and are a nice way to
use up any extra root vegetables in your refrigerator at the end of the week.

PICKLED ROOT VEGETABLES

1/3 cup (40 g) peeled and
thinly sliced rutabaga

1/4 cup (40 g) peeled and
thinly celery root

1/3 cup (40 g) peeled and
thinly sliced carrot

2/3 cup (150 ml) distilled
white vinegar

1/2 cup (120 ml) water

3 tablespoons sugar

2 sprigs thyme

ONION CREAM

3 tablespoons (70 g) plus
2 teaspoons unsalted butter

1 white onion, chopped

1/4 teaspoon baking soda

Pinch of salt

2 tablespoons Beer Vinegar
(page 30), plus more as
needed

1/4 cup (60 ml) Chicken
Stock, preferably homemade
(page 89)

3/4 cup (180 ml) heavy cream

Arctic thyme oil (page 129),
for finishing

COD CHEEKS

Scant 11/2 pounds (650 g)
cod cheeks

Salt

11/2 tablespoons rapeseed oil

To make the pickled root vegetables, place the rutabaga, celery root, and carrot in a
heatproof glass jar. Combine the white vinegar, water, sugar, and thyme in a saucepan
and bring to a boil over medium heat, stirring until the sugar has dissolved. Pour the hot
liquid over the vegetables, immersing them. Let cool to room temperature, then cover
and refrigerate for at least 4 hours before using. The vegetables will keep in the refrigerator for up to 1 month.

To make the onion cream, melt 1 tablespoon plus 2 teaspoons of the butter in a pressure cooker (see page 50) over medium heat and stir in the onion, baking soda, and salt,
mixing well. Lock the lid in place and cook at medium pressure for 14 minutes, until the

onion is caramelized. Let the pressure subside naturally. Remove the lid, add the beer vinegar, place over medium-high heat, and cook until reduced by three-fourths. Add the stock and reduce by half, and then add the cream and reduce by one-third.

Transfer the mixture to a blender and begin processing on low speed to prevent the hot mixture from splattering. Once the elements are incorporated, increase the speed to high and continue to process until smooth. Strain through a fine-mesh sieve into a small sauce-pan, place over low heat, add the remaining 2 tablespoons of butter, and stir until melted. Season with salt and beer vinegar. Reserve the thyme oil to add just before serving.

To make the cod cheeks, preheat an immersion circulator to 149°F (65°C). Trim the cheeks of any sinew and season with salt. Place the cheeks and oil in a vacuum bag and seal on the lowest setting. Cook in the circulator for 10 minutes. Remove the bag from the circulator and cool to room temperature.

To serve, add the thyme oil to the onion cream and stir until incorporated. Place the cod cheeks on a plate, garnish with the root vegetables, and dollop the cod with the onion cream.

Beer Vinegar

MAKES ABOUT 2¹/₂ CUPS (600 ML) | PREPARATION TIME: 3 TO 4 WEEKS

Beer vinegar is used to enliven a number of dishes in this book with a subtle pucker, and it's easy to make. It does take time, however, so if you cannot wait the necessary three or four weeks, any heady vinegar, such as malt vinegar, can be substituted.

A mother vinegar, which is the somewhat gummy, sometimes slimy, often wispy layer that settles on top of the container in which vinegar is fermented, is what keeps the original flavor of a vinegar alive and kicking in subsequent batches. You won't have a mother to use when you make your first batch of vinegar, but if you like the taste of that first vinegar, be sure to reserve the mother from it to make the next batch, and then continue to save a mother from every subsequent batch. That way you will sustain your vinegar's legacy.

Gunnar is the co-owner of a bistro-type restaurant that focuses on beer and has several different labels on tap. The place is called Kex, which means "biscuit" in Icelandic, and it is located in a funky former biscuit factory that also doubles as a hostel for the thousands of hipsters who converge on Reykjavík every summer. Each day, the bartenders collect the beer that overflows from the taps or glasses when they are serving customers, capturing it in a container. They introduce a mother vinegar to the beer they have collected and then let it ferment for three to four weeks, depending on the type of beer. It's a nice way to reduce waste and produce something tasty at the same time.

2¹/₂ cups (600 ml) dark beer, such as a porter or a stout

Vinegar mother, if available

Pour the beer into a clean, sterilized glass jar (see note). If you have a previous batch of vinegar and want to use the mother, decant the vinegar into a new container, being careful not to disturb the mother resting on the bottom of the jar. Add the mother to the fresh beer, top the jar with a piece of cheesecloth, and tie the cheesecloth securely to the jar rim with butcher's twine.

Keep the vinegar in a cool, dry place for 3 to 4 weeks. Check the taste of your vinegar after 1 week to see how it is doing. It should just be beginning to get tart. Also, skim off any white film growing on the surface and replace the cheesecloth with a new piece. Once the vinegar is tart and tangy enough for your liking, seal the jar with a sterilized lid. It will keep indefinitely in the refrigerator and will soon produce a mother of its own.

NOTE

To sterilize the jar, put it in a pot, cover it with water, bring the water to a boil, and boil for 10 minutes. Allow the jar to air-dry before using. You can sterilize the lid the same way.

MILK ICE CREAM, RUTABAGA and APPLE CIDER GRANITA, and SWEET-AND-SOUR DILL OIL

SERVES 4 | PREPARATION TIME: ABOUT 4 HOURS (PLUS 12 HOURS TO FREEZE
THE ICE CREAM)

When Gunnar was a teenager, he worked on farms near his hometown of Akureyri. Most of the farms are a short drive from bacalao producer Elvar Reykjalín's village. This dish is inspired by the fresh milk he used to drink on the farms, an experience he always remembers when he visits Elvar to purchase cod. The sweet-and-sour dill oil in this recipe not only adds complex, unexpected flavor but also dresses the dish in a vibrant green. Gunnar frequently pairs this oil with savory recipes, but here it works well with the creaminess of ice cream. It's also nice to drizzle over freshly whipped cream on top of a hot waffle. Rutabaga is used twice, for the granita and for the cylinders, which also call for rutabaga juice. If you don't have rutabagas on hand, parsnips or celery root will also work well.

MILK ICE CREAM

4^1/$_4$ cups (1 L) milk

1^1/$_4$ cups (250 g) sugar

^{1}/$_4$ cup (50 g) liquid glucose (see notes, page 34)

^{1}/$_2$ teaspoon salt

3 g xanthan gum (see notes, page 34)

RUTABAGA AND APPLE CIDER GRANITA

3 cups (720 ml) rutabaga juice

1^1/$_4$ cups (300 ml) apple cider

6^1/$_2$ tablespoons (80 g) sugar

BOILED, BURNED, AND PICKLED RUTABAGA CYLINDERS

2 rutabagas, peeled and each cut into 6 (1^1/$_2$-inch/4-cm) slices

^{3}/$_4$ cup plus 2 tablespoons (200 ml) cider vinegar

^{1}/$_2$ cup (120 ml) rutabaga juice

^{1}/$_4$ cup (50 g) sugar

2 tablespoons honey

SWEET-AND-SOUR DILL OIL

^{1}/$_4$ cup (60 ml) rapeseed oil

^{1}/$_2$ cup (4.5 g) fresh dill leaves

^{1}/$_4$ cup (60 ml) cider vinegar

^{1}/$_4$ cup (50 g) sugar

Dill sprigs, for garnish

To make the ice cream, prepare an ice bath. Combine the milk, sugar, and glucose in a saucepan and bring to a simmer over medium heat, stirring until the sugar has dissolved. Remove from the heat, add the salt and xanthan gum, and stir until dissolved. Nest the pan in the ice bath and let it stand, stirring occasionally, until chilled. Transfer to an ice cream maker and freeze according to the manufacturer's instructions. Scoop into an airtight container, place in the freezer, and freeze for about 12 hours, until solid.

To make the granita, prepare an ice bath. Combine all of the ingredients in a saucepan and bring to a simmer over medium heat, stirring until the sugar has dissolved. Remove from the heat, pour into a heatproof shallow container, nest the bowl in the ice bath, and let stand until chilled, stirring occasionally. Place the container in the freezer for

| continued

| Milk Ice Cream, Rutabaga and Apple Cider Granita, and Sweet-and-Sour Dill Oil, *continued*

| Milk Ice Cream, Rutabaga and Apple Cider Granita, and Sweet-and-Sour Dill Oil, *continued*

NOTES

1. Liquid glucose is not as sweet as cane sugar and does not crystallize, which makes it ideal for dessert recipes in which a smooth texture is desired. Here, it gives the ice cream an ultra-creamy consistency.

2. Xanthan gum is a food additive derived from the fermentation of naturally occurring sugars. It is commonly used as a thickening agent in products such as salad dressings and sauces. It is also used as a stabilizer to prevent ingredients from separating. Gunnar frequently uses xanthan gum to transform liquids into gels and in his ice creams. It can be purchased at specialty food stores and online.

30 minutes. Remove from the freezer, rake and stir the granita thoroughly with a fork, and return to the freezer. Repeat this process every 30 minutes for 2 to 3 hours, until the mixture is frozen and the consistency of granita. Cover and return to the freezer until serving.

To make the rutabaga cylinders, punch each rutabaga slice into a cylinder using a round 1/2-inch (13-mm) diameter cutter, then cut each cylinder on the bias on one end. Combine the vinegar, rutabaga juice, sugar, and honey in a saucepan and bring to a simmer over medium heat, stirring until the sugar has dissolved. Add the rutabaga, turn down the heat to low, and cook for about 8 minutes, until just tender. Remove from the heat and let cool to room temperature. Drain the rutabaga cylinders and place them on a heatproof platter. Using a kitchen torch, blacken the tops and sides.

To make the dill oil, combine all of the ingredients in a blender and process until smooth. Strain through a fine-mesh sieve, then transfer to a squeeze bottle.

To serve, put a scoop of granita onto a plate and top with ice cream. Arrange rutabaga cylinders around it, dot with dill oil, and garnish with dill.

RHUBARB *and* HERB SUGAR

SERVES 4 | PREPARATION TIME: 20 MINUTES

When Gunnar was a child and rhubarb was in season, his mother would give him and his brother and sister each a small bowl of sugar. They would then spend the morning wandering through the fields plucking rhubarb stalks to dip into their sugar bowls. This recipe is a twist on that memory, with the addition of lemon balm and tarragon to give the sugar an electric green color and an herbaceous hit. For a grown-up version, pair it with chilled aquavit. Indeed, on a summer's day in Iceland, there's nothing better than joining friends at an outdoor table in the sunshine, with a bowl of freshly cut rhubarb in the center, small bowls of herb sugar around it, and shot glasses filled with chilled aquavit. *Skál!*

HERB SUGAR

1/2 cup (5 g) loosely packed fresh lemon balm leaves

2 tablespoons loosely packed fresh tarragon leaves

1 cup (200 g) sugar

4 rhubarb stalks, trimmed

To make the herb sugar, rinse the lemon balm and tarragon under ice-cold running water for 30 seconds and pat dry with paper towels. In a food processor, combine the sugar and herbs and process for about 4 minutes, until the mixture is evenly green.

To serve, set out each rhubarb stalk with a small bowl of herb sugar for dipping.

THE ARCTIC CHAR SMOKER

Lake Mývatn, North-Central Iceland

∞

Kale and Buttermilk Spiced with Smoked Arctic Char 44

Parsnips Three Ways with Arctic Char Roe 48

Cured Arctic Char, Buttered Potatoes, Mixed Salad,
and Smoked Fresh Cheese 51

Butter 54

Licorice Lava 56

On the southern shore of Lake Mývatn in north-central

Iceland stands a dilapidated-looking wooden house with a pile of what looks like blocks of dirt on one side. It's not a routine stop on the tourist trail at this popular holiday destination, but it is the sweet spot for those who let their palates dictate their itineraries. It is here that Gylfi Yngvason, his wife, Audur Jónsdóttir, and their four children smoke arctic char in the same manner as their ancestors did centuries ago.

A plume of thick, gray smoke puffs up through the chimney and fills the air with a dusky earthiness whose flavor profile cannot quite be broken down at first. The fuel for this single-family operation is shaggy brown blocks of compressed hay and sheep manure, packed down over the months by the sheep themselves. They infuse the char that Gylfi neatly arranges on long wooden poles with an essence that means more than simply flavor to Icelanders.

It conjures nostalgia for an experience that is quickly succumbing to the crush of globalization and the desire for instant gratification. There was a time when almost nothing tasted better to most Icelanders than a slice of sweet rye slathered with local butter and topped with a glistening slice of smoked arctic char. Today, most of the smoked char in Iceland is processed in large, soulless buildings, where workers brush the fish with smoke oil to mask the absence of tradition.

But Gylfi persists in his time-honored work. Each morning, the quiet man with salt-and-pepper hair and a slow, discerning smile dons his bright orange fishing waders to protect his clothing from the blood and guts that are part of his work and heads to the smokehouse at the bottom of the hill from his residence, a tidy, inviting home that is now also a guesthouse. He sets out sated with rye bread his wife bakes in the nearby geothermal ovens, her homemade butter, and hot tea made from Icelandic herbs she forages. He breaks down the char in the same way he has for decades, then hangs them from wooden poles, which he carefully installs inside the smokehouse. He heaves a few of the heavy smoking blocks into a pile beneath the fish and stokes a flame that emerges meekly at first but is soon billowing with brazen energy, only to settle down into a persistent orange glow.

The fish smoke for three days and three nights while the family tends to the countless tasks necessary to maintaining the business, including caring for a small herd of sheep, a flock of chickens, and the guesthouse—and most important, a legacy that is as fundamental to who Icelanders are as the dormant volcanoes that dot the shore of Lake Mývatn.

A Conversation with Arctic Char Smoker Gylfi Yngvason

Q **How do you smoke your fish?**

I cut them lengthwise and wash them well, but I leave in the bones and a small hole at the top for hanging later. Depending on how big they are, I put them in salt for two to twenty hours. I rinse them, hang them from sticks, and put them in the smokehouse for three days and three nights. It's cold smoke, using blocks of compressed sheep manure and hay. It's a very old Icelandic tradition. The weather has to be exactly right, because the blocks must not burn, just glow. They can't be too hot.

Q **Why did you decide to become a fish smoker?**

I come from a long line of fish smokers and took over this business from my father. When I did, our smokehouse was falling down, and I thought it would be an improvement to build a new one, so I neglected the original one. My uncle was the first smoker to sell to stores in this region. Before that, we would just sell to people who were passing by. He told me not to switch houses. He said it would change the flavor of the fish. But I just laughed at him and went ahead with my plan, thinking new is always better. I smoked fish in the new smokehouse for five years, and it never tasted the same. I have no idea why that was the case. I finally gave up and returned to the first house. Yes, it is falling down, and yes, it doesn't look pretty, but it's a very good house. Its walls are thick and the temperature inside is always the same. It's perfect for my fish and results in the best flavor.

Q **Do you smoke fish year-round?**

Yes. This is my only job.

Q **Do you smoke fish other than arctic char?**

I buy and smoke rainbow trout sometimes, because we are not allowed to fish for them ourselves. I also smoke for fishermen in the area. We smoke twelve to fifteen tons of fresh fish each year. Three kilograms [6$\frac{1}{2}$ pounds] of fresh fish yields about one kilogram [2$\frac{1}{4}$ pounds] of smoked fish.

Q **Whom do you sell your fish to?**

I sell a lot of my fish to chefs. I also sell it to stores throughout Iceland. In the summertime, I sell a lot more fish because of all the people on holiday passing by. Our fish isn't exported, but it is available at the international airport, and we know that many people from around the world are buying it to take home with them. So in this way, it is finding its way out of Iceland.

Q Do you use any other parts of the fish besides what you are selling?

Some of the fish we smoke contain bones, and after we are finished with the smoking, we remove the bones, save them until winter, and then feed them to our sheep all winter long. We cold smoke our lamb for fourteen days in the same smokehouse, usually before Christmas. If you look for it, you can taste the smoked char in their meat.

Q How was smoked arctic char traditionally used in recipes?

Traditionally, it was served with just sweet rye bread and local butter. You can't find a better combination.

Q Do you find that smoking fish in the traditional way is a dying tradition?

Yes, fish has been smoked this way for centuries, but things are now changing. Only a handful of us traditional smokers are left in Iceland, maybe fewer than ten in the entire country, and the Mývatn way of using sheep dung, hay, and porous stone in the foundation of the wooden smokehouse is very specific to this region. The stone is sourced locally from the lava fields of the area and enables the smoke and outside air to slowly flow in and out. The sheep need to compress the hay and dung themselves by walking on it for at least a few months. It's impossible to do this in the new smokehouses because grates are required. We don't add anything to our fish except salt, smoke, and time.

The modern way is to put the fish in smoke for several hours and then add smoked oil to them. The fish lose a lot of flavor in this process. Modern operations also smoke fillets, whereas we keep the bones in our fish because they impart flavor. The process is more time-consuming, but it's worth it. My goal is to get the best possible taste from my smoked fish. We do everything with our hands. No machines. Fishermen could take their fish to these contemporary places, but the taste will be completely different, and so many continue to come here to have them smoked in the traditional way.

Q Is the younger generation of Icelanders interested in this technique?

No, not really. Maybe when they get older they will appreciate it. I just hope that by then it's not too late.

WHAT IS DIRT SMOKING?

In Iceland, when you hear a food described as having been dirt smoked, it usually means that the source of the smoke was a dried block of compressed hay and sheep manure. Gunnar chooses not to sugarcoat the process and calls it what it is: shit smoking. The technique infuses whatever it is smoking, usually arctic char or lamb, with an earthiness that is impossible to achieve using the more modern smoking techniques employed nowadays almost everywhere in Iceland. For an Icelander and anyone else able to overcome their misgivings about eating manure-smoked foods, the reward is flavor packed with a region's *terroir*. Its flowers, grasses, grains, and weeds are all there for those brave enough to accept the tradition.

Arctic char smoker Gylfi Yngvason explains a process he has employed to smoke his fish for decades: "The sheep compress together a mixture of hay and manure by walking over it in the barn for at least two months. We then shovel it out to dry it. It's best to move it outdoors in the early spring after the long Icelandic winter that has kept the sheep inside doing their work. The drying process is as important as the first step. It cannot be too dry or too wet or it won't smoke the fish properly. It's very hard work to remove the blocks from the barn. They're heavy and it's a tiring process, but I cannot imagine smoking my fish using anything else."

KALE *and* BUTTERMILK SPICED *with* SMOKED ARCTIC CHAR

SERVES 4 | PREPARATION TIME: ABOUT 45 MINUTES (PLUS 12 HOURS TO DRAIN
THE BUTTERMILK AND 6 HOURS TO DEHYDRATE THE ARCTIC CHAR) | PICTURED ON
PAGE 46

Gunnar is always searching for ways to use parts of vegetables that other cooks typically relegate to the trash bin. The use of kale stalks as one of the primary elements in this recipe is the perfect illustration of that. When blanched for a few seconds, they are transformed into ideal dipping vessels for the creamy buttermilk sprinkled with smoky arctic char. Of course, other vegetables, such as blanched asparagus or raw celery, can be substituted for the kale, but the stalks are a great conversation piece and are an especially clever way to use an element that rarely finds its way to the table.

The buttermilk also symbolizes the use of an element that might otherwise be discarded. The buttermilk is drained and only the solids are used here, but Gunnar reserves the whey and uses it in other recipes.

This recipe is a unique and addictive bar snack. If you're having difficulty sourcing the arctic char, salmon proves a good substitute. Either fish, once it is dehydrated and flaked, also pairs well with cream cheese for bagels or can be stirred into mayonnaise.

BUTTERMILK
1 cup (240 ml) buttermilk

ARCTIC CHAR
2¹/₂ ounces (75 g) skinned arctic char fillet

Completely dried peels from about 10 large onions, plus more if more than one smoking is desired (see note and page 250)

KALE
Stalks from 1 bunch kale

Salt

Rapeseed oil, for seasoning

NOTE
Onion peels are one of Gunnar's favorite sources of smoke, but other elements can be used in their place, such as wood chips or, in true Icelandic fashion, birch leaves or hay (see page 191).

To make the buttermilk, line a colander with a coffee filter and place the colander over a bowl. Pour the buttermilk into the colander and let drain in the refrigerator for 12 hours. Reserve the solids for plating and reserve the whey for another use such as marinating pork or beef tenderloin (see page 198).

To make the arctic char, preheat the oven to the lowest setting. Line a small baking sheet with parchment paper. Place the fish fillet on the prepared pan. Dehydrate in the oven for about 6 hours, until completely dry.

Line the bottom of a tiered steamer with the onion peels and place over high heat. Ignite the onion peels with a kitchen torch, put the steamer rack in place, and when the peels are smoking, put the dehydrated fish on the rack, cover the steamer, and leave undisturbed for about 10 minutes, until the smoldering subsides. If a more intense smokiness is desired, repeat the process once or twice. (See page 191 for an alternative homemade smoker set-up.)

Remove the fish from the steamer, let cool completely, and break apart into flakes. The flakes can be stored in an airtight container in the refrigerator for up to 1 week.

To make the kale, prepare an ice bath. Bring a saucepan of water to a boil over high heat, add the kale stalks, and blanch for a few seconds. Using a wire skimmer, transfer the stalks to the ice bath, immersing them. Let stand until chilled. Drain the stalks and pat dry with paper towels.

Season the stalks with salt and then toss them with just enough oil to make them glisten.

To serve, spoon the thickened buttermilk onto a plate and sprinkle with the char flakes. Serve the kale stalks alongside.

ABOVE: Kale and Buttermilk Spiced with Smoked Arctic Char (page 44)

OPPOSITE: Parsnips Three Ways with Arctic Char Roe (page 48)

PARSNIPS THREE WAYS
with ARCTIC CHAR ROE

SERVES 4 | PREPARATION TIME: ABOUT 1 HOUR (PLUS 24 HOURS TO PICKLE
THE PARSNIPS AND SHALLOTS AND 12 HOURS TO DEHYDRATE THE SHALLOTS)
| PICTURED ON PAGE 47

Arctic char roe is as vibrant in color as the flesh of the fish it comes from, and when added
to the caramelized puree in this recipe, it adds a briny pop of flavor. Salmon roe is a good
substitute for the sometimes difficult to source arctic char roe, and either one is a welcome
flash of vibrant color in a dish that is otherwise awash in ivory. Celery root or rutabaga
proves a good substitute for the parsnips, and no matter what root vegetable is used, be
sure to add a generous amount of vinegar to counter the natural sweetness of the puree.
You might want to double, or even triple, the volumes called for in the pickled shallot powder, as it is also terrific sprinkled over hamburgers, vegetables, fish, or nearly anything else.

PICKLED SHALLOT POWDER

1³/₄ ounces (50 g) shallots,
quartered lengthwise and
petals separated

2 tablespoons distilled white
vinegar

1 tablespoon water

2¹/₂ teaspoons sugar

PARSNIP PUREE

2 tablespoons unsalted butter

7 ounces (200 g) parsnips,
peeled and coarsely chopped

¹/₂ teaspoon baking soda

Pinch of salt

Beer Vinegar (page 30),
for seasoning

PARSNIPS

4 small parsnips, peeled

2 tablespoons unsalted butter

2 tablespoons water

Salt

TO SERVE

Arctic char roe, for garnish

Coarsely chopped fresh flat-
leaf parsley, for garnish

Fresh dill leaves, for garnish

Watercress leaves, for garnish

Rye bread crumbs, for garnish
(optional)

PICKLED PARSNIPS

1 small parsnip, peeled

¹/₂ cup (120 ml) distilled
white vinegar

¹/₄ cup (60 ml) water

2¹/₂ tablespoons sugar

To make the shallot powder, prepare an ice bath. Bring a saucepan of salted water to a boil
over high heat, add the shallot petals, and blanch for a few seconds. Using a slotted spoon,
transfer the petals to the ice bath, immersing them. Let stand until chilled. Drain, pat dry
with paper towels, and transfer to a small heatproof glass jar.

Combine the vinegar, water, and sugar in a small saucepan and bring to a boil, stirring
until the sugar has dissolved. Pour the hot liquid over the shallots, immersing them. Let
cool to room temperature, then cover and refrigerate for 24 hours.

Preheat a dehydrator to the highest setting or preheat an oven to its lowest setting. If
using an oven, line a baking sheet with parchment paper. Drain the shallots, pat dry
with paper towels, and arrange on a dehydrator tray or on the prepared baking sheet.
Dehydrate the shallots, flipping them over at the halfway point, for about 12 hours, until
they are deep golden brown. Let cool to room temperature, then grind to a coarse powder in a spice grinder (see notes). The powder will keep in an airtight container in the
refrigerator for up to 1 week.

NOTES

1. Be sure to dehydrate the shallots completely before grinding or they will become gummy.

2. Season the puree with the vinegar before adding any water to thin it. The puree is very sweet and will need the help of the vinegar to bring it to the plucky side. If too much water is mixed in before you season it, the puree may be too runny after you add the vinegar.

To make the pickled parsnip, thinly slice the parsnip lengthwise on a mandoline (see notes, page 73). Bring a small saucepan of salted water to a boil over high heat, add the parsnip slices, and blanch for a few seconds. Using a slotted spoon, transfer the slices to a small heatproof glass jar. Combine the vinegar, water, and sugar in a small saucepan and bring to a boil, stirring until the sugar has dissolved. Pour the hot liquid over the parsnip slices, immersing them. Let cool to room temperature, then cover and refrigerate for 24 hours.

To make the parsnip puree, melt the butter in a pressure cooker (see page 50) over medium heat and stir in the parsnips, baking soda, and salt, mixing well. Lock the lid in place and cook at medium-high pressure for 15 minutes, until the parsnips are caramelized to a dark golden brown and tender. Let the pressure release naturally for 15 minutes, then remove the lid.

While the parsnips are still hot, transfer them to a blender and process until a smooth, thick puree forms. Season with salt and vinegar. The puree should be smooth and easily pourable. If it is too thick, thin with a little water (see notes).

To make the parsnips, combine the parsnips, butter, and water in a saucepan and bring to a simmer over medium-low heat. Cook for 6 to 8 minutes, until all of the water evaporates and the parsnips begin to caramelize in the butter. Season with salt.

To serve, spoon some puree onto plate, top with a parsnip, and arrange some pickled parsnips alongside. Garnish with the shallot powder, roe, parsley, dill, watercress, and rye bread crumbs.

USING A PRESSURE COOKER

Pressure cooking has gained an unfortunate (and generally unwarranted) reputation as a dangerous cooking method in the home kitchen because of explosion horror stories. But any mishap is easily avoided with a little kitchen wisdom.

Every pressure cooker is different, so the first thing to do is to familiarize yourself with your cooker by reading the owner's manual from cover to cover. Some basic rules apply when using any pressure cooker, however. For example, never use less liquid than is called for in a recipe, though more liquid is generally okay. Cut the food into uniform pieces so that it will cook evenly, and if the first step is to caramelize the food, always scrape up the browned bits on the pot bottom to prevent scorching before adding liquid and moving on to the next step. Be sure to secure the lid in the locked position before you begin adding pressure to the cooker, and once the pressure is reached, moniter the time and the pressure level closely throughout the cooking process. Once the pressure is released according to the instructions in the recipe—either a quick release or by letting the pressure subside naturally—vigorously shake the cooker to lower the temperature inside before opening.

Here are a few additional tips: Fresh herbs work better in a pressure cooker than dried herbs because dried herbs are more intensely flavored and can overpower the other ingredients. When cooking legumes or grains, do not fill the pot more than half full, as they expand dramatically during cooking and can plug the vent pipe or other mechanism of the cooker. If you find that too much liquid remains after you have removed the lid, continue to cook in the open cooker until the liquid is reduced to your satisfaction.

CURED ARCTIC CHAR, BUTTERED POTATOES, MIXED SALAD, *and* SMOKED FRESH CHEESE

SERVES 4 | PREPARATION TIME: ABOUT 1 HOUR (PLUS 12 HOURS TO REFRIGERATE THE CHEESE)

Gunnar is an ardent meat and fish smoker, but he also enjoys smoking more unexpected items, such as cheese. He infuses it ever so lightly with smokiness by using a smoke gun to pipe wood smoke into it. It's a simple technique that works well with virtually anything you want to permeate with smoke, such as vegetables, sauces, or even ice creams, since the smoke carries very little heat. You can also play around with the smoking material used. For example, dried tree leaves of nearly any species or hay are good choices.

Don't be intimidated by the idea of making cheese at home. It's not as daunting as it sounds, and once you are comfortable with the technique, it's fun to mention to your guests that you made the cheese yourself. Plus, the process results in whey, which is also used here. The smoked cheese caramelizes nicely during the smoking process, which also makes it a fun and unexpected topping for ice cream. Like many Nordic chefs, Gunnar frequently cures his own fish, which, when paired with the fresh salad and the light texture of the cheese, makes for a lovely dish on a warm summer's day.

SMOKED FRESH CHEESE

1²/₃ cups (400 ml) milk

2 tablespoons plus 2 teaspoons cider vinegar, plus more as needed

Salt

Rapeseed oil, for seasoning

ARCTIC CHAR

1¹/₄ pounds (550 g) arctic char or salmon fillet (see notes, page 53)

Scant ¹/₂ cup (100 g) firmly packed light brown sugar

¹/₂ cup (80 g) rock salt (see notes, page 53)

2³/₄ ounces (80 g) mixed greens (such as birch tree leaves, dill, and angelica sprouts), finely chopped

2 tablespoons rapeseed oil

BUTTERED POTATOES

7 ounces (200 g) Yukon gold potatoes, unpeeled

2 tablespoons unsalted butter

Sea salt

MIXED SALAD

8 ounces (230 g) mixed lettuce and herb varieties that strike your fancy

Rapeseed oil, for dressing

Salt

Cider vinegar, for seasoning

Arctic char roe or salmon roe, for garnish

Rapeseed oil, for garnish

To make the smoked cheese, put the milk and vinegar in a small saucepan, stir to mix, and place over low heat. Heat to 189°F (87°C) and maintain the mixture at this temperature for about 5 minutes. The milk will separate completely into clumps of white curds and watery whey. Line a fine-mesh sieve with cheesecloth and place over a bowl. Pour the contents of the pan into the sieve and refrigerate for 12 hours.

| *continued*

| Cured Arctic Char, Buttered Potatoes, Mixed Salad, and Smoked Fresh Cheese, *continued*

NOTES

1. If your fish comes complete with skin, after you remove it, save it, cut it into bite-size pieces, and fry it up for a crunchy topping for the salad.

2. Rock salt is the workhorse of salts, ideal for curing fish, making salt crusts, and other culinary uses. It also has nonculinary uses, so look for food-grade rock salt to avoid rock salt that has been treated with chemicals.

Reserve the solids in the sieve and transfer the whey to a small, heavy saucepan. Place the pan over low heat and leave undisturbed for about 30 minutes, until the liquid begins to caramelize. Remove from the heat, pour into a heatproof bowl, and let cool to room temperature. As the liquid cools, it will stiffen to the texture of chocolate. Break it apart and reserve to use as a garnish.

Transfer the solids from the sieve to a hotel pan or deep baking pan and seal tightly with plastic wrap. Fill a smoke gun with wood chips and ignite the gun with a match. Make a small hole in the plastic wrap covering the pan, insert the nozzle of the gun through the hole, and smoke the cheese for 10 minutes. Alternatively, smoke the cheese in a wood chip–fueled homemade (see page 191) or store-bought kitchen smoker. Season the cheese with salt and drizzle with oil and vinegar to taste, then crumble to the consistency of dry ricotta.

To make the artic char, remove any skin and fat from the fish. Combine the sugar, rock salt, and greens in a bowl. Evenly distribute half of the sugar mixture in a shallow metal container just large enough to accommodate the char. Place the fish on top and cover it with the remaining curing mixture. Let stand at room temperature for 22 minutes. Remove the fish from the curing mixture and discard the mixture.

Preheat an immersion circulator to 127°F (53°C). Cut the char into 4 equal pieces, place the pieces and the oil in a vacuum bag, and seal on the medium setting. Cook in the circulator for 10 minutes. Remove the bag from the circulator, remove the fish from the bag, and keep warm. Alternatively, preheat the oven to 300°F (150°C) and line a baking sheet with parchment paper. Cut the char into 4 equal portions, rub (or spray) the bottom of each portion with rapeseed oil, and arrange on the prepared pan. Bake for 10 to 12 minutes, until medium-rare.

To make the potatoes, boil the potates in salted water to cover for 18 to 20 minutes, until just tender. Drain the potatoes, let cool just until they can be handled, and cut into disks 1/4 inch (6 mm) thick. Melt the butter in a sauté pan over medium heat, add the potatoes, and sauté for 3 to 5 minutes, until golden brown on both sides. Season with sea salt.

To make the mixed salad, toss together the lettuce and herbs with just enough oil to make them glisten. Season with salt and vinegar.

To serve, arrange the artic char, potatoes, and salad on a plate and garnish with the roe, the smoked cheese, the caramelized whey, and the oil.

Butter

MAKES ABOUT 1 POUND (450 G) | PREPARATION TIME: ABOUT 4 HOURS

Long ago, salt was an expensive commodity in Iceland (see page 256), which meant it was out of the reach of most people. The absence of easy access to salt as a preservative resulted in sour butter, a flavor favored by the palates of the time. So appealing was sour butter to the early settlers that it was used as a payment method for everything from rent to goods and services. It was also considered a nutritional powerhouse, and when stored properly, it would keep for years. There are accounts of twenty-year-old butter being sought out for its intense sour zing.

Although this recipe does not call for a twenty-year-long aging process, Icelandic butter is still highly prized by locals and visitors alike. Tourists often declare that Icelandic butter is the best butter they have ever tasted, and Icelanders are pretty sure that such testimonials are not just because visitors are invariably awestruck by the country's beauty. Icelandic dairy products are some of the richest, most nutritious in the world, and because the cows typically graze freely, eating pesticide-free hay and grasses, they produce velvety milk flush with flavor. It's no wonder that Iceland consumes more dairy per capita than almost any other country in the world. Since butter is all about the cream, it's important that you seek out organic cream with a high butterfat content for this recipe.

8$^1\!/_2$ cups (2 L) heavy cream

Sea salt (optional)

Pour the cream into the bowl of a stand mixer fitted with the whip attachment and mix on medium-high speed for about 10 minutes, until the butter solids separate from the liquid. To prevent splattering, cover the bowl with a kitchen towel. When you notice splashing in the bowl, it is time to turn off the mixer. Line a fine-mesh sieve with cheesecloth and place it over a bowl. Pour the contents of the mixer into the sieve and drain well. Reserve the liquid for another use (see note).

Transfer the butter solids to a bowl and knead with your hands for about 10 minutes to squeeze out any remaining liquid and to form a dense, shiny mass. If you want salted butter, add some salt as you knead. Form the butter into a ball or a block, put it in an airtight container, and refrigerate until chilled, about 4 hours. It will keep in the refrigerator for up to several months.

NOTE

The liquid, or buttermilk, adds a lively tang to pastry dough that calls for milk. It is also an excellent tenderizer and marinade for proteins, such as lamb and pork.

LICORICE LAVA

MAKES ABOUT 30 BITE-SIZE ROCKS | PREPARATION TIME: ABOUT 1 HOUR

Since the first day he opened Dill, Gunnar has been serving what he calls "sweet goodies." He often serves them before dinner as a way to build anticipation for the good things to come, and his Licorice Lava has been in the repertoire from the beginning. Perhaps no other sweet better represents the area of Lake Mývatn where Gylfi Yngvason smokes his arctic char. The otherworldly region is mapped by lava fields that stretch to the horizon of a world that feels more like the surface of the moon than somewhere on earth. Although the flinty texture of the Licorice Lava mirrors the porous lava stones that inspired it, don't be fooled by the airiness of this sweet. Its intense flavor will leave you wanting more.

1¼ cups (250 g) granulated sugar

½ cup (120 ml) water

1½ teaspoons egg whites

¼ cup (30 g) confectioners' sugar

3 g licorice powder (see note)

8 drops powdered black food coloring (see note)

Nonstick cooking spray

NOTE

Both licorice powder and black food coloring are available at specialty baking stores or online. The only word of warning when using the food coloring is to wear gloves, as it will stain your hands.

Combine the granulated sugar and water in a tall, heavy pot, place the pot over medium heat, and heat, stirring until the sugar dissolves. Once the sugar has dissolved, clip a candy thermometer to the side of the pan, stop stirring, and heat the mixture to 284°F (140°C).

Meanwhile, in a small bowl, whisk together the egg whites, confectioners' sugar, licorice powder, and food coloring until blended.

Line a heatproof bowl with aluminum foil, spray the oil with cooking spray, and wipe off the excess spray with a paper towel.

When the sugar mixture reaches 284°F (140°C), rapidly whisk in the egg white mixture until fully incorporated. Whisk at lightning speed to prevent the mixture from becoming a solid mass, letting the contents concurrently foam and rise to the top of the pot. As soon as it has reached its rising limit, which should take about 1 minute (including whisking time), immediately pour the mixture into the prepared bowl.

Let cool to room temperature, then break into bite-size rocks.

The rocks will keep in an airtight container at room temperature for up to 1 week.

THE RUGBRAUD BAKER

Lake Mývatn, North-Central Iceland

∞

Rye Beer Chips with Chive Skyr 66

Buttermilk Espuma, Pickled and Charred Cucumbers,
and Hay-Smoked Rye Bread Powder 68

Red Beet Pillows, Cider Vinegar Coins, Tarragon Cream,
and Rye Bread 72

Poor Man's Pear 74

Pickled Herring Ice Cream, Pickled Shallots,
and Rye Bread Crumble 76

It's easy to miss the lids. Their rusted metal surfaces blend so completely into the surrounding moonscape that only their rounded handles give them away. When lifted, the heavy covers reveal what at first appears to be nothing but a hole in the ground, until the geothermal smoke plume billowing up from inside clears to reveal more to the story. These are the geyser bread ovens of Iceland, passed down from one generation to the next, where sweet, dense rye bread known as *rugbraud*, or "geyser bread," has been baked in the same way for centuries.

The landscape on the north shore of Lake Mývatn is streaked in heaving, alluvial swirls of flaxen and rust that break at the edge of electric blue geothermal pools. The ovens rise above the lake on a gently sloping hill, where clouds of geothermal heat never subside and it is possible, even on the harshest winter day, to find warmth by standing in them. For generations, bakers of all ages have trudged through the countryside with their metal tins, waxed milk cartons, and, most recently, white plastic buckets filled with malty brown dough. In the past, every family had its own bread recipe, but modernization and inertia have battered that once-solid tradition.

Bakers still come to the geothermal ovens of Mývatn, though admittedly in smaller numbers. They do not arrive on foot as they once did, but they still carry their dough with them to their family ovens, where within twenty-four hours it is transformed from a thickened mass that looks like gingerbread into a dense rye loaf. The dough cooks slowly in the humid earth, absorbing the *terroir* of the unique topography. When the bread is ready, veteran and novice *rugbraud* bakers alike know that the best way to eat a slice is hot from the oven, slathered with creamy butter. It has been eaten this way from the beginning, and there is no point in fooling with perfection.

Gudny Halldórsdóttir was born in the remote northern village of Langanes in 1930 and, as so many young people do, left home to seek a better life. At nineteen, she spent the winter in a culinary training program at a private home in the town of Akureyri, known as the Capital of North Iceland. Her brother sold his Bible to buy her the book she needed for her studies, and with the burden of debt heavy on her shoulders, she moved farther east to Mývatn to work at a hotel run by her parents, who had relocated there a few years earlier. It was here that she learned how to bake geyser bread, walking back and forth from the ovens a few times each week with her metal baking case filled with dough.

At some point on her journey, Gudny married a local man, with whom she had five children. Today, she has eleven grandchildren and seven great-grandchildren, and although her life has changed dramatically since leaving her village more than six decades ago, one thing remains the same: she still bakes *rugbraud* in her inherited family ovens on the storied shores of Lake Mývatn.

A Conversation with Rugbraud Baker Gudny Halldórsdóttir

Q **Where did you learn to bake geyser bread?**

When I came to live in the Mývatn area in the 1950s, people were baking bread in the ground and I wanted to try it. I got a recipe for a sweet rye bread from a friend back home. I began by baking it in a standard oven, but I decided to start baking it in the ground in the late 1960s, and I have done it that way ever since.

Q **Do people in your community still bake it in the traditional way?**

Yes, people still do, even though they don't have to rely on geothermal energy any longer. Usually, if they are making *rugbraud*, they will bake it in the ground, never in a traditional oven.

Q **How do you construct an oven for geyser bread, and does each family have its own oven or do you share them?**

The walls need to be fortified with bricks, because the sides of the oven can cave in easily, and heavy metal plates are used as covers. Our family has two large ovens that my son dug in the late 1980s. Each one is about one meter [three feet] deep and one and a quarter to two meters [four by six feet] across. Each family tends to have its own oven, so there are very few bakers per oven.

Q **Do you know how old the geyser bread tradition is?**

I'm not sure how old the baking tradition is, but I do know it arose out of necessity during a time when there was no electricity and fuel was expensive. People had to rely on the heat in the ground to bake their daily bread.

Q **Has the tradition changed through the years?**

My grandfather told me that in the 1930s, teenagers were sent on foot to the ovens from as far away as five kilometers [three miles]. It was a difficult journey because there were very few roads. Today access to the ovens is easy. People also baked the bread differently. Each time they baked, they dug holes in the sulfur for holding the tightly sealed metal pots. Now we dig permanent holes in the clay.

Q **How much bread do you bake?**

We've been selling bread in local shops since the early 1980s, but we always keep a little bit for ourselves. During the busy summer months, we bake around forty kilograms [ninety pounds] of bread daily to fill the demand. But people who are just baking it for themselves make one to six kilograms [two to thirteen pounds] at a time. They then share it with their neighbors or freeze it for later use. A wax-coated paper milk carton holds just under a kilogram [two pounds] of bread, the classic size of a loaf.

Q **Do you use milk containers to bake your bread?**

No, because we produce so much, we have twenty liter-size [quart-size] sealed containers, each fitting one of our holes. People who are just baking bread for themselves tend to use milk containers. This technique has been around since the 1980s. An even more recent one is to use a round plastic bucket. Some still choose to do it like we did in the old days, using a tin or other metal pot with a good lid.

Q **Does each family have its own *rugbraud* recipe?**

Families used to but not as much nowadays. Today, many people use a standard *rugbraud* recipe that has stood the test of time.

Q **Do the seasons affect when you bake *rugbraud*?**

No, it doesn't depend on the season at all. The heat can drop temporarily if the winds get very strong, or a hole can disappear for no reason and people have to dig a new oven. But you can bake *rugbraud* even in the dead of winter.

Q **Why do you think the geyser bread tradition has endured?**

The benefits of baking bread in the ground are that it turns out softer than when you bake it in a conventional oven and it has almost no crust. It connects us to our past, too—plus, it's much more fun.

VISITING LAKE MÝVATN

Lake Mývatn, which stands in the center of northern Iceland, is one of the most mercurial places in the nation, and for a country that boasts a wealth of out-of-this-world natural beauty, that is quite an endorsement. The lake itself is surrounded by volcanoes that jut up from the dusty red terrain like a moonscape smoldering down to ashes. Algae balls that are green and soft like wet moss bob on the glassy surface of the lake. No one knows how they form or why, but because they exist only in Mývatn and one other lake in Japan, they are a rare and coveted sighting.

To the east of the lake are dozens of cone-shaped hot pots as tall as grown men, spewing blasts of geothermal steam from deep within the earth. Nothing is better on a frigid Icelandic day than to stand in a hot cloud of steam and inhale its warm, healing vapors. The nearby Mývatn geothermal baths offer another warm respite from the cold. Farther north are the geyser bread ovens, where local families bake their daily loaves of sweet rye.

RYE BEER CHIPS
with CHIVE SKYR

SERVES 4 | PREPARATION TIME: ABOUT 1 HOUR (PLUS 12 HOURS TO DEHYDRATE THE CHIPS)

Beer and bread are a natural combination, so what better way to showcase them than to combine them into one element of a recipe? Here, Gunnar adds beer to the rye bread before dehydrating it into chips. That flavor paired with the tanginess of skyr, a traditional thick, rich fresh cheese similar in consistency to Greek yogurt (see page 335), will make this one of your favorite snacks. There is a recipe for skyr in this book (page 162), but store-bought skyr, available at many major supermarkets, is a good substitute.

Chives are just one of the many flavorings that can be added to the skyr. At Icelandic Fish & Chips—an organic restaurant in downtown Reykjavík known for its fish breaded in the airiest spelt-and-barley batter—the kitchen has really upped the skyr dipping sauce game. Fish is served with seemingly endless dipping flavor options, including *tzatziki*, horseradish, honey mustard, and dill. It's an example of how fun it can be to play around with what you add to skyr, a rich and creamy ingredient that's ready for almost anything you want to stir into it. You can also add flavor to this snack by sprinkling seasonings into the bread and beer batter before you dehydrate it. Freshly grated nutmeg, dried herbs, and red pepper flakes are all excellent choices.

BEER CHIPS

7 ounces (200 g) rye or other dense, robustly flavored bread (such as pumpernickel or tangy sourdough)

1/2 cup (120 ml) India pale ale, plus more as needed

Skyr (page 162)

Finely chopped fresh chives, for garnish

To make the chips, preheat the oven to 185°F (85°C). Break up the bread into chunks, place in a food processor, and process until finely crumbled. Transfer the crumbs to a saucepan, pour in the ale, and bring to a gentle simmer over medium-low heat. Cook for about 15 minutes, until the bread is soft and has completely absorbed the beer.

Return the bread mixture to the food processor and process until smooth. Turn the batter out onto a baking sheet and spread in an even layer 3/4-inch (2-cm) thick. Bake for about 12 hours, until completely dry and crispy. Let cool to room temperature, then break into chips.

To serve, spoon skyr into a bowl and sprinkle with chives. Accompany the chips with the skyr.

BUTTERMILK ESPUMA, PICKLED *and* CHARRED CUCUMBERS, *and* HAY-SMOKED RYE BREAD POWDER

SERVES 4 TO 6 | PREPARATION TIME: ABOUT 1½ HOURS (PLUS UP TO 4 HOURS TO DRAIN BUTTERMILK AND 4 TO 6 HOURS TO AIR-DRY CUCUMBER PEEL AND FLESH) | PICTURED ON PAGE 70

Cucumbers were not cultivated by the earliest settlers in Iceland, but they are enjoyed by contemporary Icelanders, who primarily purchase those grown in the greenhouses that dot the countryside. Gunnar frequently uses cucumbers in his recipes, and because he is a stickler for never throwing away even the trimmings from a vegetable, he came up with the charred cucumber peels in this recipe. The charring brings out the natural sugars in the cucumber skins, resulting in a sweet taste reminiscent of dried orange peels. The pickled cucumber is bright and tart and pairs well with the tanginess of the buttermilk and with the nuttiness of the bread powder, which is also delicious sprinkled over ice cream.

BUTTERMILK ESPUMA

2 cups (480 ml) buttermilk

PICKLED CUCUMBER

1 large Kirby cucumber

6½ tablespoons (100 ml) malt vinegar

¼ cup (50 g) sugar

¾ teaspoon salt

CHARRED CUCUMBER

Reserved cucumber peel and flesh (from the pickled cucumber)

HAY-SMOKED RYE BREAD POWDER

1¾ ounces (50 g) rye bread, torn into bite-size pieces (2 loosely packed cups)

1 tablespoon unsalted butter, melted

Salt

About 4 handfuls of hay (see page 93)

Rapeseed oil, for garnish

To make the espuma, line a colander with a coffee filter and place over a bowl. Pour the buttermilk into the colander and let drain, refrigerated, for 4 hours, until it resembles a thickened crème anglaise. If it is too thick, whisk in some of the whey. Transfer the thickened buttermilk to a siphon and charge the siphon with 2 nitrous oxide (NO2) chargers according to the manufacturer's instructions. Shake the siphon vigorously and refrigerate until chilled (see notes).

To make the pickled cucumber, prepare an ice bath. Peel the cucumber and cut it lengthwise into sixths. Slice the seed area and a bit of the soft internal flesh into strips as long as the cucumber. Reserve the peel and soft internal flesh for the charred cucumber. Coarsely chop the external cucumber and transfer the pieces to a glass jar just large enough to

NOTES

1. A double layer of cheesecloth can be used in place of the coffee filter. If you do not have a siphon, just before serving, froth the buttermilk espuma with an immersion blender or whisk it vigorously. It will not be enough to create a true espuma (a thick foam or froth), but it will be enough to lighten and aerate the thickened buttermilk.

2. It is fine if the hay has not turned to ashes before you begin the smoking process. Billowing smoke from still-smoldering hay is sufficient.

contain them. Combine the vinegar, sugar, and salt in a small saucepan and bring to a simmer over medium heat, stirring until the sugar has dissolved. Pour the hot liquid over the cucumber, immersing it. Cover the jar loosely and place in the ice bath until chilled. Seal the jar tightly and refrigerate until ready to use.

To make the charred cucumber, thoroughly pat the reserved cucumber peel and flesh dry with paper towels. Arrange them as flatly as possible on a new set of paper towels and let them air-dry for 4 to 6 hours. Be sure the peel is completely dry, or it will curl during the charring process.

Arrange the peel and reserved soft internal flesh in a nonstick frying pan, place over low heat, and heat, turning the pieces over a few times to prevent uneven charring, for about 10 minutes, until the peel turns black and the flesh is charred. Remove from the pan and reserve.

To make the smoked bread powder, preheat the oven to 400°F (200°C). In a bowl, toss the bread pieces with the butter until evenly coated, season with salt, and arrange in a single layer on a baking sheet. Toast for 6 to 8 minutes, until the pieces are crisp on the outside but still soft and chewy on the inside. Transfer to a metal bowl.

Put the hay in a pot large enough to easily accommodate the bowl holding the bread, then ignite the hay with a kitchen torch. Once it has burned down to smoldering ashes (see notes), place the bowl on the hay to extinguish any remaining flame and cover the pot with either a tight-fitting lid or with aluminum foil. Be sure the flame is extinguished before smoking the bread or it will taste like jet fuel. Once the smoke has completely subsided, after about 5 minutes, remove the lid or foil, let the bread cool to room temperature, and then pulse to a coarse powder in a spice grinder.

To serve, dispense the espuma into a bowl and arrange the pickled and charred cucumber on top. Sprinkle with the bread powder and drizzle with oil.

OPPOSITE: Buttermilk Espuma, Pickled and Charred Cucumbers, and Hay-Smoked Rye Bread Powder (page 68)

ABOVE: Red Beet Pillows, Cider Vinegar Coins, Tarragon Cream, and Rye Bread (page 72)

RED BEET PILLOWS, CIDER VINEGAR COINS, TARRAGON CREAM, *and* RYE BREAD

SERVES 6 TO 8 | PREPARATION TIME: ABOUT 1 HOUR | PICTURED ON PAGE 71

These delightful beet pillows were inspired by Asian soup dumplings but have a strictly Icelandic flavor profile. Beets, a mainstay vegetable throughout the Nordic countries, are cleverly transformed into tiny pillows that are perfect for popping into your mouth at the start of a meal. The vinegar coins tickle the nose with their acidic aroma, while the tarragon cream mellows the dish. Such a miniature package defies the almost impossibly complex taste experience these pillows deliver and illustrates how much flavor can be realized using the most humble ingredients. At Dill, Gunnar serves his beet pillows on a stone foraged from the countryside. Stones are believed to possess healing properties in Iceland, which makes it fitting that they are paired with this renewing commencement to a meal.

RED BEET PILLOWS

1 red beet, 4 inches (10 cm) in diameter, peeled

Salt

Cider vinegar, for seasoning

Rapeseed oil, for seasoning

²/₃ cup (115 g) pickled red beets (page 298)

TARRAGON CREAM

1 egg

³/₄ cup (10 g) loosely packed fresh tarragon leaves, chopped

Dash of cider vinegar

Pinch of salt

1 cup (240 ml) rapeseed oil

VINEGAR COINS

¹/₂ cup (120 ml) cider vinegar

2 teaspoons sugar

1 g high-acyl gellan gum (see notes)

2 sprigs tarragon

CRISPY RYE BREAD

1³/₄ ounces (50 g) rye bread (1 slice)

1 teaspoon unsalted butter, melted

Salt

NOTES

1. Gellan gum is a water-soluble food additive that is often used as a thickener in place of sheet gelatin. There are two types of gellan gum: high-acyl and low-acyl. The low-acyl variety results in an extremely firm, crumbly product. High-acyl gellan gum results in a substance that is elastic and flexible, which is why high-acyl is used in this recipe. It is available online and in many specialty food stores.

To make the beet pillows, slice the beet as thinly as possible on a mandoline (see notes). Prepare an ice bath. Bring a saucepan of water to a boil over high heat, add the beet slices, and blanch for 2 seconds. Using a slotted spoon, transfer the beet slices to the ice bath, immersing them. Let stand until chilled. Drain the slices and pat thoroughly dry with paper towels.

In a bowl, toss the beet slices with a little salt, vinegar, and oil until well coated. Arrange the slices on a clean work surface to ready them for filling.

Put the pickled beets in a blender and process until they are the consistency of couscous.

To make the tarragon cream, prepare an ice bath. Bring a small saucepan of water to a lively simmer over medium-high heat. Using a slotted spoon, lower the egg into the water and cook it in the gently rolling water for 4 minutes. Transfer the egg to the ice bath and

NOTES, continued

2. A Japanese mandoline is one of the handiest tools a home cook can have in his or her kitchen arsenal. The only caveat about this inexpensive and easy-to-use tool is that you must watch out for your fingers as you slice vegetables into uniformly thin segments with the saber-sharp blades. One way to stay safe is to wear a double layer of latex kitchen gloves as you work. Another way is not to hold the vegetable with your fingers as you cut. Instead, use your palm to guide the vegetable back and forth, as it is less likely to come in contact with the blades.

3. Pouring the vinegar liquid onto a small plate rather than a larger one ensures that it will not be too thin and difficult to cut once it has set.

leave until well chilled. Remove the egg from the ice bath and immediately crack it lightly on all sides on a flat surface. Peel the egg, put it in the blender, and add the tarragon, vinegar, and salt. Process on medium-high speed until fully blended, then add the oil in a slow, steady stream and process until the consistency of a thick mayonnaise. Taste and adjust with salt and vinegar if needed.

To make the beet pillows, combine two-thirds of the tarragon cream and processed pickled beets in a bowl and mix well. Place a 1-inch (2.5-cm) dollop of the mixture in the center of a beet slice, then bring the sides up around the filling and pinch them together like a coin purse. The pillow should resemble a miniature Asian soup dumpling. Repeat with the remaining slices and filling. Refrigerate until ready to use.

To make the vinegar coins, prepare an ice bath. Combine the vinegar, sugar, gellan, and tarragon in a saucepan, place over medium heat, and heat to 185°F (85°C). Simmer at this temperature for 1 minute, skimming off any foam from the surface as it forms. Remove the pan from the heat and nest it in the ice bath until the liquid is chilled. Pour the cooled liquid into a thin layer onto a small, flat plate about 10 inches (25 cm) in diameter (see notes) and refrigerate until chilled and fully set. Using a ring cutter slightly smaller than the beet pillows (about the size of a penny), punch out disks and top each pillow with one. The coins are delicate and brittle, and a small offset spatula works best for this step, but a paring knife works well, too.

To make the crispy rye bread, preheat the oven to 325°F (165°C). Cut the bread into $1/2$-inch (12-mm) pieces and put in a bowl. Add the butter, toss until evenly coated, and season with salt. Arrange in a single layer on a baking sheet and toast in the oven for about 9 minutes, until crispy. Cool to room temperature.

To serve, using an offset spatula, top each beet pillow with a vinegar coin, dot with the remaining tarragon cream, and sprinkle with the crispy rye bread.

POOR MAN'S PEAR

MAKES 1 LARGE JAR | PREPARATION TIME: 3 WEEKS

Pears are expensive in Iceland, but rhubarb is abundant throughout the country, where the stalks grow to heights rarely seen elsewhere in the world. The outsize stalks are due to the lack of sun, which ensures a long, slow growing season. This recipe is Gunnar's exchange of a luxury item for one that is easily accessible to anyone. It is democratization of produce in action and is as appealing as a pear could ever be. The flavor is tender and sweet, with a hint of tartness from the vinegar. Ice cream is a nice companion, as is a soft fresh cheese like ricotta. Gunnar often serves his "pears" at Dill with fresh cream and crispy rye bread powder.

14 ounces (400 g) rhubarb stalks, pale, tender portion only

2 cups (480 ml) cider vinegar

1¹/₂ cups (300 g) sugar

1 sprig tarragon

Using the white portion only, trim each stalk into pieces that will fit inside a large wide-mouthed glass jar, then arrange the pieces in the jar. Combine the vinegar, sugar, and tarragon in a saucepan and bring to a boil over medium heat, stirring until the sugar has dissolved. Pour the hot liquid over the rhubarb pieces, immersing them (see note). Let cool to room temperature, then cover tightly and store in a cool, dark place for 3 weeks before using.

NOTE

If the rhubarb floats to the surface as the liquid cools, use a small bowl, plate, or kitchen weight to keep it immersed in the liquid to ensure it pickles properly.

PICKLED HERRING ICE CREAM, PICKLED SHALLOTS, *and* RYE BREAD CRUMBLE

MAKES 1 QUART (1 L) ICE CREAM AND ENOUGH GARNISH TO SERVE 4
| PREPARATION TIME: ABOUT 2 HOURS (PLUS 12 HOURS TO FREEZE THE ICE CREAM,
8 DAYS TO PICKLE THE HERRING, AND 1 WEEK TO PICKLE THE SHALLOTS)

If there is any recipe in this cookbook that might sound unappetizing, it is this one. The trick is to get over the term *ice cream* in the title and think of this as a savory dish that celebrates Iceland's most famous fish and that also happens to be a dessert. The cool creaminess of the ice cream pairs exceptionally well with the brininess of the fish, and the pickling technique employed for both the shallots and the herring adds an extra layer of whimsy. Indeed, whimsy is what this dish is all about. It's one of the first recipes Gunnar served at Dill, and it illustrates not only the playful way that he approaches his food but also his desire to showcase Iceland's most traditional ingredients in new and innovative ways. Getting over your reluctance to try something called herring ice cream promises to deliver a satisfying conversation piece that your guests will be talking about long after the ice cream has been eaten.

PICKLED SHALLOTS

2 shallots, bulbs separated and cut crosswise into thin rings

1/2 cup (120 ml) distilled white vinegar

1/4 cup (60 ml) water

3 tablespoons plus 1/2 teaspoon sugar

PICKLED HERRING

1/4 cup (65 g) salt

5 cups (1.2 L) water

8 ounces (225 g) herring fillets, cut into bite-size pieces

2 cups (480 ml) distilled white vinegar

1/4 cup (50 g) sugar

1 1/2 tablespoons yellow mustard seeds

2 tablespoons whole allspice

3 bay leaves

3 whole cloves

1 red onion, thinly sliced

1 carrot, peeled and thinly sliced

3/4 ounce (20 g) fresh dill (about 1/3 bunch)

PICKLED HERRING ICE CREAM

Pickled herring (above)

1 cup (240 ml) milk

1 cup (240 ml) heavy cream

1/4 cup (50 g) sugar

1 1/2 tablespoons liquid glucose (see notes)

2 teaspoons trimoline (see notes)

4 teaspoons ice cream stabilizer (see notes)

1 sheet gelatin, soaked in cold water to cover until softened, then squeezed to remove excess water

BUTTER

1/3 cup (80 g) unsalted butter, at room temperature

4 teaspoons buttermilk

1/4 cup (30 g) minced vegetables from herring pickling juice

Sea salt (optional)

RYE BREAD CRUMBLE

3 1/2 ounces (100 g) rye bread

1 tablespoon unsalted butter, melted

Salt

Sour cream, for garnish

NOTES

1. Glucose, trimoline (invert sugar syrup), and ice cream stabilizer are products that contribute to the sweetness and velvety creaminess of the ice cream. They can be easily sourced online or at some specialty food stores.

2. The Pacojet is a professional-restaurant kitchen appliance that purees frozen foods without thawing them, yielding a particularly creamy consistency. A home ice cream maker can be substituted. Freeze in an ice cream maker according to the manufacturer's instructions, then transfer to an airtight container, place in the freezer, and freeze for about 12 hours, until frozen solid.

To make the pickled shallots, prepare an ice bath. Bring a saucepan of salted water to a boil, add the shallots, and blanch for 1 second. Using a slotted spoon, transfer the shallots to the ice bath, immersing them. Let stand until chilled, then drain and place in a small heatproof glass jar. Combine the vinegar, water, and sugar in a small saucepan and bring to a boil over medium heat, stirring until the sugar has dissolved. Pour the hot liquid over the shallots, immersing them. Let cool to room temperature, then cover and refrigerate for at least 1 week before using. The shallots will keep in the refrigerator for up to 1 month.

To make the pickled herring, prepare an ice bath. Combine the salt and 3¾ cups (900 ml) of the water in a saucepan and bring to a boil over high heat. When the salt has dissolved, remove the pan from the heat and nest it in the ice bath until the liquid is chilled. Arrange the herring fillets in a container and pour the salted water on top, immersing them completely. Cover with a tightly fitting lid or aluminum foil and refrigerate for 24 hours.

When the herring is ready, prepare an ice bath. In a saucepan, combine the remaining 1¼ cups (300 ml) of water with the vinegar, sugar, mustard seeds, allspice, bay leaves, cloves, onion, carrot, and dill and bring to a boil over high heat. Turn down the heat to medium-high and simmer for 2 minutes. Remove the pan from the heat and nest it in the ice bath until the liquid is chilled.

Drain the herring fillets and place in a glass jar. Pour in the chilled pickling liquid, immersing the herring. Cover tightly and refrigerate for at least 1 week before using. The herring will keep in the refrigerator for up to 1 month.

To make the ice cream, drain the pickled herring, reserving the solids and liquid separately.

Separate the herring from the vegetables and reserve both. Measure 1¾ ounces (50 g) of the pickled herring for the ice cream and reserve the remainder for serving. Measure 1 cup (240 ml) of the pickling liquid, pour it into a saucepan, add the milk and cream, and bring to a simmer over medium-high heat. Add the sugar, glucose, trimoline, ice cream stabilizer, and gelatin and continue to simmer gently, stirring for about 1 minute, until all of the ingredients have dissolved and are fully incorporated. Do not allow to boil. Taste and season with additional pickling liquid if the flavor is too sweet.

| continued

| Pickled Herring Ice Cream, Pickled Shallots, and Rye Bread Crumble, *continued*

Transfer to a blender, add the 1³/₄ ounces (50 g) of pickled herring, and process until smooth.

Taste once again and season with pickling liquid as needed to create a tart and tangy flavor. Transfer to Pacojet beakers (see notes, page 77) and freeze for 12 hours. Process according to the manufacturer's instructions in a Pacojet.

To make the butter, using a stand mixer or handheld mixer fitted with the whip attachment, whip the butter on high speed until light and fluffy. Fold in the buttermilk and pickled vegetables until incorporated. Season with sea salt. Pour the butter into a shallow container and smooth the surface with an offset spatula. Cover and refrigerate until chilled, then punch out small disks using your smallest round cutter.

To make the rye bread crumble, preheat the oven to 325°F (165°C). Tear the bread into pieces, put them in the blender or a food processor, and process until crumbs form. Transfer to a bowl, add the butter, and toss until evenly coated, then season with salt. Spread on a baking sheet and toast in the oven for 4 to 6 minutes, until crisp.

To serve, spoon quenelles of the ice cream onto plates and add the pickled herring and pickled shallots alongside. Sprinkle with the rye bread crumble and dot with the butter disks and sour cream.

HERRING: SILVER OF THE SEA

Herring is more than a fish to Iceland. It is affluence, wealth, prestige, and power—or at least it was during the boom years of the first half of the twentieth century, when thousands of people flocked to Iceland's northern shores to stake their claim in a gold rush measured in gills and scales. Hundreds of ships unloaded their "silver of the sea" on the shore, where "herring girls" packed fish in brine or salt in wooden barrels, which were then shipped around the globe.

No one imagined an end to the silver shoals of herring that seemed to continuously brighten the sea. But then, in 1969, the nets came up empty and the rush was over. Overfishing shuttered the doors of the herring factories, a disaster that initiated the strict regulations the country's fishing industry follows today. Those laws ensure that there will never be another herring boom and that there will always be herring off the shores of Iceland.

THE FISHERMAN

Grímsey Island, Arctic Circle

∞

Fish Stock 88

Chicken Stock 89

Veal Stock 90

Pickled Fennel, Mustard Seeds, and Beer 91

Smoked Haddock, Dark Cod Consommé, Raw Vegetables,
and Yesterday's Bread 94

Lumpfish Roe, Smoked Mayonnaise, Beer Vinegar Jelly,
and Horseradish Cream 98

Plaice, Tarragon Tempura, and Fennel 100

Tea-Poached Skate, Braised Kale, Shallot Puree, and Skyr 104

Baked Plaice, Shrimp, Roasted Cauliflower Puree,
and Salted Almonds 108

Few people in their mid-twenties would decide to trade in their life as a university student with a promising career ahead of them to become fishermen on one of the coldest and most remote islands in the world. Sacrificing inevitable success in the comfortable city of Reykjavík for a precarious life at sea on the Arctic Circle seems a fool's game. But David Sigurdsson had an epiphany in which he realized that he did not define success by the size of the office cubicle he would work in one day or the expensive car he would likely drive if he continued studying economics.

Success was more than that, and it was worth leaving behind what was safe to pursue his dream. It had been a fleeting vision ever since he was a young boy listening to his grandfather's stories of how harrowing and rewarding a life at sea could be. It gained more clarity when his brothers recalled adventures of fishing on the Bering Sea. In time, fulfilling the dream became more important to David than anything else.

He is a descendant of a long line of fishermen, and the impulse to listen to his deepest desires eventually led him to Grímsey Island, where he met fishing-boat captain Siggi Henningsson. Siggi has changed David's life by imparting wisdom gleaned from decades at sea and by illustrating day after day that the decision to be a fisherman is a noble and dignified one.

David now thrives in his work, and even during those inevitable times when loneliness and homesickness come crashing down on him, he finds renewal each morning as he leaves the marina with Siggi, a hot cup of coffee in hand, the sun just finding its way above the horizon, and the sea stretched out before him. His days have a sense of integrity and honesty that they never had before. The memory of his past life in Reykjavík doing what everyone else expected of him but he never wanted for himself fades a little more each dawn as he sets out to find the fish.

A Conversation with Fisherman David Sigurdsson

Q **Did you always plan to be a fisherman?**

No, I was actually studying economics at the university in Reykjavík before I decided to become a fisherman. My grandfather and cousins were fishermen, but my father wasn't, so it ended up skipping a generation. My father was an electrical engineer and my mother comes from a long line of fishermen, but I think she thought I would have a better life doing something other than fishing. Once I made the decision to do it, I didn't tell her about it for four months, because I knew she would be upset. It was easy to keep the secret for a while, as she lives in Seattle. I was nervous about telling her, and at first she reacted the way I thought she would. But now she sees that I love my job, and I think she has come to peace with my decision.

Q **Why did you make the decision to move to Grímsey and fish?**

I was the youngest child, and my parents let my older brothers get away with a lot. Each one fished on the Bering Sea for ten years, and my parents were always worried about them. With me they were much more protective and wouldn't let me do anything. Now I'm a fisherman and I have all the freedom I want. The fishing tradition is engrained in our society. It's in our blood, and it's who we are. I am at peace now that I'm out on the water. I feel connected to my ancestors in a way I never would have if I had made the decision to work in a cubicle my entire life. I get back to Reykjavík three to four times a year, but that's enough. I like my life now.

Q **What is the most difficult aspect to being a fisherman on the Arctic Circle?**

The hardest part is waking up in the morning before dawn, but once I'm awake and out on the water, I love every part of it. The rocking of the boat is so soothing, and even though the work is hard, it's honest and rewarding and produces results every single day. You can't beat that kind of job. Sometimes it does get lonely here. I miss my friends and family, but it's always the people I miss, never my old lifestyle. In my other life, I always felt confused and empty. But now I feel like each day has a meaning and a purpose. I have a sense of direction I never had before, and I am calm and relaxed out here on the water.

Q How did you meet Siggi Henningsson, the owner of the fishing boat?

When I moved to Grímsey, I didn't yet have a job as a fisherman, so I was working in the local fish market. A few years ago he took me on as his first mate. It's just the two of us, and I've learned so much from him. His family owns two boats, and I feel honored to be a part of it. This boat is named after his grandfather, who was lost at sea fishing on a boat with sails. The family has a long fishing history in Grímsey, and he is so knowledgeable about every aspect of the industry. His brother Henning owns the fish-processing warehouse on the island, so I'm learning about that aspect of the business, too. I've also learned about fishing quotas from Siggi. The government regulates your taxes based on how much fish you catch and how much it's selling for at the market. It also puts a limit on how much you can catch. It's a very strict system.

Q What's a typical day like for you?

We set out at between three and four o'clock in the morning. The distance we go out varies depending on the weather and the season. Sometimes we go out from the harbor only three to four miles; other times we travel up to forty miles to find the fish. The lines used to be baited by hand, but now we use an electric baiting machine. The bait is from Asia, and we usually use squid. On average, we put out twelve lines a day in different spots, and each one contains six hundred hooks. They're dropped at between sixty and six hundred feet, and there's so much lava on the ocean floor, that it's easy for the lines to get caught up in it, which can be a real headache.

We leave the lines out for two and a half to three hours and then pull them up. We process each fish differently, depending on what it is. Skate is thrown back, as there's not much market demand for it. The exception is Christmastime, when many families traditionally eat fermented skate on December 23. Some days are boom times, with the fish flying in. On other days, we catch next to nothing, which can be depressing. But that's the life of a fisherman. You never know.

Q Do you ever miss your old life?

I do get cabin fever sometimes living on such a small island, but then I get back on the water and that feeling disappears. It's a good life.

VISITING GRÍMSEY ISLAND

Travel to remote Grímsey requires either a short plane ride from the northern mainland town of Akureyri or a longer flight from Reykjavík (daily in summer and less frequently in winter) or a three-hour ferry ride (a few times weekly in summer and less often in winter) from the northern mainland town of Dalvík, about a five-hour drive from Reykjavík. The trip through the North Atlantic can be choppy, so be prepared with motion-sickness medication, even if you're not prone to seasickness. The rocky tossing can bring down even someone with the most stalwart constitution.

Once you arrive, everything is within a short walk of the ferry terminal, including what most people come to do: visit the sign indicating the line of the Arctic Circle that slices through the island. There's one restaurant on Grímsey serving a variety of beer and spirits and local specialties like seabird, whale steaks, and seabird eggs boiled to order, plus continental offerings for the less adventurous. Next door is a sundries market, and a few steps away are the only two guesthouses on the island, both of which are inviting.

Most people arrive on the noon ferry and leave four hours later when it departs, but for those inclined to dig deeper into a place, staying overnight affords experiences that you won't soon forget. Perhaps you will take in a cake auction at the local town hall, or you'll watch a seabird-egg collector as he descends the side of an impossibly tall cliff overlooking an ominous sea. Island life can feel remote and desolate if you let the isolation of it all creep in. But if you allow yourself to marvel at the strength and kinship of the local community, your faith in the resiliency, resourcefulness, and will of the human spirit will be renewed, and you will leave yearning for another visit to Grímsey.

FISH STOCK

MAKES ABOUT 12 CUPS (2.8 L) | PREPARATION TIME: 1³/₄ HOURS

Fish stock is a natural by-product of the fish that is caught on Grímsey. In this recipe, Gunnar's addition of fennel adds a subtle anise flavor, and the celery root delivers an earthy counterpoint to the fennel. Be sure to rinse the fish bones well under cold running water to rid them of any blood and residue, or the stock will be cloudy and have an off flavor. Like the other stocks in this book, this stock can be frozen. Your future cooking self will thank you later for making a large batch of it.

1 bay leaf

2 sprigs arctic thyme

5 pounds (2.3 kg) fish bones

Rapeseed oil, for sautéing

1³/₄ ounces (50 g) coarsely chopped leek, (white and light green parts only)

1³/₄ ounces (50 g) coarsely chopped shallots

1 ounce (30 g) coarsely chopped celery

1 ounce (30 g) peeled and coarsely chopped celery root

1 ounce (30 g) coarsely chopped fennel bulb

³/₄ cup (180 ml) dry white wine

Wrap the bay leaf and thyme in a piece of cheesecloth and tightly secure with butcher's twine. Rinse the fish bones under cold running water. Pat dry with paper towels and chop coarsely.

Lightly coat the bottom of a stockpot with oil and place over medium heat. Add the leek, shallots, celery, celery root, and fennel and sauté for about 15 minutes, until tender but not caramelized. Add the bones, wine, cheesecloth bundle, and water to cover by 2 inches (5 cm) and bring to a simmer. Cook uncovered at a gentle simmer for 30 minutes. Skim the surface, then remove the pot from the heat and let sit, covered, at room temperature for 45 minutes.

Prepare an ice bath. Strain the stock through a fine-mesh sieve into a large bowl or other large vessel. Nest the bowl in the ice bath until chilled, then transfer the stock to 1 or more airtight containers and refrigerate for up to 1 week or freeze for up to 1 month.

CHICKEN STOCK

MAKES ABOUT 12 CUPS (2.8 L) | PREPARATION TIME: ABOUT 6 HOURS

This is Gunnar's go-to stock for countless recipes. Be sure to roast the bones until they are golden brown but not black, or they will impart a charred flavor to the stock.

1 bay leaf

1 sprig arctic thyme

1 whole clove

5¹/₂ pounds (2.5 kg) chicken bones, roasted (see note)

3¹/₂ ounces (100 g) leek, coarsely chopped (white and light green parts)

1³/₄ ounces (50 g) coarsely chopped shallots

1³/₄ ounces (50 g) coarsely chopped celery

1³/₄ ounces (50 g) peeled and coarsely chopped celery root

1³/₄ ounces (50 g) coarsely chopped fennel bulb

NOTE

Roasting the bones imparts a rich caramelized note to the stock. To do so, preheat the oven to 350°F (180°C) and arrange the bones on a dry baking sheet. Roast until deeply golden brown in color, about 25 minutes.

Wrap the bay leaf, thyme, and clove in a piece of cheesecloth and tightly secure with butcher's twine.

Put the bones in a stockpot, add water to cover by 2 inches (5 cm), and bring to a simmer, skimming off any residue from the surface. Add the leek, shallots, celery, celery root, fennel, and the cheesecloth bundle.

Simmer for 3 hours, uncovered, skimming the surface every 30 minutes. Remove the pot from the heat and let sit, covered, at room temperature for 2 hours. Skim the surface of any residue.

Prepare an ice bath. Strain the stock through a fine-mesh sieve into a large bowl or other large vessel. Nest the bowl in the ice bath until chilled. Transfer the stock to 1 or more airtight containers and refrigerate for up to 1 week or freeze for up to 1 month.

VEAL STOCK

MAKES ABOUT 4 QUARTS (3.8 L) | PREPARATION TIME: ABOUT 6 HOURS

In Icelandic kitchens, lamb bones are frequently substituted for veal bones. Each type contains a substantial amount of gelatin, which thickens the stock as it is leached from the bones during cooking. When sourcing the bones, try to secure a mix of feet, breast, and leg bones. The feet contain the most gelatin, so be sure to seek out as many as you can to ensure a rich and viscous result.

1 bay leaf

1 sprig arctic thyme

4 cloves

5¹/₂ pounds (2¹/₂ kg) veal bones, roasted

3¹/₂ ounces (100 g) coarsely chopped yellow onions

1³/₄ ounces (50 g) coarsely chopped shallots

1³/₄ ounces (50 g) coarsely chopped celery

1³/₄ ounces (50 g) peeled and coarsely chopped celery root

1³/₄ ounces (30 g) coarsely chopped fennel bulb

Wrap the bay leaf, thyme, and cloves in a piece of cheesecloth and tightly secure with butcher's twine. Put the bones in a pot, add water to cover by 2 inches (5 cm), and bring to a simmer, skimming off any residue from the surface. Add the onion, shallots, celery, celery root, fennel, and the cheesecloth bundle. Simmer for 3 hours, uncovered, skimming the surface every 30 minutes. Remove the pot from the heat and let sit, covered, at room temperature for 2 hours. Skim the surface of any residue.

Prepare an ice bath. Strain the stock through a fine-mesh sieve into a large bowl or other large vessel. Nest the bowl in the ice bath until chilled. Transfer the stock to 1 or more airtight containers and refrigerate for up to 1 week or freeze for up to 1 month.

PICKLED FENNEL, MUSTARD SEEDS, *and* BEER

MAKES ABOUT 1 QUART (960 ML) | PREPARATION TIME: ABOUT 30 MINUTES (PLUS 1 WEEK TO PICKLE THE FENNEL)

Fennel pickled in beer mellows the anise flavor of the vegetable and infuses the liquid with a subtle licorice note. Gunnar uses a dark Icelandic beer called Móri that has a hint of caramel running through it, but any dark porter will work. This side dish is delightfully flexible, pairing well with everything from duck breast, beef roast, or pork loin to roasted chicken. It's also nice with mashed potatoes or fish from Grímsey, which is Gunnar's preference. Onions are a good substitution for the fennel and can be prepared in the same manner.

1 pound (450 g) fennel bulbs

1 to 3 sprigs dill

1 cup (240 ml) cider vinegar

2/3 cup (150 ml) dark beer (such as porter or stout)

1 cup (200 g) sugar

1 1/2 tablespoons brown mustard seeds

1 1/2 tablespoons yellow mustard seeds

Salt

Prepare an ice bath. Bring a saucepan of salted water to a boil over high heat. While the water is heating, cut off the stalks and fronds from each fennel bulb and trim the bottom. Cut each bulb in half lengthwise, leaving the core intact so the halves hold together. Drop the halved bulbs into the boiling water and simmer for about 4 minutes. Using a slotted spoon, transfer the bulbs to the ice bath, immersing them. Let stand until chilled. Drain the bulbs, place them in a large, widemouthed glass jar, and add the dill.

Combine the vinegar, beer, and sugar in a saucepan and bring to a boil over medium heat, stirring until the sugar has dissolved. Add the mustard seeds, remove from the heat, season with salt, and pour the hot liquid over the fennel and dill, immersing them. You may need to weight the fennel down with a small bowl, plate, or kitchen weight to keep it immersed in the liquid as the liquid cools. Let cool to room temperature, then cap tightly and store in a cool place for 1 week before using.

HAY SMOKING

Hay has been a fundamental part of Icelandic agriculture since the arrival of the first settlers in their longships. Gunnar transports the pastoral aroma of the Icelandic countryside into his kitchen by hay smoking everything from arctic char and cheese to lamb and oil. The technique is a simple one, but the resulting flavor and aroma are immense. Sometimes for dramatic effect, Gunnar will fill a barrel to the brim with hay, position it in front of Dill's floor-to-ceiling windows, with the restaurant's bird sanctuary visible behind it, and then ignite the hay. It's a sight to behold, as the senses awake to the sweet smell of hay filling every corner of the restaurant.

If you live outside of a metropolitan area, sourcing hay may not be as difficult as you might think. A local farmer will likely be happy to sell you a bale of hay, and it's a good way to make friends with a neighbor. A bale is a large amount of hay to contend with, but if you have a garage, store it there and then just grab a few handfuls whenever you want to to do a little hay smoking. If you live in a city, going on a day trip in search of a hay supply can be a challenging and fun experience.

SMOKED HADDOCK, DARK COD CONSOMMÉ, RAW VEGETABLES, *and* YESTERDAY'S BREAD

SERVES 4 | PREPARATION TIME: ABOUT 2 HOURS | PICTURED ON PAGE 96

One of the workhorse fish of Icelandic cuisine, haddock is enjoyed both fresh and smoked. Smoked haddock should be easy to source from most fishmongers, but if finding it proves a challenge, any smoked white fish can be used in this recipe. Just before serving, the fish is broken into pieces and added to the consommé, which warms it and infuses it with flavor. The hay smoked oil is not necessary, but the hay does impart a pleasing pastoral note. Dried leaves or wood chips can be used in place of the hay. Gunnar uses cod bones in his consommé, but the bones from the smoked haddock will suffice. Using the bread from yesterday (or any stale bread you have on hand) is a good way to use up an ingredient that might otherwise be tossed out and reflects Gunnar's resourceful nature.

DARK COD CONSOMMÉ

Head and bones from 1 small cod (about 8 ounces/225 g), cut into small pieces

1 small carrot, peeled and coarsely chopped

1/2 small celery root, peeled and coarsely chopped

1/4 fennel bulb, thinly sliced

2 celery stalks, thinly sliced

2 shallots, thinly sliced

5 sprigs lemon thyme

Salt

YESTERDAY'S BREAD

1 1/2 ounces (40 g) day-old bread, torn into bite-size pieces

1 1/2 teaspoons unsalted butter, melted

Salt

RAW VEGETABLES

Celery root, peeled and coarsely chopped

Radishes, thinly sliced

Small carrot, peeled and thinly sliced

Green (unripe) strawberries (see notes)

Sorrel leaves, torn

Rapeseed oil, for seasoning

Salt

Cider vinegar, for seasoning

SMOKED HADDOCK

8 ounces (225 g) smoked haddock fillet

1 tablespoon rapeseed oil

Salt

Hay-Smoked Oil (page 233), for drizzling

To make the consommé, place a frying pan over medium-high heat. When the pan is hot, add the cod head and bones and fry, stirring often, until very dark but not burned. Transfer the contents of the frying pan to a saucepan, add water to cover by 2 inches (5 cm), and bring to a boil over medium-high heat, skimming any residue that forms on the surface. Lower the heat to medium to maintain a slow, steady simmer and add the carrot, celery root, fennel, celery, shallots, and lemon thyme. Continue to simmer, uncovered, for 45 minutes, skimming the surface as necessary.

Prepare an ice bath. When the consommé is ready, remove the pan from the heat and nest it in the ice bath until the consommé is chilled, skimming the surface as it cools. Strain through a fine-mesh sieve into a container, season with salt, cover, and refrigerate, then reheat gently just before serving (see notes).

NOTES

1. When it is time to reheat the consommé, place it over very low heat to prevent it from boiling or even simmering. If the consommé is agitated, foam will form on the surface and cloud its clarity.

2. Unripe (green) strawberries are frequently used in Iceland, and although they are not necessary for this dish, they do impart a bright flavor note. If you cannot find them, any tart fruit, such as a green apple or barely ripe plums or peaches, will work.

To make yesterday's bread, preheat the oven to 350°F (180°C). In a bowl, toss the bread with the butter until well coated. Spread the bread in a single layer on a baking sheet and toast for about 5 minutes, until the edges of the pieces are just starting to crisp. Season with salt and let cool to room temperature.

To make the raw vegetables, combine the celery root, radishes, carrot, strawberries, and sorrel in the amounts desired in a bowl, then toss with just enough oil to make them glisten. Season with salt and vinegar.

To make the smoked haddock, break up the fish into small flakes, removing any errant bones or skin. In a bowl, toss the fish with the oil until well coated, then season with salt.

To serve, spoon the warmed consommé into a bowl with a wide lip and drizzle with the hay smoked oil. Arrange the bread, vegetables, and haddock on the lip and invite guests to mix them into their consommé as they like.

ABOVE: Smoked Haddock, Dark Cod Consommé, Raw Vegetables, and Yesterday's Bread (page 94)

OPPOSITE: Dried onion peels (page 250)

LUMPFISH ROE, SMOKED MAYONNAISE, BEER VINEGAR JELLY, *and* HORSERADISH CREAM

SERVES 4 | PREPARATION TIME: ABOUT 4 HOURS

Everything is saved at Dill and that includes onion peels. The staff dries them by collecting them in a container near the oven and letting the oven's residual heat do the work. It takes a few days to dry the peels completely. If you live in a humid area, it will probably take longer. Garlic peels work well, too.

The vinegar jelly in this recipe makes for an elegant presentation, but if you want to forgo this step, reducing the vinegar by half and drizzling it over the finished dish is an easy alternative. Salmon roe can be substituted for the lumpfish roe in the smoked mayonnaise, and the mayonnaise, with or without the roe, is also delicious on sandwiches. The use of grated fresh horseradish in this recipe reflects Gunnar's desire to create dishes with big flavors. Be conservative when grating, as the horseradish can really make your nose tickle if you add too much.

SMOKED OIL

1 cup (240 ml) rapeseed oil

Completely dried peels from about 6 large onions, plus more if more than one smoking is desired (see page 250)

SMOKED MAYONNAISE WITH LUMPFISH ROE

1 egg yolk

1 cup (240 ml) smoked oil (above)

Salt

Beer Vinegar (page 30), for seasoning

3¹/₂ ounces (100 g) lumpfish roe

BEER VINEGAR JELLY

³/₄ cup (180 ml) Beer Vinegar (page 30)

¹/₄ cup (60 ml) water

¹/₄ cup (50 g) sugar

1.2 g powdered agar agar (see note)

5 sheets gelatin, soaked in cold water to cover until softened, then squeezed to remove excess water

HORSERADISH CREAM

2¹/₂ tablespoons finely chopped shallot

1 bay leaf

Leaves from 1 sprig arctic thyme

4 teaspoons Beer Vinegar (page 30), plus more for seasoning

³/₄ cup (180 ml) heavy cream

Grated fresh horseradish, for seasoning

Salt

0.5 g xanthan gum (optional; see note, page 34)

Mixed fresh herbs and peppery salad leaves (such as chicory and arugula), for garnish

To make the smoked oil, pour the oil into a glass container. Put the onion peels in a second metal container large enough to contain the container holding the oil. Place the containers over high heat. Ignite the onion peels with a kitchen torch, quickly set the oil container on top, and cover the larger container with either a tight-fitting lid or with aluminum foil, which will cut off the oxygen and reduce the flame to a smoldering cloud of onion aroma. Remove the lid or foil after 30 minutes, when the smoke has subsided. If a more intense smokiness is desired, repeat the process once or twice. Let the oil cool to room temperature, then transfer to a squeeze bottle. It will keep at room temperature for up to 1 month.

NOTE

Agar agar is a naturally occurring thickener derived from seaweed available in both powdered and liquid form. Look for it in specialty food stores and online.

To make the mayonnaise, in a bowl, whisk the egg yolk until blended. Then, whisking constantly, slowly add the smoked oil, drop by drop, until the mixture begins to thicken. Add the remaining oil in a slow, steady stream while whisking vigorously to form a mayonnaise. Season with salt and vinegar. The mayonnaise will keep in an airtight container in the refrigerator for up to 1 week. Gently fold in the roe when ready to use.

To make the vinegar jelly, combine the vinegar, water, and sugar in a saucepan and bring to a boil over medium heat, stirring until the sugar has dissolved. Add the agar agar while whisking constantly. Boil for 1 minute, then remove from the heat, add the gelatin, and whisk until completely dissolved. Pour into a 9 by 13-inch (23 by 33-cm) baking sheet, forming a layer 1/8 inch (3 mm) deep. Be sure the bottom of the pan is completely flat and even or the jelly will be difficult to remove from it. Cover and refrigerate until well chilled and set.

Cut the jelly into 2-inch (5-cm) squares, then, using a small offset spatula, carefully transfer the squares to a large tray. Spoon a small amount of the smoked mayonnaise down the center of each square. Using the offset spatula to lift the edge, roll up the square into a cylinder. Place the cylinders, seam side down, on a clean tray, cover, and refrigerate until ready to serve.

To make the horseradish cream, put the shallot, bay leaf, and thyme in a dry saucepan over medium heat and toast until the bay is aromatic and the shallots have begun to sweat. Add the vinegar and simmer over medium-high heat for about 1 minute, until the vinegar has almost completely evaporated. Add the cream and cook until reduced by half. Remove from the heat and grate in horseradish to taste. Be judicious with this step, as the flavor of fresh horseradish is very intense and might overwhelm some palates. Strain through a fine-mesh sieve into a bowl and season with salt and more vinegar. Just before serving, whisk in the xanthan gum to thicken.

To serve, place the vinegar jelly rolls on a plate, top them with the mix of herbs and salad leaves, and pour the horseradish cream on top.

PLAICE, TARRAGON TEMPURA, *and* FENNEL

SERVES 4 | PREPARATION TIME: 1 HOUR (PLUS 12 HOURS TO REFRIGERATE THE OIL FOR THE MAYONNAISE)

Plaice is the largest commercially caught flatfish in Europe and is a prominent item on the Dill menu. Gunnar loves it for its delicate flavor and the versatility it affords. Plaice grows quite large in the frigid waters surrounding Iceland, but its smaller incarnations are widely available throughout America and Europe. Should you have trouble sourcing it, flounder makes an excellent substitute. Virtually any large-leaved herb such as sage or chicory, or even bitter greens such as arugula or mizuna, can be used in place of tarragon for the tempura, which is a fun and unexpected way to showcase herbs in a dish. The silky, herbaceous character of the tarragon mayonnaise brings everything together. The mayonnaise also makes a nice addition to burgers or wraps.

TARRAGON MAYONNAISE

3 tablespoons packed fresh tarragon leaves

$^1/_2$ cup (120 ml) rapeseed oil

1 egg yolk

Salt

Beer Vinegar (page 30), for seasoning

PLAICE

14 ounces (400 g) skinned plaice fillet, cut into 4 equal pieces

2 teaspoons rapeseed oil

Sea salt

TARRAGON TEMPURA

Rapeseed oil, for frying

$6^1/_2$ tablespoons (50 g) all-purpose flour

$^3/_4$ teaspoon baking powder

$^1/_2$ teaspoon potato starch (see note)

4 or 5 fresh tarragon leaves per person

Salt

FENNEL SALAD

2 small fennel bulbs

Rapeseed oil, for seasoning

Salt

Beer Vinegar (page 30), for seasoning

NOTE

Potato starch helps keep the tempura batter from becoming too wet by absorbing some of the liquid into its thirsty cells. Plus, the combination of the potato starch and the baking powder gives the batter a light and airy texture that will not weigh down the delicate herb leaves.

To make the tarragon mayonnaise, combine the tarragon and oil in a blender and process at high speed for 7 to 9 minutes, until steaming hot. Cover and refrigerate for 12 hours, then strain through a fine-mesh sieve.

In a bowl, whisk the egg yolk until blended. Then, whisking constantly, slowly add the tarragon oil, drop by drop, until the mixture begins to thicken. Add the remaining oil in a slow, steady stream while whisking vigorously to form a mayonnaise. Season with salt and vinegar. Transfer to a squeeze bottle and refrigerate until chilled.

To make the plaice, preheat the oven to 325°F (165°C). Arrange the plaice portions on a baking sheet and drizzle evenly with the oil. Cover with plastic wrap, pressing it directly onto the surface of the fish, and bake for 14 to 16 minutes, until cooked through. Season with salt and keep warm.

To make the tempura, pour the oil to a depth of 4 inches (10 cm) into a heavy, deep pot and heat to 325°F (165°C). Line a plate with paper towels. While the oil is heating, sift together the flour, baking powder, and potato starch into a bowl. Whisking constantly, gradually add the water and then whisk until the batter is smooth.

One at a time, dredge the tarragon leaves in the batter, coating evenly and shaking each leaf to remove any excess. Working in batches, drop the leaves into the hot oil and fry for about 2 minutes, until crispy and just starting to turn golden brown. Using a slotted spoon, transfer to the towel-lined plate to drain, then season with salt.

To make the fennel salad, cut the fennel bulbs in half lengthwise and remove the core. Thinly slice the fennel halves lengthwise on a mandoline (see note, page 73), season with oil, salt, and vinegar, and toss to coat evenly.

To serve, arrange the warm plaice on a plate, squeeze the tarragon mayonnaise over it, and arrange the fennel salad on top. Finish with the tarragon tempura.

TABOO FOODS

Horse meat and whale meat are consumed in many house-holds in Iceland. They are extremely controversial foods that incite emotional responses from tourists who see items such as horse sausage, horse steaks, smoked whale, and whale steaks on restaurant menus or discover whale jerky for sale in souvenir shops. Gunnar makes the argument that these meats are consumed as a means of survival in many remote villages, and that eating them does not strike the same emotional cord with Icelanders as it does with most visitors, because they have long been part of the national table.

Whale hunting is highly regulated in Iceland, and every portion of the whale is used. It is illegal to hunt whale species that are endangered or threatened. This book does not endorse whale hunting, but it is important that readers understand how Icelanders view the hunt and the consumption.

The people on Grímsey Island regularly consume whale meat. It is one of the few proteins, along with fish and sea-birds, that is accessible to residents on this remote sliver of land surrounded by a raging sea. In other words, it is con-sumed there for survival, just as it has been for centuries.

TEA-POACHED SKATE, BRAISED KALE, SHALLOT PUREE, and SKYR

SERVES 4 | PREPARATION TIME: ABOUT 2 HOURS | PICTURED ON PAGE 106

When Grímsey Island fisherman Siggi Henningsson fishes on the Arctic Circle, he tries to keep everything he catches. Unfortunately, there is so little demand for skate (a member of the ray family) that he usually tosses any that turn up on his lines back into the sea. Skate is seen as high-maintenance compared with other ocean fish. In fact, it is so reviled by some that it has been called a garbage fish. Not surprisingly, Gunnar, who is always seeking out foods that others have deemed a waste of time, is a big fan of skate, insisting that once cooks learn how to handle skate properly in the kitchen, they will be rewarded with its great flavor.

One of the biggest time-saving steps you can take is to ask your fishmonger to sell you a skate wing (preferably skinned), so you avoid the task of removing the spine and other bones—a big kitchen headache. Should your fishmonger really like you, he or she might also remove the gristle located inside the wing, which acts like a giant pin bone separating a single wing into two pieces. If you get your skate home and the gristle is still there, simply remove it by cutting it away with a sharp boning knife. With the skin and spine removed and the wing separated, you are ready to enjoy skate as much as Gunnar does. One thing you might never want to do with skate though is ferment it the way Icelanders do on December 23 to commence the Christmas season. The smell is enough to give skate a bad name all over again.

SKATE WING

14 ounces (400 g) skate wing

8 cups (2 L) herbal tea (see note)

Salt

BRAISED KALE

1 bunch kale

1 tablespoon unsalted butter

1 shallot, finely chopped

Salt

Powdered seaweed (see notes, page 310), for seasoning

SHALLOT PUREE

4 shallots, chopped

Powdered seaweed (see notes, page 310), for seasoning

Rapeseed oil, as needed to cover

Salt

Beer Vinegar (page 30), for seasoning

SKYR FOAM

Unsalted butter, for sautéing

1 shallot, chopped

1 clove garlic, chopped

Leaves from 2 sprigs arctic thyme

1 tablespoon Beer Vinegar (page 30)

1/3 cup (80 ml) dry white wine

1/2 cup (120 g) Skyr (page 162)

1/2 cup (120 ml) milk

Salt

1 g soy lecithin (see notes, page 27)

To make the skate wing, rinse the skate under cold running water to remove any residue, then pat dry with paper towels. Wrap a baking sheet with plastic wrap. Put the skate in a large pot, add the tea, and pour in enough water to cover the skate by 2 inches (5 cm). Place over high heat, bring to a simmer, reduce to medium-low and gently simmer for 8 to 10 minutes, until the flesh is falling from the bones. The timing depends on the

NOTE

For this recipe, Gunnar uses a tea blend of Icelandic herbs called Witch's Brew, but any herbal tea you like will work. Herbal tea is big business in Iceland, where the terrain is covered with herbal treasures like sorrel, arctic thyme, and angelica. Most tea lovers in the nation have their own blend that they forage and dry themselves. It's a good project for any tea aficionado with access to wild herbs.

thickness of the skate wing. Drain the skate, pat dry, and while it is still hot, place it on the plastic wrap–covered baking sheet. Cover well with a second sheet of plastic wrap and let stand at room temperature for 6 minutes. This step will loosen the skin from the flesh. Peel the skin away, if it has not already been removed by your fishmonger, then remove the flesh from the bones with an offset spatula. Season the flesh with salt.

To make the braised kale, bring a saucepan of salted water to a boil. While the water is heating, separate the kale stems from the leaves, then coarsely chop the leaves. Reserve the stems and leaves separately. Add the stalks to the boiling water, blanch for 30 seconds, and then drain well and chop finely. Melt the butter in a pot over medium heat. Add the shallot and sauté for about 7 minutes, until caramelized. Add the kale leaves and stems and sauté for a few minutes until tender and bright green. Season with salt and powdered seaweed. Keep warm.

To make the shallot puree, preheat the oven to 200°F (95°C). Arrange the shallots in a single layer a small baking dish, sprinkle with powdered seaweed, and add just enough oil to barely cover them. Seal the dish with aluminum foil and bake for 1 to 1^1/$_2$ hours, until the shallots are tender. Remove from the oven and drain carefully, reserving the shallots and oil separately. Put the shallots in a blender and process at high speed, adding enough of the reserved oil to form a smooth puree. Season with salt and vinegar.

To make the skyr foam, melt enough butter in a saucepan over medium-high heat to coat the pan bottom lightly. Add the shallot, garlic, and thyme and sauté for about 7 minutes, until the shallots and garlic are caramelized. Add the vinegar and continue to cook until the vinegar has evaporated. Add the wine and cook until reduced by three-fourths. Meanwhile, in a small bowl, whisk together the skyr and milk. Once the wine has reduced, turn down the heat to medium, add the skyr mixture, and continue to simmer, stirring constantly. The skyr and milk will separate during this step but will come back together in the next.

Transfer the mixture to a blender and begin processing on low speed to prevent the hot mixture from splattering. Once the elements are incorporated, increase the speed to high and continue to process until smooth. Season with salt, add the soy lecithin, and process on high speed to create a foam.

To serve, put a spoonful of the the shallot puree on a plate, arrange the skate and kale around the puree, and garnish with the skyr foam.

OPPOSITE: Tea-Poached Skate, Braised Kale, Shallot Puree, and Skyr (page 104)

ABOVE: Baked Plaice, Shrimp, Roasted Cauliflower Puree, and Salted Almonds (page 108)

BAKED PLAICE, SHRIMP, ROASTED CAULIFLOWER PUREE, *and* SALTED ALMONDS

SERVES 4 | PREPARATION TIME: ABOUT 1¹/₂ HOURS | PICTURED ON PAGE 107

No, Gunnar is not calling for a dinosaur part when he includes pterygiophores in an ingredients list. A pterygiophore is actually the place where the fish fin connects to the body in most species. It is something that most others would never consider cooking, but Gunnar knows that a little roasting can turn it into an addictive snack. Here, he uses pterygiophores for garnish, but they are also wonderful paired with one of the mayonnaise recipes in this book. Your fishmonger might give you a quizzical look when you first request pterygiophores, but it's a safe bet that after he or she gets past the initial shock, you will get them at a steep discount—or perhaps even for free, which is what happened when they were sought out for testing this recipe. The other elements in this dish are not as unusual, and when all of them are brought together on a plate, they form a perfectly orchestrated mélange of creamy, briny, salty, sweet, and crunchy.

PLAICE

1 pound (450 g) skinned plaice or flounder fillet, cut into 4 equal pieces

2 tablespoons rapeseed oil

Salt

SHRIMP

6 ounces (180 g) small shrimp, peeled (shells reserved), deveined, and tail segments removed

1 tablespoon rapeseed oil

3 tablespoons cider vinegar

Salt

ROASTED CAULIFLOWER PUREE

3 tablespoons unsalted butter

¹/₂ head (7 ounces/200 g) cauliflower, florets coarsely chopped and core reserved

Salt

Cider vinegar, for seasoning

4 teaspoons milk, plus more if needed

RAW CAULIFLOWER

Reserved cauliflower core (above)

Rapeseed oil, for seasoning

Cider vinegar, for seasoning

Salt

SALTED ALMONDS

40 blanched almonds

2 teaspoons water

2¹/₂ teaspoons sugar

¹/₂ teaspoon salt

SHRIMP SAUCE

1¹/₂ tablespoons unsalted butter

Reserved shrimp shells (above)

3 tablespoons peeled and chopped carrot

2 tablespoons chopped shallot

2 tablespoons chopped fennel bulb

3 tablespoons chopped celery

2¹/₂ tablespoons chopped fresh dill

2 sprigs thyme

¹/₃ cup (80 ml) Beer Vinegar (page 30), plus more for seasoning

¹/₂ cup (120 ml) water

¹/₂ cup (120 ml) fish stock, preferably homemade (page 88)

³/₄ cup (180 ml) heavy cream

Salt

4 roasted plaice pterygiophores, for garnish (see notes)

Old man's pepper, for garnish (see notes)

To make the plaice, preheat the oven to 325°F (165°C). Arrange the plaice portions on a baking sheet and drizzle evenly with the oil. Cover with plastic wrap, pressing it directly onto the surface of the fish, and bake for 14 to 16 minutes, until cooked through. Season with salt.

NOTES

1. Pterygiophores length will vary
depending upon the fish, and
since they are used as a garnish,
it does not matter all that much
how long they are. Roast them
on a baking sheet at 350°F
(180°C) until golden brown and
crispy, season with salt, and cool
to room temperature.

2. Old man's pepper, also
known as yarrow, has a strong,
distinctive flavor and has long
been been revered for its healing
properties. It is available in some
specialty food stores and as an
herbal supplement in health
food stores.

To make the shrimp, in a bowl, toss the shrimp with the oil, cider vinegar, and a little salt. Let stand at room temperature for about 30 minutes, until the shrimp turn pink and the acid has "cooked" the shrimp as for ceviche.

To make the cauliflower puree, preheat the oven to 350°F (180°C). Melt 3^1/$_2$ tablespoons of the butter. In a bowl, toss the cauliflower florets with 2 tablespoons of the butter, coating evenly, then season with salt and cider vinegar. Spread the cauliflower on a small baking sheet, place in the oven, and roast for about 25 minutes, until charred and deeply caramelized on the outside.

Transfer the cauliflower to a blender, add the milk and the remaining 1^1/$_2$ tablespoons butter, and process on high speed until smooth. Taste and adjust with salt and cider vinegar if needed.

To make the raw cauliflower, prepare an ice bath. Using a mandoline (see notes, page 73), slice the cauliflower core as thinly as possible. Reserve the slices in the ice bath until ready for serving to prevent browning. Just before serving, drain, pat dry with paper towels, and season with oil, cider vinegar, and salt.

To make the almonds, preheat the oven to 325°F (165°C). Combine the almonds, water, sugar, and salt in a bowl, toss to mix well, then spread out on a small baking sheet. Roast the nuts, tossing them every few minutes to prevent burning, for about 10 minutes, until all of the liquid has evaporated. Pour onto a plate to cool.

To make the shrimp sauce, melt the butter in a saucepan over medium-high heat. Add the shrimp shells and fry until they begin to caramelize. Add the carrot, shallot, fennel, celery, dill, and thyme and sauté for about 5 to 8 minutes, until the vegetables are caramelized and the herbs are aromatic. Add the beer vinegar and simmer until almost evaporated. Add the water, stock, and cream and simmer for 20 minutes, until rich, thick, and deeply flavorful. Strain through a fine-mesh sieve and season with salt and beer vinegar. Keep warm. Just before serving, froth with an immersion blender, if desired.

To serve, arrange the plaice, shrimp, cauliflower puree, and raw cailiflower on a plate and sprinkle with the almonds. Garnish with the pterygiophores and old man's pepper and drizzle with the warm shrimp sauce.

THE SEABIRD EGG COLLECTOR

Grímsey Island, Arctic Circle

∞

After a day of fishing that begins at 3:00 a.m. and concludes at around 4:00 p.m., fishing-boat captain Siggi Henningsson's day is not over yet. He lives on Grímsey Island; the Arctic Circle passes through this three-mile-wide speck of land at the top of the world and the thrashing wind has shaped the terrain into watermelon-size mounds of earth. There is an urgency to Siggi's work as he spryly navigates a summer's day that is precious when you live on the Arctic Circle. In a few short months, the sun will set for the last time, the bitter cold will set in, the fishing will conclude for the season, and the fewer than ninety residents of Grímsey will wait out the darkness and the cold in lonely isolation.

But Siggi does not see his life on Grímsey as isolated. There are relationships to foster with the other residents of the island, a motley family of longtime inhabitants and newcomers hoping to settle down in one of the most remote spots on earth. After cleaning up from fishing, Siggi meets with his brother and nephews on the edge of a cliff. There he dons a climbing suit, harness, and helmet, loops one end of a rope through the harness, and then attaches the rope to the back of a tractor. He does not flinch as he hops over the side of the cliff with a collecting bag, waving good-bye to his family, and descending to collect seabird eggs. It's something he has been doing since he was a small boy. It is dangerous work, but it's just another afternoon well spent for Siggi, who collects hundreds of eggs that he then delivers to a collective refrigerator that anyone on the island can use.

He keeps three eggs for himself for a dinner later that night. It will be a classic island meal of boiled eggs, whale steak, seabird breasts, and a salad covered in a béchamel sauce that Gunnar will prepare for the feast. The chef and the fisherman have become close friends over the years. Gunnar says he visits Grímsey to clear his head and get away from it all. The orderly, ambitious life that Siggi leads inspires him and recharges him, and his optimism is infectious.

Later that night, after the dishes have been done, the hour is late and another 3:00 a.m. wake-up call looms, but Siggi has no plans to sleep. He has just purchased a new Jet Ski and invites his dinner guests to go for a ride in the marina. He plays like a kid in the frigid waters, and the next day when we are out fishing with him, he tells us that he used to travel back and forth between Grímsey and Akureyri, the largest town in northern Iceland. We mention that it is a forty-mile trip over a sea so choppy that the ferries sometimes suspend service because of the danger—that a man and his Jet Ski are no match for an ocean ready to swallow them up in its icy waves. He just grins his fresh, knowing grin and says, "You have to take chances in life. You have to really live it, feel it, and challenge yourself. Otherwise, what's the point?"

A Conversation with Seabird Egg Collector Siggi Henningsson

Q **What do you enjoy most about living on Grímsey?**

I like how remote it is. I think because of the isolation, people here are very supportive of one another and we are a really tight-knit community. We have to be to get through the long winters. We need to take care of one another in ways that many communities do not but perhaps should. I live away from the town, though, because there are a few too many people there for me. I like being away from it all, and while you might say just being on the island is being away from it all, I like having even more space than most folks who live here.

Q **You are not a native of Grímsey. When did you move here?**

I was around ten when my family moved here from Hjalteyri, a town in western Iceland. We are a family of fishermen, and fishing had decreased in our region, so we moved farther north where the fish were still abundant. Today, I live here with my wife and young son. My two brothers also live on the island with their families, and my parents are here too. I like having everyone nearby.

Q **Seabird egg collecting is a hobby of yours but fishing is your career. What do you enjoy most about fishing?**

I like the challenge and the hard work. I also like being out on the water where it's quiet and you can clear your head to the sound of nothing but the wind, birds, and water. But then there is a rush when the fish start coming in, and it is very rewarding to bring home a good catch. I feel connected out here to my family, who were fishermen as far back as anyone can remember. It makes me feel close to them, and I like knowing that I am carrying on a legacy.

Q **When did you start collecting seabird eggs?**

I've done it ever since I moved to the island. My brother and uncle always made me go, and at first I didn't like it. But then I developed a love for it. Few people collect them on the island any longer, and it's a tradition that will die out unless we continue to do it. It's a part of who we are here on Grímsey, and it's important to maintain it. If we don't, nothing will be left but the stories of the people who used to collect eggs, and the knowledge of how to do it will have been forgotten. It must be passed down from generation to generation to keep it alive.

Q What is the most challenging part of collecting the eggs?

The hardest part of collecting eggs is not to get the rope stuck between the rocks. If you're not careful, the rocks will wear it down and it will break. We are hundreds of feet above the sea, and a fall from that height into the water will surely kill you. Falling rocks are another danger. It's why we wear helmets. We have lost men in recent years to egg collecting, but it is part of life here on the island and a risk that some are willing to take. Life on Grímsey can be dangerous, and with fewer than ninety people living here, losing one is a tremendous loss. Last winter, one of my friends died when he was walking on the top of one of the cliffs bringing in his sheep. He fell on the ice and shot out into the sea on an ice chute that had formed. We never found him.

Q What are the required tools for egg collecting?

You must always wear a helmet, a harness, and a suit for protection. There is the rope, of course, and the tractor is required for letting the rope down and pulling it back up the cliff. We used to do this without the use of a tractor and a rope by climbing up the cliff sides from a boat, but too many men died that way. I use a stick to collect the eggs once I'm near them, and I put them in a bag attached to my harness. The eggs are very durable, with a much thicker shell than a chicken egg, so they do not break during the collection process. They are also cone-shaped, thanks to clever mother nature, to prevent them from rolling off the cliffside. We use radios to communicate, which is helpful.

Q When does the season begin?

We start collecting eggs on around May 10. The birds will continue to lay eggs until a bird hatches, and in this way we are not affecting the population by taking a few of their eggs. The birds lay the eggs directly on the cliff sides rather than build nests. We go out to collect about three times per season and then we stop. We take the eggs to a collective cooler in the center of town for anyone to eat when they have a craving for one. We also sell them to the one restaurant in town. Tourists seem to like eating them. It's something different for them—something they have never experienced before.

Q How do you like to prepare your seabird eggs?

I eat only about five eggs per season, and I prepare them by boiling them until they are hard, peeling them, and sprinkling them with a little salt and sugar. It's not complicated. I find in life that the simple way is usually the best way.

PUFFIN

Seabirds, such as the puffin, the guillemot, and the razorbill, are plentiful in Iceland, and although it is not as common as it once was to find their eggs and meat on the nation's table, Icelanders still have a fondness for them, with many restaurant menus featuring items such as smoked puffin and guillemot breasts. Iceland has one of the most plentiful puffin populations in the world, at an estimated nine million birds. Like the razorbill and guillemot, they nest in cliffside nooks and crannies high above the pounding sea.

Puffins were once most common in the Westman (Vestmannaeyjar) Islands in southern Iceland, but as a result of global warming, they are migrating farther north to places like the remote Westfjords in the northwest and to Grímsey Island on the Arctic Circle, where their meat is often smoked to sustain the small island population through the harsh winters.

The birds are caught using what looks like a giant butterfly net, and in many parts of Iceland where they nest, locals host hunting parties in midsummer, at which hundreds of birds are caught in just a few days. Local cooks prize this small bird with its Technicolor beak not only for its tender breast but also for its heart and liver.

CAULIFLOWER, SEABIRD EGGS, *and* BURNED BUTTER

SERVES 4 | PREPARATION TIME: ABOUT 40 MINUTES | PICTURED ON PAGE 120

This recipe is one of those dishes that Gunnar frequently surprises his guests at Dill with when they don't expect much from a bowl of cauliflower, butter, and an egg. And then they taste it and the bowl is emptied in a flash, because the combination of the creamy egg, the crunchy raw cauliflower, and the caramelized sweetness of the burned butter delivers much more flavor and texture than they're expecting in such an unfussy dish. When seabird eggs are in season, Gunnar requests them for this recipe, always showing his guests the large cone-shaped turquoise eggs speckled with black before he prepares them. A standard chicken egg is a good substitute, but should you ever find yourself with a seabird egg in your kitchen, be sure to use it in this easy but magnificent recipe.

CAULIFLOWER PUREE

2¹/₂ cups (250 g) cauliflower florets (from about ¹/₂ head cauliflower)

¹/₄ cup (60 ml) milk

¹/₄ cup (60 ml) heavy cream

2 tablespoons unsalted butter

Salt

Beer Vinegar (page 30), for seasoning

NOTES

1. Tapioca maltodextrin is described on page 23. If you wish to omit it here, you can simply drizzle burned butter on top of the egg and cauliflower.

2. An alternative to using an immersion circulator is to steam the cauliflower until tender, then combine the milk and cream in a small saucepan, bring to a gentle simmer over medium heat, add the cauliflower, and cook until warmed through. Drain and reserve the cauliflower and liquid separately, then proceed to the next step.

BURNED BUTTER POWDER

3 tablespoons burned butter (see page 119)

¹/₂ cup (10 g) tapioca maltodextrin (see notes)

Salt

4 eggs

2 to 3 cauliflower stalks, thinly sliced on a mandoline (see notes, page 73)

To make the cauliflower puree, preheat an immersion circulator (see notes) to 181°F (83°C). Place the cauliflower, milk, and cream in a vacuum bag and seal on the highest setting. Cook in the circulator for about 20 minutes, until the cauliflower is tender. Test if the cauliflower is done by pinching it through the bag. If it is tender and easily breaks apart, it is ready. If it still feels woody and tough, it requires an extra 1 to 2 minutes. Remove the bag from the circulator and drain the contents of the bag, reserving the liquid and cauliflower separately.

Transfer the cauliflower to a blender, add the butter, and process on high speed, adding the reserved liquid as necessary to form a smooth puree. Season with salt and vinegar.

To make the burned butter powder, in a bowl, vigorously whisk together the butter and tapioca maltodextrin for about 20 seconds, until a fine powder forms. Season with salt.

To make the eggs, prepare an ice bath. Bring a saucepan of water to a vigorous boil. Carefully lower 1 egg into the water and cook at a vigorous boil for 3¹/₂ minutes. Transfer the egg to the ice bath and leave until well chilled. Repeat this process with the remaining eggs, bringing the water up to a boil each time before adding the next egg. Remove each egg from the ice bath and immediately crack it lightly on all sides on a flat surface. Carefully peel away the shell, then remove the egg white and reserve for another use.

Carefully place the egg yolk in the bottom of a bowl that will be used for serving. The yolk will be hot, so use caution when handling it. Repeat with the remaining eggs.

To serve, spoon the puree around the yolk, arrange a wispy cloud of raw cauliflower on top, and sprinkle with the burned butter powder.

BURNED BUTTER

Burned butter is not really burned. Instead, it is deeply caramelized butter that adds a toasty sweetness to whatever it is cooked with or drizzled over. To make it, melt butter in a pan over medium heat and cook until it becomes a rich chestnut brown, stirring every once in a while to prevent scorching. Do not let it go past this color or it will indeed taste burned.

ABOVE: Cauliflower, Seabird Eggs, and Burned Butter (page 118)

OPPOSITE: Baby Potatoes, Angelica Mayonnaise, and Pickled Shallot Powder (page 122)

BABY POTATOES, ANGELICA MAYONNAISE, *and* PICKLED SHALLOT POWDER

SERVES 4 | PREPARATION TIME: ABOUT 1 HOUR (PLUS 36 HOURS TO PICKLE AND DEHYDRATE THE SHALLOTS) | PICTURED ON PAGE 121

Gunnar's family owns a home in eastern Iceland near the town of Egilsstadir that has been in the extended family for generations. He stays there with his wife and children whenever they venture east. Its cozy bedrooms invite the weary traveler to rest deeply and awaken to surround the large wooden dining room table for a breakfast feast.

During the research for this book, we arrived at the house late enough to see the Northern Lights streaking across the sky. We were ravenous and there was little to eat, so Gunnar told us to put on our shoes, then he pulled his truck up to the door and drove us to the expansive garden on the edge of the property, where we did a little midnight potato picking in our pajamas. We ate the potatoes for dinner that night and also the next morning, when he prepared this recipe for an on-the-go breakfast in plastic cups, picking angelica from just outside the door to flavor the mayonnaise that he dolloped on top of the boiled potatoes.

When in season, Gunnar uses seabird eggs in the mayonnaise for their bright golden color and decidedly eggy flavor. In this recipe, the potatoes and mayonnaise are gussied up with other elements, but should you find yourself in need of comfort food or of a quick and easy snack for your kids, head straight for the potato-mayonnaise combination and omit the rest.

PICKLED SHALLOT POWDER

1³/₄ ounces (50 g) shallots, quartered lengthwise and petals separated

2 tablespoons distilled white vinegar

1 tablespoon water

2¹/₂ teaspoons sugar

CREAM CHEESE FOAM

3¹/₂ ounces (100 g) cream cheese, at room temperature

4 teaspoons milk

0.3 g xanthan gum (see notes, page 34)

Cider vinegar, for seasoning

Salt

POTATOES

16 small new potatoes (or more if the potatoes are extremely small), unpeeled (see notes)

2¹/₂ tablespoons unsalted butter, melted

Salt

RYE BREAD POWDER
(*see* NOTES)

2³/₄ ounces (80 g) rye bread

2¹/₂ teaspoons unsalted butter, melted

Salt

ANGELICA MAYONNAISE

1³/₄ ounces (50 g) angelica sprigs (see notes, page 19)

¹/₂ cup (120 ml) rapeseed oil

1 egg yolk

Salt

Beer Vinegar (page 30), for seasoning

Fresh angelica leaves, for garnish

To make the shallot powder, prepare an ice bath. Bring a small saucepan of salted water to a boil over high heat, add the shallots, and blanch for a few seconds. Using a slotted spoon, transfer the petals to the ice bath, immersing them until chilled. Drain, pat dry with paper towels, and transfer to a small heatproof glass jar.

NOTES

1. If possible, use small new potatoes in an array of colors for added interest and a diversity of flavors.

2. Rye bread powder is good for sprinkling over everything from baked potatoes with sour cream to salads to fish.

3. Feel free to skip the siphon if you don't have one. The cream cheese is tasty simply dolloped on top of the potatoes, although it will not be as light and airy.

Combine the vinegar, water, and sugar in a small saucepan and bring to a boil over medium heat, stirring until the sugar has dissolved. Pour the hot liquid over the shallots, immersing them. Let cool to room temperature, then cover and refrigerate for 24 hours.

Preheat a dehydrator to the highest setting or preheat an oven to its lowest setting. If using an oven, line a baking sheet with parchment paper. Drain the shallots, pat dry with paper towels, and arrange on a dehydrator tray or on the prepared baking sheet. Dehydrate the shallots, flipping them over at the halfway point, for about 12 hours, until they are deep golden brown. Let cool to room temperature, then grind to a coarse powder in a spice grinder. The powder willl keep in an airtight container in the refrigerator for up to 1 week.

To make the cream cheese foam, in a bowl, whisk together the cream cheese, milk, and xanthan gum until smooth, free of lumps, pourable, and resembling melted ice cream. (This can also be done in a stand mixer fitted with the whip attachment.) Season with vinegar and salt. Transfer to a siphon and charge the siphon with 2 nitrous oxide (NO_2) chargers according to the manufacturer's instructions. Shake the siphon vigorously and refrigerate until chilled (see notes).

To make the potatoes, boil the potatoes in salted water to cover for 12 to 15 minutes, until tender. Drain the potatoes, let cool just until they can be handled, then cut the larger potatoes in half crosswise. In a bowl, combine the potatoes and butter and stir gently to coat evenly. Season with salt. Keep warm.

To make the rye bread powder, preheat the oven to 325°F (165°C). Tear the bread into pieces, put them in a blender or food processor, and process until crumbs form. Spread the crumbs in an even layer on a baking sheet, drizzle with the butter, and season with salt. Bake for 8 to 10 minutes, until toasted. Let cool to room temperature, then process in a blender on high speed until a fine powder forms.

To make the angelica mayonnaise, using the angelica sprigs and oil, prepare the angelica oil as directed on page 126; strain but don't freeze. In a bowl, whisk the egg yolk until blended. Then, whisking constantly, slowly add the oil, drop by drop, until the mixture begins to thicken. Add the remaining oil in a slow, steady stream while whisking vigorously to form a mayonnaise. Season with salt and vinegar.

To serve, arrange the potatoes on a plate, spoon the mayonnaise on top, dispense the cream cheese foam alongside the potatoes, and sprinkle everything with the shallot powder and bread crumbs. Garnish with angelica leaves.

CURED, SMOKED, *and* DRIED PORK BELLY

MAKES 2 CUPS PORK BELLY SEASONING, PLUS 1³/₄ POUNDS (800 G) BELLY FOR USE
AS BACON | PREPARATION TIME: 1 MONTH

On the Arctic Circle where the winters are fierce, the residents of Grímsey are isolated for
months at a time. They require pantries stocked with preserved items like this pork belly
to see them through the long cold season. The good news is that this recipe is not only
practical but also addictively good. Gunnar transforms his pork belly into a ground seasoning that is like a grown-up version of bacon bits. He uses it to flavor pastas, salads, and
potatoes and other vegetables. Of course, a single family can use only so much pork belly
seasoning in a year (unless you want everything to taste like pork, which is not necessarily
a bad thing), so here part of the belly is used for making the seasoning and the rest is saved
for some of the best breakfast bacon you will ever fry up.

2¹/₄ pounds (1 kg) pork belly

CURING MIX (*see* NOTES)

**1 tablespoon plus 2 teaspoons
salt**

**¹/₂ teaspoon pink curing salt
No. 1**

**Pinch of freshly grated
nutmeg**

**2¹/₂ tablespoons light brown
sugar**

2 cloves garlic, minced

**4 fresh bay leaves, finely
chopped (or crumbled dried
bay leaves)**

**Leaves from 5 sprigs thyme,
chopped**

**Leaves from 2 sprigs
rosemary, chopped**

4 handfuls wood chips or
completely dried onion peels
from 10 onions (see page 250)

NOTES

1. You must make two batches of
this curing mix. Do not double
the ingredients to make one big
batch and save half of it for the
second curing. The herbs must
be fresh each time the cure is
applied to the pork.

2. If you do not have a perforated hotel pan, you can put the
wood chips or onion peels in a
deep hotel pan or baking pan
lined with foil, set a rack inside
the pan, and put the pork on the
rack. Ignite, cover, and smoke as
directed.

Cut the skin off the pork belly. In a small bowl, stir together the salt, curing salt, nutmeg,
sugar, garlic, bay leaves, thyme, and rosemary, mixing well. Rub the mixture evenly over
the entire surface of the pork, then wrap the pork tightly in plastic wrap, making sure that
it is airtight. Place the pork in a tray deep enough to collect the juices that will be released
during the curing process. Set another tray on top of the pork along with a weight (soup
cans work well) to compress it during curing. Wrap the whole set-up in plastic wrap,
securing it tightly, and refrigerate for 3 weeks.

Remove the plastic wrap and brush off the curing mix. Make a second batch of the curing mix (see notes). Once again, rub the entire surface of the belly with the curing mix,
wrap tightly in plastic wrap, place in a deep tray, weight down the belly, and refrigerate
for 1 more week.

Remove the plastic wrap and brush off the curing mix. Wrap the belly in cheesecloth and hang in a cool, dry place for 1 day before smoking.

Arrange wood chips on the bottom of a deep hotel pan or similar vessel lined with foil. Place the cheesecloth-wrapped belly in a perforated hotel pan that fits inside the first pan. Place over high heat. Ignite the chips with a kitchen torch, top with the perforated pan, and seal the entire set-up securely with aluminum foil. Allow the smoke to smolder out completely, about 45 minutes, before removing the foil. If a more intense smokiness is desired, repeat the process once or twice.

Remove the belly from the smoker, unwrap the cheesecloth, and hang it in a cool, dry place for 3 days.

Preheat the oven to the lowest setting. Cut one-fourth of the belly against the grain into thin slices. Arrange the belly slices in a single layer on a baking sheet, place in the oven, and dehydrate them, turning once during the dehydration process, for 12 hours, until completely dry.

Break up the dehydrated slices and process them in a spice grinder to a fine powder. Transfer to an airtight container and store in the refrigerator. The powder will keep for up to 1 month. Use the remaining cured and smoked pork belly as bacon. It will keep well wrapped in the refrigerator for up to 2 weeks.

FROZEN OIL: ANGELICA

MAKES 1¹/₂ CUPS (360 ML) | PREPARATION TIME: ABOUT 15 MINUTES

Angelica oil is a bright spot on any winter plate longing for spring. This easy storage method using larger plastic freezer bags provides a large amount of oil in the dead of a winter freeze, just when you need it most.

20 sprigs (100 g) young angelica (page 333)

1¹/₂ cups (360 ml) rapeseed oil

Put the angelica in a colander and rinse for a few seconds under ice-cold running water. Do this step quickly or the water will strip the angelica of its flavor. Pat the sprigs thoroughly dry with paper towels and transfer them to a blender. Add the oil and process on high speed for 4 to 6 minutes, until steaming hot and the angelica is completely incorporated into the oil.

Strain the oil through a fine-mesh sieve, transfer to a vacuum bag, and seal at the lowest setting. Alternatively, transfer to a ziplock heavy-duty freezer bag, press out the air, and secure closed. Freeze until ready to use, up to 3 months. Thawed, the oil will keep at room temperature for a further 1 week and in the refrigerator for up to 3 weeks.

INFUSED OILS

Spring and summer are fleeting in Iceland, especially on a remote island like Grímsey, where the temperature rarely climbs high enough to induce a sweat. Although Iceland is warmer in the winter months than its name implies because of its position on the Gulf Stream, its growing season is still short.

Gunnar takes full advantage of the gardening time available by coaxing dozens of herbs and root vegetables, such as parsnips, potatoes, beets, and carrots, from the box gardens he has built between the bird sanctuary and his restaurant. To carry the flavor of the Icelandic summer into the dark winter months, he has devised a clever way to preserve his herbs by infusing them in oil and then freezing the oil in vacuum-sealed bags (see recipe this page) or ice-cube trays (see page 128) until he is ready to add a little brightness to his moontime dishes. The oils freeze well for up to 3 months.

FROZEN OIL: LOVAGE

MAKES 1¹/₂ CUPS (360 ML) | PREPARATION TIME: ABOUT 30 MINUTES
(PLUS 12 HOURS TO REFRIGERATE THE OIL)

Freezing your infused oils in ice-cube trays is a convenient way to have a single serving of 2 tablespoons on hand whenever you need one.

LOVAGE OIL

2 cups (100 g) tightly packed fresh lovage leaves, with stalks reserved

1 cup (240 ml) rapeseed oil

PICKLED LOVAGE STALKS

Reserved stalks from oil (above)

²/₃ cup (150 ml) distilled white vinegar

¹/₃ cup (75 g) sugar

To make the oil, put the lovage leaves and stalks in a colander and rinse for a few seconds under ice-cold running water. Do this step quickly or the water will strip the lovage of its flavor. Pat the leaves and stalks thoroughly dry with paper towels. Set the stalks aside.

Put the leaves and oil in a blender and process on high speed for 4 to 6 minutes, until steaming hot and the lovage is completely incorporated into the oil. Prepare an ice bath. Transfer the infused oil to a saucepan and heat to 221°F (105°C), until the solids separate from the oil. Stir frequently during this step to prevent the solids from scorching on the bottom of the pan. Nest the pan in the ice bath and let stand until the oil is chilled. Transfer to an airtight container and refrigerate for 24 hours.

To make the pickled stalks, slice the stalks into thin rings and place the rings in a heat-proof container with a lid. Combine the vinegar and sugar in a small saucepan and bring to a simmer over medium heat, stirring until the sugar has dissolved. Pour the hot liquid over the lovage rings, immersing them. Let cool, cover, and let stand at room temperature for 2 hours.

Strain the oil through a fine-mesh sieve. Drain the lovage rings and distribute them evenly among the sections in a 12-section ice-cube tray. Divide the oil evenly among the sections, then place the tray in the freezer and freeze until solid.

To use, pop out as many cubes as desired and thaw at room temperature.

FROZEN OIL: ARCTIC THYME

MAKES ABOUT 1¹/₂ CUPS (360 ML) | PREPARATION TIME: ABOUT 1 HOUR
(PLUS 12 HOURS TO REFRIGERATE THE OIL)

The arctic thyme in this recipe can be replaced with regular thyme or any other herb you prefer. Follow any of the freezing methods in this section for a fresh pop of summer in the middle of winter.

2 bunches (2¹/₂ ounces/ 75 g) arctic thyme sprigs with blossoms

1 cup (240 ml) rapeseed oil

To make the oil, preheat an immersion circulator to 131°F (55°C). Place the thyme and oil in a vacuum bag and seal on the lowest setting. Cook in the circulator for 45 minutes. Meanwhile, prepare an ice bath. When the oil is ready, transfer the bag to the ice bath until chilled. Refrigerate for 12 hours.

The oil will keep well for 1 month. Before using, strain the oil through a fine-mesh sieve and discard the thyme. Alternatively, you can strain the oil, discard the thyme stems, and put the oil and thyme leaves and blossoms in a blender, and process on high speed for 4 to 6 minutes, until steaming hot and the thyme is completely incorporated into the oil. Strain through a fine-mesh sieve and freeze using the freezer bag method (see page 126) or the ice cube tray method (see page 128).

FROZEN OIL: FENNEL

MAKES ABOUT 1¹/₄ CUPS (300 ML) | PREPARATION TIME: ABOUT 30 MINUTES
(PLUS 12 HOURS TO REFRIGERATE THE OIL)

Onions or shallots can be used in place of the fennel.

7 ounces (200 g) young fennel bulbs, coarsely chopped

1 cup (240 ml) rapeseed oil

2 teaspoons salt

Put the fennel, oil, and salt in a blender and process at high speed for 4 to 6 minutes, until steaming hot and the fennel is completely incorporated into the oil, stopping to scrape down the sides of the blender as needed. Prepare an ice bath. Transfer the infused oil to a saucepan and heat to 221°F (105°C), until the solids separate from the oil. Stir frequently during this step to prevent the solids from scorching on the bottom of the pan. Nest the pan in the ice bath and let stand until the oil is chilled. Transfer to an airtight container and refrigerate for 24 hours.

Strain the oil through a fine-mesh sieve. Transfer to a vacuum bag and seal at the lowest setting. Alternatively, transfer to a ziplock heavy-duty freezer bag, press out the air, and secure closed. Freeze until ready to use up to 3 months.

THE BARLEY FARMER

Vallanes, Eastern Iceland

∞

Herb Mayonnaise and New Small Vegetables 136

Pickled Angelica 137

Pickled Angelica Butter 137

Angelica Mustard 139

New Potatoes Two Ways with Grill Oil
and Pickled Onions 140

Fried Calf's Liver, Cabbage Puree, Kale,
and Beer Vinaigrette 144

Rapeseed Oil Cake, Cider Apples, Buttermilk Ice Cream,
and Pine Tree Oil 150

Skyr, Fennel Sorbet, and Roasted Barley 154

There was no forest surrounding Eymundur Magnússon's barley farm on the shores of Lake Lagarfljót in eastern Iceland. He had to grow his own. The dairy farmer turned organic farm pioneer who now owns Modir Jord (Mother Earth), one of the most successful organic food companies in all of Iceland, started growing barley more than a quarter century ago.

At the time, no one was eating barley in Iceland. It shared a common tale of woe with other Icelandic resources: people assumed expensive imports were superior to their own products and ignored the potential around them. Eymundur made it his mission to convince Icelanders to eat their own barley once again, and along they way, he planted over one million trees on his little slice of nirvana called Vallanes Farm.

The farmer's shock of red hair hints at the Celtic lineage that runs in the veins of many Icelanders, and his soft-spoken nature mirrors that of most of his countrymen. When Icelanders told him he was crazy to plant barley, he quietly continued his work, seed by seed, tree by tree. Now that his forest surrounds him, he has started building trails through the trees so that visitors can wander around in his paradise.

As they meander through the birch forest, they might catch a glimpse of "the monster house," the canteen in which aspiring farmers who flock to Vallanes from around the world enjoy three meals a day made from produce freshly harvested from the fields. Eymundur prefers to bike around his massive farm, where in the summer the sun bathes the barley stalks in a shimmering gold. He is a self-made man who is happy to share his bounty and his wisdom with others—over a bowl of barley, of course.

A Conversation with Barley Farmer Eymundur Magnússon

Q **Do chefs like Gunnar inspire you?**

We work together and inspire each other. It's rewarding to see my products being used by chefs I admire like Gunnar. Seeing his excitement for my work and knowing he supports it helps me keep going. In the end, it doesn't matter how good the product is if a chef or home cook doesn't use it properly. There's no salvation for it.

Q **Do you find that Icelanders know what to do with what you produce?**

At first they didn't, and it was very frustrating. During my grandmother's generation, barley was typically used in a preparation similar to gruel. It wasn't appetizing and the barley flavor was lost during the long cooking. People didn't have a fondness for barley because of it, and it was hard to convince them to try my barley.

I started selling it at a local market, and people who I convinced to try it would report back to me the next week that it tasted the same in their gruel as it always did. It was frustrating to know that they were still preparing it in the same tired way, and I really had to make an effort to show people how to showcase my barley in its best light. I started preparing dishes at my stand for people to try, and eventually I won them over by convincing them to start cooking the barley in a lighter, healthier way.

No one was eating barley in Iceland twenty years ago. Today Icelanders consume over sixty tons of it annually, and much of it is mine. There was a long tradition here of eating rice, which makes absolutely no sense at all. But for a long time, Icelanders always thought imports were superior to local resources, and I now love hearing from my customers that they have replaced rice with barley. Today my barley is for sale in stores throughout Iceland, and I am very proud of this. Icelandic barley is some of the best in the world, and knowing I contributed to its return is very gratifying.

Q **What makes it the best?**

Our growing season is short, and even during the spring and summer, it takes a lot of time for vegetables and grains to grow because the weather is always slightly cold here, even at the height of summer. This slow growing gives the plants time to build flavor, and by the time they're harvested, they are packed with it. I might be biased, but I truly do believe our barley is some of the best in the world. It has a sweet, nutty taste that you can't find in other barleys.

Q **What other products do you make?**

We make chutneys, jams, pancake mixes, crackers, vegetable burgers, and many other products that are for sale throughout Iceland. Icelandic people eat oat porridge instead of barley porridge, and I'm now working on trying to convince them to switch from oats to barley. My wife is instrumental in this. We married in 2010. She's been working in the food business for several years and was the founder of Slow Food in Iceland, so she was very lucky to find an organic farmer, and I was very lucky to find her.

Q **How many trees have you planted at Vallanes?**

I've planted over one million trees on my property. When I started farming here over twenty-five years ago, people told me I was crazy. The elevation is high here, and they told me there wasn't enough oxygen to sustain a healthy farm. So, I told them that I would have to make my own, and that's why I started planting trees. When you look out over the property now, most of the trees that you see were planted by me and my family. If you ask me at the end of my lifetime what I am proudest of, I will say reintroducing barley to Iceland and growing my own forest.

Q **How did the economic collapse affect your barley sales?**

People say you should eat what grows in the same environment where you live, and it makes perfect sense. After the economic collapse, my barley sales jumped 50 percent, since Icelanders could no longer afford to purchase expensive imports. At first they bought it out of necessity, but now they do it because they want to. We have always been proud of being Icelandic, but we didn't see the value in the things we can grow here. Now we do.

When I sell in Reykjavík, people come up to me and thank me for what I'm doing, and that is extremely gratifying. I feel like a pioneer who works hard to make his dreams come true. I'm very happy with my work, and I love that people also enjoy and appreciate it. We now invite people to come from around the world to stay at the farm, to learn about our work, to walk along the trails that we have created through our forest. People are used to walking on concrete. Here they walk on untouched land and run their fingers through the barley. For me, there is nothing more satisfying.

HERB MAYONNAISE *and* NEW SMALL VEGETABLES

MAKES 1 GENEROUS CUP (240 ML) | PREPARATION TIME: ABOUT 25 MINUTES

Spring is the time to revel in the sunshine after a harsh winter. This recipe celebrates the spring vegetables that emerge on farms and gardens throughout Iceland after a long, dark season. Guests enjoy watching Gunnar harvest the baby vegetables from his raised gardens just outside the front window of Dill, and sometimes they are even invited to pick their own vegetables. Dressed up with a cheerful green herb mayonnaise, this recipe is the perfect way to greet the spring.

HERB MAYONNAISE
(*see* NOTES)

1/2 cup (50 g) fresh young angelica leaves

1/2 cup (50 g) fresh Spanish chervil leaves (see notes)

1/4 cup (25 g) fresh lovage leaves

1 1/2 cups (360 ml) rapeseed oil

1 egg yolk

2 teaspoons Dijon mustard

Salt

Beer Vinegar (page 30), for seasoning

2 tablespoons sour cream

New small vegetables, any variety, raw, trimmed and peeled if necessary

NOTES

1. Substitute one of the herb-infused oils on pages 126 to 129 for the herb oil.

2. Spanish chervil, also known as cicely, sweet cicely, and sweet chervil is a fernlike herb with an intense anise aroma. Parsley, tarragon, or dill can be substituted.

To make the mayonnaise, prepare an ice bath. Put the angelica, chervil, lovage, and oil in a blender and process on high speed for 6 to 8 minutes, until steaming hot and the herbs are fully incorporated into the oil. Strain through cheesecloth or a fine-mesh sieve into a bowl, forcing out as much oil from the herb mass as possible so no flavor is lost. You should have about 1 cup (240 ml). Nest the bowl in the ice bath until the oil is well chilled.

Put the egg yolk and mustard in a blender and process just until blended. With the motor running on medium speed, add the herb oil in a slow, steady drizzle. When about half of the oil has been added and the mixture has begun to emulsify, you can begin to add the remaining oil slightly faster, processing for about 6 to 8 minutes total, until a thick mayonnaise forms. Alternatively, make the mayonnaise by hand: In a bowl, whisk together the egg yolk and mustard until blended. Then, whisking constantly, slowly add the herb oil, drop by drop, until the mixture begins to thicken. Add the remaining oil in a slow, steady stream while whisking vigorously, until a thick mayonnaise forms. Season the mayonnaise with salt and vinegar, whisking until incorporated. Cover and refrigerate until chilled.

To serve, whisk the sour cream into the mayonnaise. Serve a small bowl of mayonnaise alongside the vegetables. Keep this dish as unadulterated and wild as you can. It is a celebration of spring and, in this case as in most, the season knows best.

PICKLED ANGELICA

MAKES ABOUT 1¹/₂ PINTS (720 ML) | PREPARATION TIME: ABOUT 30 MINUTES

Angelica flourishes nearly everywhere in Iceland, and its large, hollow stalks are perfect for pickling. When the pickled stalks are thinly sliced, they yield miniature rings that are wonderful sprinkled on fish, salads, or vegetables for a burst of taste and color. Gunnar uses pickled angelica frequently in his dishes, and should you be able to source it fresh, this recipe is highly recommended for its versatility and flavor.

9 ounces (250 g) angelica stalks with their seeds

2 cups (480 ml) distilled white vinegar

¹/₄ cup (50 g) sugar

4 teaspoons sea salt

Combine the stalks, seeds, and vinegar in a small saucepan and bring to a gentle simmer over medium heat. Remove from the heat, add the sugar and salt, and stir until dissolved. Let cool to room temperature.

Transfer to a glass jar, cap tightly, and refrigerate until chilled. Use the stalks, seeds, and pickling juice to add zing to recipes. The angelica will keep in the refrigerator for up to 1 month.

PICKLED ANGELICA BUTTER

MAKES A SCANT 2 CUPS (450 G) | PREPARATION TIME: ABOUT 20 MINUTES

At Dill, Gunnar serves this butter, along with pine butter and sea salt butter, on a rustic wooden board, accompanied by a rough-hewn wooden knife. He pairs the butters with powdered seaweed (see notes, page 310) and homemade sea salt (see page 258). It's a butter service to remember, especially when served with warm rye bread baked in-house. The color of the angelica butter is mossy green, and because of the pickled flavor, it's a feisty addition to sandwiches or served on top of fresh-from-the-grill steak.

1 cup (225 g) unsalted butter, at room temperature

¹/₃ cup (80 g) Skyr (page 162)

4 teaspoons pickling juice from Pickled Angelica (above)

¹/₃ cup (50 g) minced stalks from Pickled Angelica (above)

Sea salt

In a stand mixer fitted with the whip attachment, whip the butter on high speed until it is light and fluffy.

Add the skyr and continue to whip until incorporated. Stir in the pickling juice and stalks and season with salt. Cover and refrigerate until chilled before using.

The butter will keep in an airtight container in the refrigerator for up to 1 week. If not used immediately after preparation, rewhip just before service to perk it up.

ANGELICA MUSTARD

MAKES 1 CUP (250 G) | PREPARATION TIME: ABOUT 20 MINUTES (PLUS 1 MONTH
REFRIGERATION BEFORE USE)

Gunnar has an extensive mustard program at Dill. He incorporates a wide variety of herbs
and spices into his concoctions and stores them in jumbo-size glass jars that he keeps in
a cool, dark corner of the restaurant's basement until they are needed. Any herb can be
substituted for the angelica, and when packaged in small glass jars, the mustard makes a
great gift.

3 tablespoons black mustard
seeds

3 tablespoons yellow mustard
seeds

3¹/₂ tablespoons dry mustard

³/₄ cup (180 ml) pickling juice
from Pickled Angelica
(page 137)

2 juniper berries

2 whole allspice berries

3 tablespoons minced fresh
angelica

3 tablespoons minced stalks
from Pickled Angelica
(page 137)

1 tablespoon plus 2 teaspoons
cider vinegar

2 tablespoons tightly packed
dark brown sugar

2 tablespoons sea salt

Bring a small saucepan of water to a boil, add the black and yellow mustard seeds, and
simmer for 15 seconds. Drain immediately and let the seeds cool to room temperature.

In a small bowl, stir together the dry mustard and pickling juice, mixing well. Let stand
at room temperature for 10 minutes, stirring a few times to prevent the mixture from
separating. Stir in the cooled mustard seeds.

In a spice grinder, grind together the juniper and allspice to a powder. Add to the mustard
mixture along with the fresh angelica, angelica stalks, vinegar, sugar, and salt. Whisk until
well mixed and the sugar and salt have dissolved.

Transfer to a small glass jar or other nonreactive airtight container and refrigerate for
1 month before using. The mustard will keep in the refrigerator for up to 3 months.

NEW POTATOES TWO WAYS *with* GRILL OIL *and* PICKLED ONIONS

SERVES 4 | PREPARATION TIME: ABOUT 1 HOUR (PLUS 1 WEEK TO PICKLE THE ONIONS) | PICTURED ON PAGE 142

The potatoes cultivated in eastern Iceland are some of the best grown in the country. In this recipe, they are both pureed and boiled and then paired with pickled shallots. In keeping with his reduce-waste philosophy, Gunnar frequently employs what he calls "grill oil" in his recipes. This is oil that has already been used to cook something, which means that it is filled with tasty browned bits. When it is used in a new recipe, it imparts a deep, nutty flavor to the dish. Once you try reusing oil in this manner, you will never want to throw away your grill oil again. It can be collected as you cook and stored in an airtight container (in order to prevent it from imparting its flavor to other items) in the refrigerator. Gunnar recommends sheep tallow for this recipe. But since sheep tallow will prove almost impossible to source, lard or rendered duck fat make good substitutes.

PICKLED ONIONS

4 white pearl onions, halved lengthwise and petals separated

4 red pearl onions, halved lengthwise and petals separated

$^1/_2$ cup (120 ml) distilled white vinegar

$^1/_4$ cup (60 ml) water

$2^1/_2$ tablespoons sugar

POTATO PUREE

2 medium new potatoes, unpeeled

2 tablespoons unsalted butter, at room temperature

$^1/_4$ cup (60 ml) heavy cream

Salt

BOILED POTATOES

8 very small new potatoes, unpeeled

2 teaspoons sheep tallow, lard, duck fat, or unsalted butter, melted

Salt

GRILL OIL

$3^1/_2$ tablespoons rapeseed oil

$^1/_4$ leek (white part only), chopped

$^1/_2$ shallot, chopped

$^1/_4$ cup (60 ml) cherry vinegar

1 leek (green part only), incinerated (see note)

2 tablespoons black truffle oil

Salt

Sea-salted potato chips (page 310), for garnish

To make the pickled onions, prepare an ice bath. Bring a saucepan of salted water to a boil, add the white onions, and blanch for about 1 minute. Using a slotted spoon, transfer the onions to the ice bath, immersing them until chilled.

Blanch and chill the red onions the same way. Drain the onions and put the white onions and red onions in separate small heatproof glass jars. Combine the vinegar, water, and sugar in a saucepan and bring to a boil over medium heat, stirring until the sugar dissolves. Pour the hot liquid over the onions, dividing it evenly between the jars to immerse the onions. Let cool to room temperature, then cap tightly and refrigerate for 1 week before using.

NOTE

Leek ash makes frequent appearances at Dill and is easy to make. Preheat the oven to the highest setting. Line a baking sheet with a nonstick baking mat. Separate the leek greens into individual leaves and arrange them in a single layer on the prepared pan. Place in the oven for about 8 minutes, until charred. Let cool, transfer to a spice grinder, and grind to a powder. The powder will keep in an airtight container at room temperature for up to 1 week.

To make the potato puree, boil the potatoes in salted water to cover for 18 to 20 minutes, until tender. Drain the potatoes, let cool just until they can be handled, then pass them through a ricer or food mill into a bowl. Stir in the butter and cream and season with salt. Keep warm.

To make the boiled potatoes, boil the potatoes in salted water to cover for 18 to 20 minutes, until tender. Drain the potatoes, let cool just until they can be handled, then pat dry with paper towels and halve lengthwise. In a bowl, toss the potatoes with the sheep tallow, coating evenly. Season with salt. Keep warm.

To make the grill oil, heat $1^1/_2$ tablespoons of the rapeseed oil in a small sauté pan over medium-high heat, add the white portion of the leek and the shallot, and heat just until the vegetables begin to sweat. Add the vinegar and cook until reduced by three-fourths. Remove from the heat, transfer to a blender, add the incinerated leek, the remaining 2 tablespoons of rapeseed oil, and the truffle oil and process on medium speed until smooth. Season with salt.

To serve, arrange the boiled potatoes on a plate and spoon potato purée alongside. Sprinkle with pickled onions and drizzle with grill oil. Garnish with the potato chips.

OPPOSITE: New Potatoes Two Ways with Grill Oil and Pickled Onions (page 140)

ABOVE: Fried Calf's Liver, Cabbage Puree, Kale, and Beer Vinaigrette (page 144)

FRIED CALF'S LIVER, CABBAGE PUREE, KALE, *and* BEER VINAIGRETTE

SERVES 4 | PREPARATION TIME: ABOUT 1 HOUR | PICTURED ON PAGE 143

The original version of this recipe calls for reindeer liver, a luxury item in Iceland because hunting reindeer is regulated by a strict and limited lottery system (see page 146). Reindeer herds flourish in the eastern part of the country and sightings are common against a backdrop of retreating glaciers and icebergs making their way to sea. Although the reindeer liver Gunnar prepares at Dill is rich and flavorful, it is also difficult to source, so calf's liver is substituted here. It is paired with kale, cabbage puree, and an herb puree, making it an ideal dish for a cold winter's eve when you just might be thinking about reindeer pulling a heavily laden sleigh across the sky.

CABBAGE PUREE

3 tablespoons unsalted butter

7 ounces (200 g) green cabbage, chopped

2 tablespoons chopped shallot

Salt

Beer Vinegar (page 30), for seasoning

KALE

Rapeseed oil, for sautéing

Unsalted butter, for sautéing

1 bunch kale leaves, chopped into bite-size pieces

Salt

HERB PUREE

$2/3$ cup (35 g) chopped fresh dill

$2/3$ cup (35 g) chopped fresh flat-leaf parsley

4 teaspoons water, plus more as needed

Salt

0.5 to 1 g xanthan gum (see notes, page 34)

FRIED LIVER

About 1 tablespoon unsalted butter

About 1 tablespoon rapeseed oil

1 sprig dill, finely chopped

Leaves from 2 sprigs arctic thyme

1 calf's liver, $1^{1}/4$ to $1^{3}/4$ pounds (550 to 800 g), trimmed of excess fat and sinew

Sea salt

BEER VINAIGRETTE

$1^{1}/2$ tablespoons sugar

Reserved pan juices from frying liver

$1/2$ cup (120 ml) Beer Vinegar (page 30)

Salt

To make the cabbage puree, melt $1^{1}/2$ tablespoons of the butter in a sauté pan over medium-low heat. Add the cabbage and shallot and sauté for about 12 minutes, until caramelized. Season with salt and vinegar and process with the remaining $1^{1}/2$ tablespoons of butter in a blender until smooth, adding additional vinegar or water as needed to form a smooth puree.

To make the kale, heat the oil and melt the butter in a pan. Sauté the kale leaves until tender and season with salt.

To make the herb puree, combine the dill, parsley, and water in a blender and process until smooth. Strain through a fine-mesh sieve into a bowl and season with salt. Whisk in the smaller amount of xanthan gum until thickened. Evaluate the consistency of the puree and whisk in more xanthan gum as needed to create a thickened yet glossy sauce.

To make the calf's liver, melt enough butter with some oil in a sauté pan over high heat to coat the pan bottom generously. Add the dill and thyme and sauté for 30 seconds. Add the liver and fry, turning once, for 9 to 12 minutes, until golden brown on all sides and medium rare in the center. Using a slotted spatula, transfer the liver to a plate. Pour the pan juices into a small heatproof bowl. Keep warm. Reserve the pan unrinsed for making the beer vinaigrette.

To make the beer vinaigrette, return the pan to low heat, add the sugar, and heat, without stirring, until caramelized. Add the reserved liver pan juices and the vinegar, increase the heat to medium-high, and cook for about 15 minutes, until the mixture is thick and syrupy. Season with salt.

To serve, thinly slice the liver crosswise and arrange a quarter of it on a plate. Top with the kale and cabbage and herb purees. Drizzle everything with the beer vinaigrette.

GEOTHERMAL GREENHOUSES

It's hard to grow vegetables in many parts of Iceland because of the amount of lava in the soil and the short growing season, but Icelanders have devised a way to grow vegetables year-round. Throughout the countryside, greenhouses are a common feature, lighting up the long winter nights like neon-yellow spaceships. They are fueled by geothermal electricity and the plants are usually watered with geothermal water, making these greenhouses nearly 100 percent sustainable operations.

Fridheimar is on the tourist route of the Golden Circle, which is about an hour from Reykjavík. The famed three-hour drive includes Iceland's iconic waterfall Gullfoss; its geyser field Geysir (after which all other geysers around the world are named); and Thingvellir, which up until a century ago was the gathering spot of Iceland's government, until it relocated to Reykjavík (Iceland bears the distinction of having the longest continuously running government in the world). If all these impressive sights are not enough, there is Fridheimar, one of the best places to witness geothermal greenhouses. The family-owned operation grows organic tomatoes that have become fixtures on Icelandic supermarket shelves. The tomatoes are also transformed into jams, Bloody Mary mix, and soups that can be purchased to take home or sampled in Fridheimar's welcoming café, right in the center of one of the greenhouses.

REINDEER

Reindeer were introduced to Iceland from Norway in the eighteenth century. Small herds now run wild in eastern Iceland, and it's an extraordinary joy to see a herd roaming through the countryside. Sightings are common at the base of the retreating Vatnajökull glacier, where a herd gathers on a channel of land between the ocean and the glacier.

Reindeer hunting is for the privileged few who win a limited lottery each year, and the meat is extremely precious and expensive. It is enjoyed both fresh and smoked, and its flesh is similar to venison in its leanness but richer and darker.

RAPESEED OIL CAKE, CIDER APPLES, BUTTERMILK ICE CREAM, *and* PINE TREE OIL

SERVES 6 TO 8 | PREPARATION TIME: ABOUT 2 HOURS (PLUS 12 HOURS TO FREEZE THE ICE CREAM) | PICTURED ON PAGE 152

Pine trees are much more common in eastern Iceland than anywhere else in the country, and Gunnar frequently incorporates their needles into his recipes. They impart the flavor of strong juniper and are a festive ingredient to use during the winter holiday season. After sourcing your pine twigs from a nearby tree, rinse them well under cold running water to rid them of any sap and residue, then dry them well before using. Pine is called for three times in this recipe, and when paired with the tangy buttermilk ice cream and the tartness of the cider apples, it creates a unique flavor profile that your guests will love, especially on a cold, dark winter's night when everyone's mood needs lightening.

BUTTERMILK ICE CREAM

3/4 cup (180 ml) heavy cream

3/4 cup (150 g) sugar

1/4 cup (50 g) liquid glucose (see notes, page 34)

2 sheets gelatin, soaked in cold water to cover until softened, then squeezed to remove excess water

2 cups (480 ml) buttermilk

RAPESEED OIL CAKE

4 eggs

1 cup (220 g) firmly packed light brown sugar

1 1/3 cups (315 ml) rapeseed oil (see notes)

2 1/2 cups (300 g) all-purpose flour

3/4 teaspoon baking soda

2 1/2 teaspoons baking powder

1 teaspoon salt

CIDER APPLES

2 green apples (such as Granny Smith), peeled, halved, cored, and immersed in acidulated water to prevent browning

1/2 cup (120 ml) apple cider (see notes)

1 sprig pine

APPLE FOAM

1 1/4 cups (300 ml) apple cider

2 1/2 tablespoons superfine sugar

0.5 g citric acid

4 g soy lecithin (see notes, page 27)

PINE TREE OIL

1 3/4 cups (75 g) pine tree needles, rinsed well under ice-cold water to remove residue and sap and coarsely chopped (see notes)

1 1/4 cups (300 ml) rapeseed oil

Salt

PINE TREE POWDER

2 tablespoons tapioca maltodextrin (see notes, page 23)

1/4 teaspoon salt

2 teaspoons liquid glucose (see notes, page 34)

1 teaspoon pine tree oil (at left)

To make the ice cream, prepare an ice bath. Combine the cream, sugar, and glucose in a saucepan over low heat and stir until the sugar has dissolved. Remove from the heat, add the gelatin, and stir until dissolved. Add the buttermilk and process with an immersion blender until smooth. Strain through a fine-mesh sieve into a bowl. Nest the bowl in the ice bath and let stand until chilled, stirring occasionally. Transfer to an ice cream maker and freeze according to the manufacturer's instructions. Scoop into an airtight container, place in the freezer, and freeze for about 12 hours, until solid.

NOTES

1. Olive oil is a good substitute for the rapeseed oil, though it will impart a stronger flavor than neutral rapeseed oil.

2. Store-bought apple cider with sugar works well.

3. Be sure to coarsely chop the pine needles (depending on their size) to prevent them from being caught in the blades of the blender.

To make the cake, preheat the oven to 350°F (180°C). Butter a 9 by 5-inch (23 by 12-cm) loaf pan. In the bowl of a stand mixer fitted with the whip attachment, combine the eggs and brown sugar and beat on high speed until frothy. Add the oil in a slow, steady stream, beating until incorporated. In a bowl, stir together the flour, baking soda, baking powder, and salt. Add the dry ingredients to the egg mixture and stir until incorporated. Transfer the batter to the loaf pan.

Bake for 40 to 45 minutes, until golden brown and a cake tester inserted into the center comes out dry. Let cool in the pan on a wire rack to room temperature, then turn out of the pan.

To make the cider apples, preheat an immersion circulator to 147°F (64°C). Combine all of the ingredients in a vacuum bag and seal on the highest setting. Cook in the circulator for 20 minutes, until the apples are tender. Meanwhile, prepare an ice bath. When the apples are ready, transfer the bag to the ice bath until chilled. Remove the apple halves from the bag and cut into thirds. As an alternative to the immersion circulator, place the apples in a pot and add enough apple cider to cover the apples. Bring to a simmer over medium-high heat, reduce heat to medium, and simmer until the apples are tender, about 12 minutes.

To make the apple foam, combine about one-third of the apple cider and the superfine sugar in a saucepan and bring to a simmer over medium heat, stirring until the sugar dissolves.

Add the remaining apple juice, the citric acid, and the soy lecithin and stir until dissolved. Remove from the heat and let cool to room temperature. Just before serving, process with an immersion blender until frothy.

To make the pine tree oil, combine the needles and oil in a food processor and process on high speed for about 8 minutes, until smooth. Strain through a fine-mesh sieve into a bowl and season with salt. Transfer to a squeeze bottle. The oil will keep in the refrigerator for up to 1 month.

To make the pine tree powder, combine the maltodextrin, salt, and liquid glucose in a food processor and process while adding the oil in a slow, steady stream. Continue to process until a powder forms. Transfer to an airtight container and store at room temperature until ready to use. The powder will keep at room temperature for up to 1 week.

To serve, break the cake up into pieces and arrange some pieces on a plate. Place a scoop of the ice cream and a spoonful of the apples alongside the cake and drizzle with the oil. Spoon the foam on top of everything and sprinkle with pine tree powder.

OPPOSITE: Rapeseed Oil Cake, Cider Apples, Buttermilk Ice Cream, and Pine Tree Oil (page 150)

ABOVE: Skyr, Fennel Sorbet, and Roasted Barley (page 154)

SKYR, FENNEL SORBET, *and* ROASTED BARLEY

SERVES 6 TO 8 | PREPARATION TIME: ABOUT 1 HOUR (PLUS 4 HOURS TO FREEZE THE SORBET) | PICTURED ON PAGE 153

Gunnar's desserts are rarely heavy, and this recipe, showcasing farmer Eymundur Magnússon's barley, is the perfect example of his use of vegetables in desserts, a practice that prevents the jarring contrast that sometimes occurs when moving from a savory course to a sugary dessert. The barley is nutty and crunchy, adding a nice counterpoint to the bright flavor and smooth texture of the sorbet and the tanginess of the skyr. If you like, carrot or cucumber can be substituted for the fennel.

FENNEL SORBET

2 cups (480 ml) freshly squeezed fennel juice (see notes)

3/4 cup (150 g) sugar

2 tablespoons liquid glucose (see notes, page 34)

1/4 teaspoon salt

4 teaspoons cider vinegar

FROTHY SKYR

2/3 cup (150 ml) heavy cream

1/4 cup (30 g) confectioners' sugar

2 sheets gelatin, soaked in cold water to cover until softened, then squeezed to remove excess water

1²/3 cups (475 g) Skyr (page 162)

FENNEL SALAD

1 fennel bulb, halved lengthwise, cored, and thinly sliced

1 teaspoon rapeseed oil

Pinch of salt

ROASTED BARLEY

1/2 cup (100 g) pearl barley (see notes)

1/4 cup (50 g) sugar

1/2 teaspoon salt

2¹/2 to 3¹/2 cups (600 to 840 ml) water

1 cup (240 ml) rapeseed oil

Dried apricots, for garnish

Prunes, for garnish

NOTES

1. Cut the fennel just before juicing and place in acidulated water to prevent browning.

2. Pearl barley is barley that has been processed to remove the hull and bran, resulting in small, ivory spheres.

3. If you do not have a siphon, just before serving, froth the skyr mixture with an immersion blender or whisk it vigorously. It will not be as light and airy as with the siphon method, but it will be just as tasty.

To make the sorbet, prepare an ice bath. Combine one-fourth of the fennel juice, the sugar, the glucose, and the salt in a saucepan and bring to a simmer over medium heat, stirring until the sugar has dissolved. Add the vinegar and the remaining fennel juice and mix well. Remove from the heat, nest the pan in the ice bath, and let stand stand until chilled, stirring occasionally. Transfer to an ice cream maker and freeze according to the manufacturer's instructions. Scoop into an airtight container, place in the freezer, and freeze for about 4 hours, until frozen solid.

To make the frothy skyr, combine the cream and sugar in a saucepan and bring to a simmer over medium heat, stirring until the sugar has dissolved. Remove from the heat, add the gelatin, and stir until the gelatin has dissolved. Whisk in the skyr until creamy and smooth. Transfer to a siphon and charge the siphon with 2 nitrous oxide (NO_2) chargers according to the manufacturer's instructions. Shake the siphon vigorously and refrigerate until chilled (see notes).

To make the fennel salad, in a bowl, toss together the fennel and oil until the fennel glistens. Season with salt and refrigerate until chilled.

To make the roasted barley, line a baking sheet with parchment paper. In a saucepan, combine the barley, sugar, salt, and 2^1/$_2$ cups (600 ml) of the water and bring to a gentle simmer over medium-low heat. Cook, stirring frequently, for about 30 minutes, until all of the water has evaporated. The barley should be almost fully tender. If it is not, add a little more water and continue cooking. When the barley is ready, transfer it to the prepared baking sheet, spread in an even layer, and let cool to room temperature.

In a heavy pot, heat the oil to 350°F (180°C). Add the barley a handful at a time and fry, stirring constantly to prevent scorching, for 10 to 15 seconds, until golden brown. Don't worry if the barley clumps together. Once it has cooled, it will be easy to break the clumps apart. Using a slotted spoon, transfer the barley to paper towels to drain. Let cool to room temperature, then transfer to an airtight container and store at room temperature until ready to use. The barley will keep at room temperature for up to 1 week.

To serve, spoon the sorbet and fennel salad into a bowl and dispense the frothy skyr on top. Garnish with the roasted barley and dried fruits.

THE DAIRY FARMER

Egilsstadir, Eastern Iceland

∞

Skyr 162

Custard with Blueberries and Cinnamon Sugar 163

Crispy Pork Skin, Juniper Skyr, and Rosemary Salt 165

Crispy Oats Cooked in Beer with Malt Cream 168

Fennel Salad, Cottage Cheese, and Spiced Nuts 171

Skyr, Blueberries, and Cream 172

Birch Meringue, Buttermilk Pudding, and Birch Granita 174

Stone Bramble and Cottage Cheese with Whey Caramel
and Whey Granita 177

There is a small family farm in eastern Iceland that has been owned by the same family for generations. The cows are lovingly looked after by Vigdís Sveinbjörnsdóttir and her husband, Herdís Jónsson, whose farming lineage stretches back longer than anyone can trace. Passing on a family tradition is a common occurrence in Iceland, but as the younger generations yearn for more urban lifestyles, there is the constant fear that farms such as Landbunadur will disappear. The husband-and-wife team produces both beef and dairy products, such as skyr and butter, which they serve at the small café and visitor's center at the entrance to the farm.

They want people to fall in love with the taste of beef and milk that has been produced from cows that are allowed to roam freely in the countryside, where they fortify themselves on the pesticide-free grasses and hay that flourish in the spring and summer months. They also hope that one of their three children will fall enough in love with farm life to forgo a career elsewhere and instead take over the farm, ensuring its survival.

Dairy farmers in Iceland face the same issues that many dairy farmers around the world face. They are required to pasteurize their milk, rather than sell it raw to the general consumer, and they must send it to a regional facility, where it is processed collectively with the rest of the milk in the area. Vigdís chooses to sell as much of the farm's dairy production as she can at her café, so that guests to the farm have the opportunity to taste products, such as butter and skyr, produced solely from the farm's milk.

This is the only way that people are able to taste the unique *terroir* of the farm—a *terroir* that Vigdís worries will be lost if her children decide to leave the land. For now, the family continues to raise its cows with the same love and integrity that past generations showed their charges.

A Conversation with Dairy Farmer Vigdís Sveinbjörnsdóttir

Q **Have you always been a dairy farm?**

This farm has been in my husband's family for generations and used to be a sheep farm, as well. But in the late 1980s, it became strictly a dairy and beef farm. It was due to a disease that broke out in this area, and while our sheep were not infected, they were slaughtered anyway as a precaution to prevent further outbreaks. No one in this area was allowed to have sheep for five years. We were compensated for it, but following that period, we decided to convert solely to a dairy and beef farm.

Q **How many dairy cows do you have?**

We have room for seventy-two dairy cows but right now we have seventy. We are close to maximum capacity.

Q **What do you produce?**

We produce around thirty tons of beef each year and also quite a bit of dairy, which we sell as both milk and skyr. We sell our cattle to local farmers who slaughter them for us and distribute our beef, but I also buy some of it back to sell in our store at the farm. I don't make a lot of money on this, but I like knowing that we are selling beef that is of the highest quality and was treated in a humane way.

Q **Whom do you sell your milk to?**

We sell it to a local collection plant that processes our milk with the rest of the milk in the region. In Iceland, we are not allowed to sell raw milk. It must be pasteurized and then processed in a controlled facility with milk from other farms. We pasteurize the milk ourselves. The pasteurization requirement was introduced in the 1950s, and the policy has not changed. We drink raw milk at home, but unfortunately it is illegal to sell it to the general public.

Q **What are the biggest challenges that you face?**

The weather is one of the biggest challenges that every Icelandic farmer faces. It is so unpredictable, and because it is, some years are much more successful and productive than others. That means we must plan for hard times long before they happen or we won't survive from year to year. This is the story of Iceland and its people and has been ever since the land was settled.

Q **Were you affected by the economic crisis?**

Farmers on the whole were the first to have the interest rates on their loans increased to begin paying back the newly incurred national debt, which hurt farmers in general a great deal. Fortunately, we did not have large loans, so the rates did not affect us. But the governments also lowered the subsidies farmers received for their products, and this affected all farmers, including us. All Icelanders are expected to help pay off the national debt, which can be frustrating because we were not personally responsible for it. But it's the reality and you have to face it, deal with it, and move on without letting it affect you too much or you will not be able to move forward with your work and your life.

Q **Where do you sell your dairy products?**

I only sell our dairy products on the farm, because the main purpose of producing milk is to bring people here to experience the life of the farm, to see the animals, and to understand where their milk comes from. Always buying something prepackaged in the store breaks the connection between the farmer and the consumer, and we are trying to reconcile it. In the summer months, we have many visitors, which is encouraging.

Q **How many people do you employ at the farm?**

There are only two of us along with my daughter, who takes care of the cows in the summer. I have three children, and they all have other plans for their lives. But they also want this farm to endure, so either they have to do something about it or let it go. Hopefully, they are all planning to do something about it in order to keep it in the family. Sometimes it seems their other plans are getting in the way, but we always remind them that if that happens, we will have to sell the farm. I have hope that at least one of them will decide to keep it going.

SKYR

MAKES 5 POUNDS (2.3 KG) WITH WHEY, JUST OVER 2^1/$_2$ POUNDS (1.1 KG) WITHOUT
WHEY | PREPARATION TIME: ABOUT 1 HOUR (PLUS 30 MINUTES TO COOL TO ROOM
TEMPERATURE AND 12 TO 15 HOURS TO SET)

Skyr, a thick and creamy cheese that is similar in flavor and texture to Greek yogurt, is a
fundamental ingredient in Icelandic cuisine, and virtually every home refrigerator in the
country holds a container of it (for more information, see page 335).

The healthful, flavorful whey that remains after draining the milk is used in several
recipes in this book. The "old skyr" called for here is similar to a sourdough starter, in that
it carries the active yeasts and bacteria from the region in which it was first produced.
You do not need the starter to make skyr, but it is a good idea to keep a little each time to
incorporate into the next batch. Once you see how easy it is to make skyr, it might become
as fundamental to your diet as it is that of an Icelander.

10^1/$_2$ cups (2^1/$_2$ L) skim milk

2 tablespoons old skyr,
if available (see headnote)

NOTE

A nonstick pan will prevent the
skyr from scorching during the
lengthy time it takes to heat it
up and keep it at temperature. If
you do not have a nonstick pan,
a regular heavy saucepan will
work, but you must be prepared
to monitor the skyr closely
throughout the entire process.

In a nonstick saucepan (see note), heat the milk over low heat to 200°F (95°C) and keep
it at this temperature for 10 minutes. It's crucial to keep the temperature steady, not
allowing it to drop below or rise above, or the skyr will either scorch or not set properly.
Stir the milk throughout this process to prevent it from sticking on the pan bottom.
Remove the pan from the heat and set aside at room temperature. Let cool to 102°F
(39°C). This entire process takes a substantial amount of time, over 1 hour to heat the
milk and almost 30 minutes for it to cool to room temperature.

Add the old skyr, if using and whisk until well blended. Cover with a kitchen towel and
let stand at room temperature for 12 to 15 hours (up to 24 hours), until thickened to the
consistency of Greek yogurt and the curds have separated from the whey.

At this point, you can either stir the whey into the skyr to thin it, or drain the skyr through
cheesecloth for a thicker consistency. Cover tightly and refrigerate until chilled. The skyr,
either thinned with the whey or strained, will keep in the refrigerator for up to 1 week. The
whey will keep in an airtight container in the refrigerator for up to 1 week.

CUSTARD *with* BLUEBERRIES *and* CINNAMON SUGAR

SERVES 4 | PREPARATION TIME: ABOUT 1 HOUR (PLUS 3 TO 4 HOURS TO CHILL THE CUSTARD)

Áabrystir (colostrum), the first milk produced after a cow gives birth, is one of the Icelandic products that is virtually impossible to source outside of the country. It is buttercup yellow and loaded with fat, vitamins and minerals, and flavor. Gunnar says it's like an instant crème anglaise without the hassle. Unfortunately, it's only sold at traditional markets in Iceland. That means that most of the rest of the world will have to make due with heavy cream thickened with gelatin, which makes a fine substitute. The custard is a good way to conclude a meal, especially when paired with macerated blueberries and sprinkled with cinnamon sugar.

CUSTARD

1¹/₂ cups (360 ml) heavy cream

1 sheet gelatin, soaked in cold water to cover until softened, then squeezed to remove excess water

BLUEBERRIES

Scant 1 cup (125 g) blueberries

1¹/₂ tablespoons superfine sugar

CINNAMON SUGAR

2¹/₂ tablespoons Demerara sugar

2¹/₄ teaspoons ground cinnamon

To make the custard, set up a bain-marie. Place a wide saucepan on the stove top and put a heatproof bowl in the pan. Add the cream to the bowl, pour water into the pan to reach halfway up the sides of the bowl, and turn on the heat to medium-low. Heat the cream to 158°F (70°C). This will take about 18 minutes.

Add the gelatin to the warm cream and stir to dissolve completely. Transfer the cream to 4 ramekins, each 4 inches (10 cm) in diameter, and let cool slightly. Cover each custard with plastic wrap pressed directly onto the surface to prevent a skin from forming and refrigerate for 3 to 4 hours, until chilled and set. (It may take longer if the ramekins are deep.)

To make the blueberries, in a bowl, toss together the blueberries and sugar until the blueberries are fully coated. Set aside at room temperature for 30 minutes before serving to soften and sweeten the berries.

To make the cinnamon sugar, in a small bowl, combine the sugar and cinnamon until incorporated.

To serve, top the ramekins with the blueberries and sprinkle with the cinnamon sugar.

CRISPY PORK SKIN, JUNIPER SKYR, *and* ROSEMARY SALT

SERVES 6 TO 8 | PREPARATION TIME: ABOUT 18 HOURS (INCLUDES 1¹/₂ HOURS TO REFRIGERATE AND 12 HOURS TO DEHYDRATE THE SKIN)

The fried pork skin in this recipe is feather light and addictively crunchy, and when dipped into the tangy skyr and sprinkled with rosemary salt, it becomes a tempting indulgence. Most of the preparation time is devoted to the inactive steps of simmering, chilling, and dehydrating, so don't let the large number of hours scare you away from what has the potential to become a go-to game-day indulgence. Rosemary pairs particularly well with the skyr, but herbs such as thyme, tarragon, or savory make fine substitutes. To seriously pursue the juniper theme and embrace your inner Icelander, replace the herbs altogether with the needles from a 3-inch (7.5-cm) pine twig. Just be sure to rinse the needles well under ice-cold running water to remove excess sap and residue before using.

ROSEMARY SALT

Leaves from 3 sprigs rosemary

Scant ¹/₄ cup (65 g) sea salt (see notes)

CRISPY PORK SKIN

1 pound (450 g) pork skin

Vegetable oil, for deep-frying

JUNIPER SKYR

¹/₃ cup (100 g) honey

3 tablespoons plus 1 teaspoon (50 ml) cider vinegar

1 sprig rosemary

¹/₄ cup (70 g) Skyr (page 162)

2 juniper berries, ground to a powder

NOTES

1. If possible, make your own sea salt for this recipe (page 258), just as Gunnar does.

2. If you're looking for a new addition to your cocktail repertoire, double the ingredients for the honey mixture, whisk half of the strained liquid into the juniper skyr, and use the other half to drizzle into highballs of bourbon splashed with tonic.

To make the rosemary salt, in a spice grinder, combine the rosemary and salt and grind until evenly ground and almost a powder.

To make the pork skin, place the skin in a saucepan, add water to cover by 3 inches (7.5 cm), and bring to a boil over medium-high heat. Boil uncovered, adding water as needed to keep the skin covered, for about 2 hours, until tender.

Remove from the heat and let stand for about 45 minutes. At this point, the skin should be cool enough to handle. Drain it and, using a razor blade, gently scrape off any hair and fat from the skin. (Any hair will scorch and any fat will splatter when you deep-fry the skin.) Cut the skin into playing card–size pieces and refrigerate the skin in an airtight container for 1¹/₂ hours.

Preheat a dehydrator to 147°F (64°C). Arrange the skin on a dehydrator tray and dehydrate for 12 hours, until completely dry.

Pour oil to a depth of 2¹/₂ inches (6 cm) into a heavy, deep pot and heat to 320°F (160°C). Working in batches, add the skin pieces to the hot oil and fry for about 30 seconds, until

| continued

they puff up. Using a slotted spoon or wire skimmer, transfer them to paper towels to drain, then sprinkle with the rosemary salt. Repeat with the remaining skin pieces.

To make the juniper skyr, combine the honey, vinegar, and rosemary in a saucepan and bring to a boil. Remove from the heat, cover with aluminum foil, and let stand at room temperature for 10 minutes (see notes). Prepare an ice bath.

Strain the liquid into a bowl and nest the bowl in the ice bath until the liquid is well chilled. In a bowl, whisk together the skyr and juniper, then whisk in the chilled liquid. Cover and refrigerate until chilled.

To serve, set out the puffed pork skin with bowls of the juniper skyr for dipping and the rosemary salt for sprinkling.

PORK IN ICELAND

The first settlers in Iceland introduced pigs along with goats, cows, chickens, sheep and horses. By the sixteenth century, pigs had become extinct, however, and were not introduced again until the nineteenth century. As a result, few traditional pork recipes exist from the earliest days. But since its reintroduction, pork has become a darling of both chefs and home cooks and holds a prominent place on the Icelandic table.

It is especially appreciated on special occasions like Christmas, when some families enjoy pork belly with crispy skin studded with aromatics such as juniper, cloves, and bay leaves.

BEER IN ICELAND

The tradition of cultivating barley in Iceland died out in the Middle Ages and with it went Iceland's earliest beer traditions. Beer was reintroduced a few hundred years later on a limited scale. Then, in 1915, all alcoholic beverages were banned in Iceland, a prohibition that continued until 1935, when the restriction was lifted on all beverages except beer. The prohibition against beer remained in force until 1989, when its consumption was finally legalized. As a result, the first beers made in Iceland in recent times were simple pilsners and ales, with Viking and Gull being standout brands.

In recent years, with the advent of Iceland's culinary renaissance, brewers are becoming more creative, as they look to their native ingredients for inspiration. Arctic thyme, angelica, and sorrel are emerging in new types of Icelandic beer, such as porters, stouts, Indian pale ales, and red ales. It's an exciting time to be a brewer in Iceland, and an exciting time to be a beer drinker, too.

CRISPY OATS COOKED *in* BEER *with* MALT CREAM

SERVES 4 TO 6 | PREPARATION TIME: ABOUT 1 HOUR (PLUS 12 HOURS TO DEHYDRATE THE OATS)

Gunnar incorporates a spiced wheat beer called Freyja into this recipe. Freyja is not only the revered goddess of love, beauty, war, and death in Norse mythology but is also the name of Gunnar's lovely wife. Any high-quality wheat beer is a good substitute for the Icelandic brew. Malt is another important ingredient in Iceland, where locals so appreciate the flavor that the carbonated beverage Maltextrakt, made by Egils, is available through-out the country. Malt extract is used in this recipe, and when incorporated into cream, it creates a delicious dip. The crispy oats, a fun spin on humdrum porridge, are the perfect vehicle for it.

OATS COOKED IN BEER

2 teaspoons unsalted butter

²/₃ cup (100 g) steel-cut oats

2 cups (480 ml) wheat beer

¹/₄ cup (60 ml) heavy cream

MALT CREAM

¹/₄ cup (70 g) Skyr (page 162)

1¹/₂ teaspoons malt extract syrup

1¹/₂ teaspoons honey

Salt

Beer Vinegar (page 30), for seasoning

Malt extract reduced by half, for garnish

NOTES

1. Be sure to simmer the oats over low heat, or they will take on the bitterness of the beer.

2. The starch in the oats must be broken down completely, or they will not dehydrate properly. The oats can also be dehydrated for about 12 hours in an oven set to the lowest setting.

To make the oats, melt the butter in a saucepan over medium heat, add the oats, and sauté for 5 to 7 minutes, until lightly golden. Add the beer, stir well, cover, and simmer over low heat (see notes), adding more beer if needed to prevent scorching, for about 30 minutes, until the mixture is the consistency of coarse porridge. Remove from the heat and stir in the cream. Transfer to a food processor and pulse to break down the oats completely (see notes). Let cool to room temperature.

Preheat a dehydrator (see notes) to 155°F (68°C). Line a dehydrator tray with a nonstick baking mat. Using an offset spatula, spread the cooled oats in a thin, even layer onto the mat. Dehydrate for about 12 hours, until completely dry and crispy. Break into dipping-size crackers and store between sheets of parchment paper in an airtight container until ready to serve. The crackers will keep at room temperature for up to 3 days.

To make the malt cream, in a bowl, whisk together the skyr, malt extract, and honey. Season with salt and vinegar, transfer to a piping bag fitted with a 1-inch (2¹/₂-cm) tip, and refrigerate until chilled.

To serve, pipe out generous dollops of the malt cream and dot them with reduced malt. Serve the oat chips alongside.

FENNEL SALAD, COTTAGE CHEESE, *and* SPICED NUTS

SERVES 4 | PREPARATION TIME: ABOUT 1 HOUR

This simple recipe combines the creaminess of cottage cheese, freshness of raw fennel contrasted with a fennel puree, and spicy crunch of toasted nuts. It's a wonderful way to kick off a meal, or makes a nice vegetarian main course.

COTTAGE CHEESE

$^1/_2$ cup (100 g) large-curd cottage cheese

2 tablespoons full-fat sour cream

Salt

Beer Vinegar (page 30), for seasoning

SPICY NUTS

$1^1/_2$ tablespoons hazelnuts

$1^1/_2$ tablespoons walnuts

$1^1/_2$ tablespoons peanuts

1 whole clove

1 teaspoon fennel seeds

$^1/_2$ teaspoon dill seeds

1 star anise pod

$^3/_4$ teaspoon ground cinnamon

Sea salt

Rapeseed oil, for seasoning

FENNEL PUREE

2 fennel bulbs, cored and finely chopped

$^1/_2$ cup (120 ml) milk

$^1/_2$ cup (120 ml) heavy cream

$^1/_2$ teaspoon sugar

2 tablespoons unsalted butter

Salt

FENNEL SALAD

1 fennel bulb, halved lengthwise and cored

Salt

Rapeseed oil, for seasoning

Beer Vinegar (page 30), for seasoning

To make the cottage cheese, combine the cottage cheese and sour cream and mix well. Season with salt and vinegar, cover, and refrigerate until chilled.

To make the spicy nuts, preheat the oven to 350°F (180°C). Spread all of the nuts on a baking sheet and toast in the oven for 7 to 8 minutes, until golden brown. While the nuts are still warm, put them in a kitchen towel and then rub them between your palms to remove the skins. Finely chop the nuts and let cool to room temperature.

Combine the clove, fennel seeds, dill seeds, and star anise in a small frying pan over medium-low heat and toast, shaking the pan often, for 5 to 6 minutes, until fragrant and nicely toasted. Remove from the heat, stir in the cinnamon, and let cool to room temperature. Transfer to a spice grinder and grind to a fine powder. Transfer the ground spices to a small food processor, add the nuts, and pulse until ground to a fine powder. Season with salt and a few drops of oil.

To make the fennel puree, combine the fennel, milk, cream, and sugar in a saucepan and bring to a simmer over medium-low heat. Cook for 8 to 10 minutes, until the fennel is tender. Drain, reserving the liquid and fennel separately. Transfer the fennel to a blender, add the butter, and process on high speed until a puree forms, adding the cooking liquid as needed to achieve a smooth consistency. Season with salt.

To make the fennel salad, thinly slice the fennel on a mandoline (see notes, page 73). Season with salt, oil, and vinegar.

To serve, spoon the cottage cheese onto plates along with the fennel puree and salad. Sprinkle with the spicy nuts.

SKYR, BLUEBERRIES, *and* CREAM

SERVES 4 | PREPARATION TIME: ABOUT 15 MINUTES

Skyr is a favorite breakfast item for Icelanders, and this dual-purpose recipe can be served for breakfast or for dessert. Gunnar often serves it to his four children as a comforting wake-up call.

²/₃ cup (120 g) blueberries

Superfine sugar, for sweetening

1¹/₂ **cups (430 g) Skyr** (page 162)

³/₄ **cup (180 ml) heavy cream**

In a bowl, sprinkle the blueberries with sugar and let stand at room temperature for about 30 minutes to soften and sweeten the berries.

To serve, spoon the skyr into a bowl, spoon the berries over the skyr, and drizzle with a little cream.

BIRCH MERINGUE, BUTTERMILK PUDDING, *and* BIRCH GRANITA

This dessert is a fun conversation piece for guests who will be dazzled by the unexpected appearance of birch in many of the elements. A few years ago, Gunnar and one of his business partners, Ólafur Örn Ólafsson, started distilling a birch schnapps called Birkir and a liqueur called Björk in conjunction with the artisanal spirits maker Foss Distillery. It's just one of many artisanal spirits emerging in recent years.

The meringue could take a bit longer to set than indicated, depending on the humidity level where you live, but give it time and it will firm up for you. This dessert is a celebration of Iceland's national tree, an element that is stitched into every bite in whimsical and unexpected ways.

BIRCH MERINGUE

2¹/₂ tablespoons egg white powder

2 tablespoons water

2 tablespoons (30 g) Birkir schnapps (see notes)

¹/₄ cup (40 g) sugar

DRIED BIRCH

Generous handful of birch leaves

BIRCH TREE GRANITA

2 cups (480 ml) water

1 cup (200 g) sugar

2 (8-inch/20-cm) leafy birch twigs, cut into 1-inch (2.5-cm) pieces

BUTTERMILK PUDDING

1¹/₂ cups (360 ml) buttermilk

2 (14.5-g) packets unflavored gelatin

¹/₃ cup (50 g) finely chopped blanched almonds

¹/₂ cup (100 g) sugar

¹/₂ cup (140 g) Skyr (page 162)

¹/₂ cup (120 ml) whipped cream

BIRCH TREE HONEY

¹/₃ cup (100 g) honey

2 tablespoons water

2 (8-inch/20-cm) leafy birch twigs, cut into 1-inch (2.5-cm) pieces

To make the birch meringue, preheat a dehydrator to the lowest setting (see notes). Line a dehydrator tray with a nonstick baking mat. In a small bowl, whisk together the egg white powder and water until aerated, then transfer to the small bowl of a stand mixer fitted with the whip attachment (see notes). Add the schnapps and whip on high speed until light and frothy. Still on high speed, add the sugar in a slow, steady stream until incorporated, then continue to whip until stiff peaks form, stopping to scrape down the sides of the bowl as needed.

Transfer the egg white mixture to a piping bag fitted with a 1-inch (2.5-cm) plain tip and pipe lines 2 inches (5 cm) long onto the lined tray. Dehydrate for about 12 hours (see notes), until the mixture is the texture of meringue. The meringue will keep in an airtight container at room temperature for up to 1 week. Break into pieces just before serving.

NOTES

1. Gunnar laces the meringue with his schnapps, but if you cannot locate it (it is sold everywhere in Iceland but is difficult to find outside of the country), a dark spiced rum is a good substitute.

2. The meringue must first be whisked by hand to aerate it enough to give the whip enough volume to catch and begin doing its job.

3. The meringue and the dried birch can also be dehydrated for about 12 hours in an oven set to the lowest setting.

4. If you have a dehydrator capable of drying on two settings at the same time, dehydrate the meringue and dried birch simultaneously.

To make the dried birch, preheat the dehydrator to the lowest setting (see notes). Spread the birch leaves on a dehydrator tray and dehydrate for about 12 hours, until dry. Transfer to a spice grinder and pulse to a fine powder.

To make the granita, combine the water and sugar in a saucepan and bring to a boil over medium-high heat, stirring until the sugar has dissolved. Remove from the heat, add the birch, and let stand at room temperature for 30 minutes. Strain through a fine-mesh sieve into a shallow container. Place in the freezer for 30 minutes. Remove from the freezer, rake and stir the granita thoroughly with a fork, and return to the freezer. Repeat this process every 30 minutes for 4 to 6 hours, until the mixture is frozen and the consistency of granita.

To make the pudding, pour half of the buttermilk into the stand mixer fitted with the whip attachment and the remaining half into a saucepan. Sprinkle the gelatin over the buttermilk in the pan and let stand for 3 to 5 minutes, until it blooms. Place the pan over low heat and heat, stirring frequently, just until fully dissolved. Remove from the heat and let cool to room temperature.

Whip the other half of the buttermilk on medium speed for about 3 minutes, until frothy. Add the almonds, sugar, and skyr and whip until incorporated, about 2 minutes more. Add the buttermilk-gelatin mixture and whip for 1 minute. Add the whipped cream and whip just until incorporated. Transfer to a 9-inch (23-cm) round nonstick cake pan and refrigerate for about 4 hours, until chilled and firmly set. Cut into slices just before serving.

To make the birch honey, combine the honey and water in a saucepan and bring to a gentle simmer over medium heat, whisking continuously, for 2 to 3 minutes, until smooth. Remove from the heat, add the birch, and let cool to room temperature. Strain through a fine-mesh sieve into a small bowl.

To serve, place a slice of the pudding on a plate and set a spoonful of the granita beside it. Sprinkle the meringue over the pudding, then drizzle with the honey and garnish with the dried birch.

STONE BRAMBLE *and* COTTAGE CHEESE *with* WHEY CARAMEL *and* WHEY GRANITA

SERVES 4 TO 6 | PREPARATION TIME: ABOUT 1¹/₂ HOURS (PLUS 12 HOURS TO MACERATE THE BERRIES AND 4 TO 6 HOURS TO FREEZE THE GRANITA)

Gunnar loves foraging for berries, and stone bramble berries are a special treat. They are more elusive than the dark blue crowberries (page 334) that flourish throughout the country, so finding a bush of the tart red berries is a rare treasure. They are used throughout Scandinavia in both savory and sweet dishes and also grow in temperate regions of Asia and Europe. Cranberries or lingonberries are good substitutes.

The whey caramel and granita in this recipe are made with *mysa*, the whey left over from making skyr. It is sold in quart (liter) containers in Icelandic supermarkets (Icelanders really like their whey).

STONE BRAMBLE BERRIES

¹/₂ cup (100 g) sugar

²/₃ cup (150 ml) water

¹/₄ cup (60 ml) cider vinegar

7 ounces (200 g) stone bramble berries, rinsed in ice-cold water

COTTAGE CHEESE

1¹/₂ cups (300 g) large-curd cottage cheese

¹/₄ teaspoon salt

1¹/₂ tablespoons sugar

¹/₄ cup (60 ml) rapeseed oil

NOTE

Reduce the stone bramble liquid by half and drizzle over ice cream or over meats, such as venison or pork. It is also tasty in a cocktail based on a neutral spirit like vodka or gin.

WHEY CARAMEL

1 cup (240 ml) skyr whey (see page 162)

¹/₄ cup (50 g) sugar

WHEY GRANITA

1 cup (240 ml) skyr whey (see page 162)

¹/₂ cup (100 g) sugar

Honey, for garnish

To make the stone bramble berries, prepare an ice bath. Combine the sugar and water in a saucepan and bring to a simmer over medium heat, stirring until the sugar has dissolved. Remove from the heat and nest the pan in the ice bath until the liquid is chilled. Stir in the vinegar and the berries, transfer to an airtight container, cover, and refrigerate for 12 hours. Drain just before serving, reserving the liquid for another use (see notes).

To make the cottage cheese, in a bowl, combine all of the ingredients and stir to mix well. Cover and refrigerate until chilled.

To make the whey caramel, combine the whey and sugar in a saucepan over low heat and heat, stirring, until the sugar has dissolved. Continue cooking over low heat for about 1 hour, until thick and syrupy. Remove from the heat and let cool to room temperature.

To make the whey granita, prepare an ice bath. Combine the whey and sugar in a saucepan over medium heat and bring to a simmer, stirring until the sugar has dissolved. Remove from the heat and nest the pan in the ice bath until the liquid is chilled. Pour into a shallow container and place in the freezer for 30 minutes. Remove from the freezer, rake and stir the granita thoroughly with a fork, and return to the freezer. Repeat this process every 30 minutes for 4 to 6 hours, until the mixture is frozen and the consistency of granita.

To serve, sprinkle the stone bramble berries onto plates and spoon the cottage cheese, caramel, and granita on top. Drizzle generously with the honey and add additional berries.

THE BIRCH AND MUSHROOM FORAGER

Egilsstadir, Eastern Iceland

∞

Most visitors to Iceland who don't venture beyond the lava fields surrounding Reykjavík on their way to such nearby tourist hot spots as the waterfall of Gullfoss or the geysers of Geysir National Park assume the country is a land of jagged black volcanic rock with sparse stands of trees heroically growing in the shadow of soaring mountains. They would never guess that eastern Iceland boasts vast green forests and a bountiful sun that rarely finds its way to Reykjavík. This is the land that reminds Icelanders of what once existed in many parts of the country before the trees were felled by their ancestors to build wooden houses.

Birch, the national tree of Iceland, grows in abundance in the eastern forests. Its sap was once a staple for Icelanders, who boiled it down to syrup in the same way that maple sap is processed in the United States. The tradition has long been lost, save for a few stalwarts who never forgot the importance of birch on the Icelandic table.

Today, Bergrún Arna Thorsteinsdóttir sells birch syrup, mushrooms, and other traditional Icelandic culinary products through her company Holt og Heidar. The birch schnapps and liqueur company that Gunnar and a partner founded in 2009 (see page 174) uses birch for infusing their spirits from Bergrún, adding a birch twig to every bottle.

As she wanders through the lush green forests of eastern Iceland, Bergrún taps birch trees and forages for mushrooms. It is another country altogether from the mossy lava fields of the west, reminding Icelanders who visit the area of what their ancestors likely experienced as they inhaled the oxygen-rich air of the forests. Her company's products are an easy way to transport the past into the contemporary Icelandic kitchen. They are an edible reminder of what once was, and if conservation and reforestation efforts succeed, a symbol of what can be again.

A Conversation with Birch and Mushroom Forager Bergrún Arna Thorsteinsdóttir

Q **How do you make your birch syrup and other products?**

It requires 125 liters of birch sap to make a single liter of birch syrup. The process is very labor-intensive and calls for a tremendous amount of raw ingredients. We add 25 percent sugar to each jar of birch syrup that we sell. Otherwise, the tannins are so bitter that the syrup would not appeal to the consumer. Making birch syrup was a tradition that disappeared centuries ago, but we are trying to revive it. Last year we produced 300 kilograms [660 pounds] of birch syrup, and this year we hope to produce even more.

Q **Whom do you sell your products to?**

We used to sell them only in Iceland, but now there is interest abroad, and we have started selling our products to Norway, with other countries hopefully on the horizon. Tourists seem very interested in what we make, and more and more Icelanders are interested in what we do, too. That makes me happy, because it is their heritage that we are trying to preserve.

Q **How much land do you use to produce your products?**

We are allowed to use the entire birch forest as long as we use it responsibly. We are very conscientious and do not exploit the forest in any way. We replant seedlings to replace the trees that we take, and tapping the trees for sap does no harm to them. We do everything here in a sustainable way, because we have learned lessons from the past. Our ancestors deforested much of Iceland for their timber needs, and today we consider these forests to be precious and deserving of protection.

Q **Have you tried Gunnar's liqueur and schnapps?**

Yes, I like them very much. It's nice to see our birch transformed into something so beautiful. We had been trying to make birch juice, but it wasn't working out. When we were contacted about using our birch to make spirits, we were excited to see if someone else could make a go of infusing liquids with birch, and we are happy that it was a success.

Q **How many people do you employ?**

There are only two of us, and then we have seasonal workers throughout the year to help us. We tap trees beginning around April, and once it begins, it lasts for about three weeks. It's a short season and we need to move quickly to obtain as much sap as we can.

Q **Do you handle other Icelandic ingredients in addition to the birch?**

Yes, we also collect mushrooms and sell them both dried and fresh. We harvest berries and sell them fresh or turn them into jams and juices. The same goes for rhubarb. We try to use as many of Iceland's natural products as we can to show people just how delicious and special they are.

VISITING EASTERN ICELAND

Eastern Iceland is one of the farthest locations to visit from Reykjavík, but the few days of driving time or the hour-long plane ride you must undertake to get there is well worth it. Egilsstadir, the largest town of the region, is not far from the lush birch forests and large barley farm of Vallanes, where owner Eymundur Magnússon is always happy to welcome visitors to his little piece of Icelandic heaven on the shores of picturesque Lake Lagarfljót (see page 133). It is said that a monster similar to the one in Loch Ness surfaces every so often in the lake, so keep your eyes open for a sighting.

The region boasts many guesthouse, hotel, and cozy cabin accommodations, perfect base camps for the horseback riding, river rafting, and hiking opportunities that abound in the area. South of Egilsstadir, along a shoreline drive that will leave you mesmerized by the natural beauty of its waterfalls, cliffs, and soaring mountains, is Iceland's largest glacier, Vatnajökull, which covers 8 percent of the country.

Here is where you can view (even take a boat ride through) the massive turquoise blue icebergs that have broken off from the glacier and are making their way out to sea. This is also the area where reindeer herds roam freely. They are plentiful, and should you be watching for their velvet antlers on the horizon, you are very likely to spot some.

ONION PEEL–SMOKED BONE MARROW, BEETS, *and* BEET–CHERRY VINEGAR PUREE

SERVES 4 | PREPARATION TIME: ABOUT 4 HOURS (INCLUDES 3 HOURS TO PICKLE THE BEETS)

Gunnar's tableside presentations at Dill are sometimes dramatic affairs that are as beautiful as his food is exquisite, and this recipe is a nice illustration of that quality. The marrow is smoked over onion peels, a technique explained on page 250. When served tableside directly from the oven, the striking contrast of the long pieces of halved bone, bubbling from caramelization, resting on a bed of onion peels and accompanied with red and yellow beets, yields a riot of colors that elicits gasps of appreciation from the diners. Another version of this dish calls for smoking the marrowbones over a bed of dried birch leaves, an option that is just as striking, and perfect for a brisk autumn day. The beet–cherry vinegar puree and the red and yellow beets are the ideal chromatic counterpoints for an enticing dish you will want to make again and again.

SMOKED BONE MARROW

4 nice beef marrowbones, each about 8 inches (20 cm) long, cut in half lengthwise (canoe cut) and soaked in ice water for at least 2 hours (see notes, page 190)

Salt

Completely dried peels from at least 10 large onions (see page 250)

BEETS

1 yellow beet, peeled

1 red beet, peeled

1/2 cup (120 ml) cherry or raspberry vinegar

1/4 cup (60 ml) water

2 1/2 tablespoons sugar

1 sprig rosemary

BEET–CHERRY VINEGAR PUREE

3/4 cup (180 ml) cherry or raspberry vinegar

1 3/4 cups (420 ml) freshly squeezed red beet juice (see notes, page 190)

1 cup (200 g) sugar

1 1/2 teaspoons powdered agar agar (see note, page 99)

Salt

To make the smoked bone marrow, season the marrowbones with salt. Arrange the onion peels on the bottom of a deep hotel pan or similar vessel lined with foil and place over high heat. Evenly arrange the bones in a perforated hotel pan that fits inside the first pan. Ignite the peels with a kitchen torch, top with the perforated pan, and seal the entire set-up securely with aluminum foil. Allow the smoke to smolder out completely, about 30 minutes, before removing the foil.

To make the beets, cut the yellow and red beets into planks 1 inch (2.5 cm) thick. Using a round cutter 1/2 inch (12 mm) in diameter, cut each plank to yield a cylinder 1/2 inch (12 mm) in diameter and 1 inch (2.5 cm) long. Bring a saucepan of salted water to a boil, add the yellow cylinders, and cook for 5 to 5 1/2 minutes, until just tender. Using a slotted

| continued

NOTES

1. Soaking the bones in ice water for at least 2 hours before using will remove any excess blood and impurities.

2. Save the beet scraps created when preparing different elements in this recipe for the beet juice required for the vinegar. They will not yield enough juice for the whole recipe, but it is nevertheless a good way to avoid waste.

3. The yellow and red beets can be cooked in the same water as long as the yellow beets are cooked first.

spoon, transfer to paper towels to drain. Repeat the process with the red cylinders. Place each color in a separate heatproof bowl (see notes).

Combine the vinegar, water, sugar, and rosemary in a saucepan and bring to a gentle simmer over medium-low heat, stirring until the sugar has dissolved. Remove from the heat, discard the rosemary, and pour half of the liquid over the red cylinders and half over the yellow cylinders. Let stand at room temperature for 3 hours before using, or cover and refrigerate until ready to use.

To make the beet–cherry vinegar puree, combine the vinegar, half of the red beet juice, and the sugar in a saucepan and bring to a boil over medium heat, stirring until the sugar has dissolved. Remove from the heat, add the agar agar, and process with an immersion blender until smooth. Season with salt, then return to low heat and cook, stirring, for about 1 minute, until the mixture starts to thicken. Strain through a fine-mesh sieve into a small heatproof bowl and let cool to room temperature. It will be the texture and thickness of fluid gel.

Transfer the mixture to a blender and process on high speed, adding the remaining beet juice in a slow, steady stream. Continue to process until the puree is the consistency of a glossy gel. Transfer to a squeeze bottle and refrigerate until chilled. The puree will keep in the refrigerator for up to 2 days.

Meanwhile, preheat the oven to 400°F (200°C). Once you have removed the foil, finish the marrow in the oven for 2 minutes. Finally, caramelize the surface of the marrow with a kitchen torch or place under the broiler for 2 to 3 minutes.

To serve, arrange 2 marrowbone halves and a spoonful of beet cylinders on a plate. Drizzle them both with the vinegar puree.

HOW TO ASSEMBLE
A HOMEMADE SMOKER

Constructing a smoker is not as difficult as it sounds. The only tools required for a basic smoker are a bottom compartment that can handle direct heat and has a tight-fitting lid (or aluminum foil), the smoking material, a kitchen torch or matchstick to light the smoking material, and a top compartment to hold what is being smoked. A deep hotel pan (or deep baking pan), a perforated hotel pan (or a wire rack), and aluminum foil work well. A vegetable steamer—a pan with a rack insert and a lid—is also a good option.

Put a bed of hay, leaves, wood chips, or onion peels in the bottom compartment and arrange what you are smoking in the top compartment and place over high heat. Ignite the smoking material and get a good flame going by gently blowing on it. Then set the top compartment in the bottom compartment and seal the entire set-up securely with the lid (foil). The lid will cut off the oxygen supply, resulting in a smoldering fire that will infuse the food with smokiness. The smoke will take about 5 to 10 minutes to subside, depending upon the intensity of the flame and the smoking material used. At this point, repeat the process once or twice more, depending on the smokiness desired.

WHERE IS THE CHICKEN?

Iceland has a number of animals that were introduced with the first settlers (see page 290). Among them was the chicken, but its popularity decreased over the centuries because of a preference for fattier meats, such as lamb, pork, and beef.

The species was nearly extinct until renewed interest prompted some Icelanders to start raising chickens for both their meat and their eggs. Nowaday, chicken is beginning to appear more frequently on the national table.

MUSHROOMS, CHEESE, *and* BIRCH

SERVES 4 | PREPARATION TIME: ABOUT 2¼ HOURS

This lovely little appetizer, with its bubbling cheese and mushrooms prepared two ways, is easy to create. Collecting mushrooms appeals to Gunnar's love of foraging, and one of the prime spots to look for them is in eastern Iceland, where they flourish in the birch forests. Elsewhere in the country they are less commonly encountered because of past deforestation.

Gunnar likes to use larch mushrooms, one of the most common species in Iceland, for this dish. They can be difficult to find elsewhere, so just use your favorite mix of fresh mushrooms in their place. For the cheese, he uses the funky smelling Ísbúi, but that, too, is a challenge to find outside of Iceland. Aged Gouda or raclette make a fine substitute.

MUSHROOM AND BIRCH FOAM

14 ounces (400 g) mushrooms (such as shiitake, morel, chanterelle, or cremini)

3 cups (720 ml) water, plus more if needed

2 (8-inch/20-cm) leafy birch twigs, leaves removed and twigs halved

¾ cup (180 ml) milk

Salt

Beer Vinegar (page 30), for seasoning

3 g soy lecithin (see notes, page 27 and below)

MUSHROOM PUREE

Reserved mushrooms from the foam

Scant ½ cup (120 ml) heavy cream

2 tablespoons unsalted butter

Salt

Beer Vinegar (page 30), for seasoning

4 large, thick slices Ísbúi, aged Gouda, or raclette cheese

NOTE

Alternatively, omit the soy lecithin and whisk vigorously instead. Although this will not create a true foam, it will produce an aerated sauce.

To make the mushroom and birch foam, combine the mushrooms, water, and birch in a saucepan and bring to a vigorous simmer. Turn down the heat to low, cover partially, and simmer gently for 1½ hours. Keep an eye on the water during this step and add more as needed to prevent scorching. Drain the mixture through a fine-mesh sieve, reserving the liquid and solids separately. Return the liquid to the saucepan, bring to a boil, and reduce by half. Add the milk and reduce by one-fourth, stirring frequently to prevent the milk from foaming over the sides of the pan. Strain once more through a fine-mesh sieve, as the milk can produce a film on the surface of the liquid. Season with salt and vinegar. When ready to serve, add the soy lecithin and process with an immersion blender until foamy (see note).

To make the mushroom puree, discard the birch twigs from the reserved mushrooms. Put the mushrooms in a blender or food processor and process to a chunky paste. Combine the cream and butter in a small saucepan and bring to a boil over medium-high heat. Add the mushrooms and stir until most of the liquid has evaporated and the mushrooms have thickened. Season with salt and vinegar.

To serve, spoon the mushroom puree onto a plate and place a slice of cheese on top to cover the puree completely. Ignite the cheese with a kitchen torch until it is golden brown and bubbly, then top with a generous spoonful of the foam.

PINE-SAUTÉED REDFISH, SALSIFY, PINE TREE SAUCE, *and* BURNED BUTTER VINEGAR

SERVES 4 | PREPARATION TIME: ABOUT 1 HOUR (PLUS 12 HOURS FOR THE PINE TREE OIL) | PICTURED ON PAGE 196

Salsify, a root vegetable with white, creamy flesh and sturdy skin, is also known as the oyster plant because its flavor recalls the brininess of that shellfish. A member of the dandelion family, salsify can be used in the same way as other root vegetables, such as parsnip, celery root, and rutabaga, and is a favorite of Gunnar's, who prizes its long shelf life and pronounced flavor.

Here, it is paired with redfish, pine, birch tree schnapps, and burned butter for an interesting flavor marriage that melds the virtues of the woods and the sea. Gunnar likes redfish for its lean flavor and flaky texture, but should you have trouble finding it, flounder, trout, smelt, or tilapia are good substitutes. This dish represents eastern Iceland especially well because the region is one of the few in the country where the forest meets the sea.

PINE TREE SAUCE

3 tablespoons distilled white vinegar

2 tablespoons Chicken Stock, homemade (page 89) or store-bought

3 (6-inch/15-cm) pine tree twigs, rinsed well under ice-cold water to remove residue and sap

1/3 cup (80 ml) egg yolks

1/2 cup (120 ml) skyr whey (see page 162)

1/2 cup (50 g) minced shallots

1/4 cup (60 ml) Beer Vinegar (page 30)

3 tablespoons pine tree vinegar, plus 1 tablespoon for seasoning (optional, see note)

1 cup plus 1 1/2 tablespoons (250 g) unsalted butter, melted

Salt

PINE TREE ASH

Needles from 1 (6-inch/15-cm) pine tree twig, rinsed well under ice-cold water to remove residue and sap

SAUTÉED REDFISH

1 1/2 tablespoons unsalted butter

1 teaspoon rapeseed oil

2 (8-inch/20-cm) pine tree twigs, rinsed well under ice-cold water to remove residue and sap

1 (14-ounce/400-g) skinned redfish fillet, cut into 8 equal pieces

Salt

BURNED BUTTER VINEGAR

1 1/2 tablespoons Beer Vinegar (page 30)

1 teaspoon sugar

0.3 g xanthan gum (see notes page 34)

1/4 cup (55 g) burned butter (see page 119)

1 1/2 teaspoons finely chopped shallot

1 tablespoon chopped fresh chives

1 tablespoon pine tree oil (page 150)

Salt

SALSIFY

1 1/2 tablespoons unsalted butter

1 teaspoon rapeseed oil

2 (10-inch/25-cm) salsifies, unpeeled, washed and scrubbed rigorously, and halved lengthwise

1 tablespoon Birkir schnapps (see page 174)

Salt

To make the sauce, combine the white vinegar, stock, and 1 pine twig in a saucepan, bring to a gentle simmer over low heat, and cook for 5 minutes. Strain through a fine-mesh sieve into a small heatproof container and discard the pine twig. Let cool to room temperature.

NOTE

To make pine tree vinegar, bring white wine vinegar to a simmer and add the pine twigs. Remove from the heat and cool to room temperature. Strain through a fine-mesh sieve and discard the twigs.

Preheat an immersion circulator to 149°F (65°C). Place the cooled liquid and the egg yolks in a vacuum bag and seal on the lowest setting. Cook in the circulator for 30 minutes.

Meanwhile, place the whey, shallots, beer vinegar, and the remaining 2 pine twigs in a saucepan, bring to a simmer over medium heat, and cook for about 8 minutes, until reduced by about two-thirds. Strain through a fine-mesh sieve into a blender and add the 3 tablespoons of pine vinegar. With the blender on low speed, add the butter in a slow, steady stream until thickened to the consistency of hollandaise sauce. Season with salt to taste and 1 tablespoon of pine vinegar, if desired.

To make the pine tree ash, heat a dry frying pan over high heat, add the pine needles, and toast until completely charred. Let cool to room temperature, then grind in a spice grinder to a powder.

To make the redfish, melt the butter with the oil in a sauté pan over medium heat. Add the pine twigs and sauté for 30 seconds. Season the redfish pieces on both sides with salt, add to the pan, and sauté over medium heat for 4 to 5 minutes on the first side, spooning the sizzling butter and oil on top as they cook. Flip the pieces over and cook the same way on the second side for 4 to 5 minutes, until just cooked through. Repeat the process. Using a spatula, transfer to paper towels to drain. Keep warm.

To make the burned butter vinegar, combine the vinegar and sugar in a small, heavy saucepan and bring to a simmer. Cook until the sugar dissolves, then add the xanthan gum and stir until thickened. Add the butter, shallot, chives, and pine tree oil and season with salt. Remove from the heat and keep warm.

To make the salsify, melt the butter with the oil in a pan over medium-high heat. Add the salsifies and sauté for 8 to 10 minutes, until tender. The timing will depend on their thickness. Add the schnapps and continue cooking until the liquid evaporates. Season with salt.

To serve, arrange the salsify and fish on a plate, drizzle with the burned butter vinegar and the pine tree sauce. Sprinkle the pine tree ash on top.

OPPOSITE: Pine-Sautéed Redfish, Salsify, Pine Tree Sauce, and Burned Butter Vinegar (page 194)

ABOVE: Whey-Glazed Pork Belly, Caramelized Parsnip Puree, and Herb Emulsion (page 198)

WHEY-GLAZED PORK BELLY, CARAMELIZED PARSNIP PUREE, *and* HERB EMULSION

SERVES 4 | PREPARATION TIME: ABOUT 1 HOUR (PLUS 12 HOURS TO REFRIGERATE
AND 12 HOURS TO COOK THE PORK BELLY AND DEHYDRATE THE PORK SKIN)
| PICTURED ON PAGE 197

Eastern Iceland is filled with welcoming country hotels that serve buffets of traditional
dishes. This recipe is the refined version of some of those buffets; it calls for slow cooking
spice-studded pork belly, glazing it with a cap of herbaceous whey, and accompanying it
with crispy pork skin, caramelized parsnips, and celery root puree. The dish is finished
with an elegant herb emulsion and mountain spinach, an amethyst-colored herb also
known as orach. Mountain spinach, which has long flourished in the temperate climates
of central Europe, has recently found its way to the greenhouses of Iceland, where it has
quickly become a favorite of Gunnar's, who values it for both its pronounced flavor and its
jewel-box color.

PORK BELLY

1 (1¹/₂-pound/680-g) piece of
boneless pork belly

2 cups (480 ml) water

2 tablespoons plus 1 teaspoon
salt

2¹/₂ tablespoons sugar

1 cinnamon stick

5 juniper berries

4 whole cloves

1 sprig rosemary

CRISPY PORK SKIN

Reserved pork skin

Vegetable oil, for deep-frying

Salt

Ground cinnamon, for
seasoning

Ground cloves, for seasoning

Ground juniper berries, for
seasoning

WHEY GLAZE

¹/₃ cup (80 ml) skyr whey
(see page 162)

3 tablespoons unsalted butter

2 tablespoons rapeseed oil

3 tablespoons chopped shallot

¹/₂ cinnamon stick

1 sprig rosemary

2 whole cloves

¹/₃ cup (80 ml) Beer Vinegar
(page 30), plus more for
seasoning

³/₄ cup (180 ml) Chicken
Stock, preferably homemade
(page 89)

Salt

CARAMELIZED PARSNIP

1 parsnip, peeled and halved
crosswise

Unsalted butter, for sautéing

1 teaspoon rapeseed oil,
for sautéing

Salt

PARSNIP PUREE

2 tablespoons unsalted butter

1¹/₂ cups (200 g) peeled and
coarsely chopped parsnips

¹/₂ teaspoon baking soda

Salt

Beer Vinegar (page 30), for
seasoning

CELERY ROOT PUREE

1¹/₂ cups (200 g) peeled and
coarsely chopped celery root

4 teaspoons milk

4 teaspoons heavy cream

1¹/₂ tablespoons unsalted
butter

Salt

Cider vinegar, for seasoning

HERB EMULSION

2¹/₂ teaspoons stone-ground
mustard

2 teaspoons Beer Vinegar
(page 30), plus more for
seasoning

1 teaspoon chopped garlic

2 tablespoons chopped shallot

¹/₂ cup (30 g) chopped
fresh dill

¹/₃ cup (20 g) chopped fresh
flat-leaf parsley

¹/₄ cup (60 ml) water, plus
more if needed

1 cup (240 ml) rapeseed oil

Salt

Fresh mountain spinach, for
garnish

NOTE

To remove the pork skin easily, grasp the edge of the skin with one hand and, using a razor-sharp boning knife in the other hand, deftly cut the skin away from the fat.

To make the pork belly, cut the skin off (see note) and save it to make the crispy pork skin. Combine the water, salt, sugar, cinnamon, juniper, cloves, and rosemary in a saucepan and bring to a boil over high heat, stirring until the sugar has dissolved. Remove from the heat and let cool to room temperature. Place the pork belly in a vacuum bag, pour the brine over it, and seal on the lowest setting. Refrigerate for 12 hours.

Preheat an immersion circulator to 167°F (75°C). Place the bag in the circulator and cook for 12 hours. Remove the bag from the circulator and keep warm.

To make the crispy pork skin, prepare as directed on page 165, crisping in the oil and seasoning with the salt, cinnamon, cloves, and juniper.

To make the glaze, reduce the whey in a small saucepan over medium heat until only 1 tablespoon remains. Set aside. In a separate small saucepan, melt 1 tablespoon of the butter with half the oil over medium-high heat. Add the shallot, cinnamon, rosemary, and cloves and cook, stirring, for 5 to 7 minutes, until the shallot is caramelized and the spices are aromatic. And the vinegar and reduce by three-fourths. Add the stock and reduce by half. Add the remaining 2 tablespoons of butter and stir until melted. Strain through a fine-mesh sieve into the saucepan holding the whey and whisk together. Season with salt and vinegar.

To finish the pork belly, remove the belly from the bag and cut into 8 equal pieces. Heat a large sauté pan over medium heat. When the pan is hot, arrange the belly, fat side down, in the pan. Let the fat render until it begins to turn a light golden brown. Spoon some of the glaze into the pan and then, using tongs, turn the belly pieces over to coat them in the glaze. Cook for a minute or two more before adding more glaze and turning once more. Continue this process until the pork belly is lacquered, glossy, and well coated in glaze.

To make the caramelized parsnip, bring a saucepan of salted water to a boil. Add the parsnip and cook for about 5 minutes, until almost tender. The timing will depend on the size of the parsnip. Drain and pat dry with paper towels. Melt enough butter with some oil in a sauté pan over medium-high heat to form a thin film on the pan bottom. Add the parsnip and sauté until deeply caramelized. Remove from the heat, and when cool enough to handle, slice thinly crosswise on a mandoline (see notes, page 73).

| continued

| Whey-Glazed Pork Belly, Caramelized Parsnip Puree, and Herb Emulsion, *continued*

To make the parsnip puree, melt the butter in a pressure cooker (see page 50). Add the parsnips, baking soda, and salt, lock the lid in place, bring to medium-high pressure, and cook for 15 minutes, until the parsnips are caramelized and tender. Let the pressure release naturally for 15 minutes. Remove the lid, transfer the contents of the cooker to a blender, and process until smooth. Season with salt and add a generous amount of beer vinegar. The parsnips are very sweet and require a substantial splash of vinegar for balance. If the mixture is too thick after seasoning, add water to thin it to the desired consistency.

To make the celery root puree, preheat the immersion circulator to 183°F (84°C). Place the celery root, milk, and cream in a vacuum bag and seal on the lowest setting. Cook in the circulator for about 8 minutes, until tender. Test for doneness by pinching the celery root through the bag. If it is tender and breaks apart easily, it is ready. The timing will depend on how fine the cut is. Remove the bag from the circulator and drain the celery root, reserving the solids and cooking liquid separately. Transfer the celery root to a blender, add the butter, and process on high speed to a puree, adding a little of the cooking liquid if necessary to achieve a smooth consistency. Season with salt and cider vinegar.

To make the herb emulsion, in a blender, combine the mustard, beer vinegar, garlic, shallot, dill, parsley, and water and process on high speed to a puree while adding the oil in a slow, steady stream. Add more water, if necessary, to achieve a smooth consistency. Season with salt and more vinegar, if desired.

To serve, arrange 2 pork belly slices fat side-up on each plate. Spoon the parsnip and celery root purees alongside. Arrange a few pieces of the caramelized parsnips next to the purees and drizzle everything with the herb emulsion. Garnish with mountain spinach.

FRIED GOOSE BREAST, CELERY ROOT TWO WAYS, *and* PARSLEY *and* DILL OIL

SERVES 4 | PREPARATION TIME: ABOUT 1^1/$_2$ HOURS (PLUS 12 HOURS TO REFRIGERATE THE OIL) | PICTURED ON PAGE 204

Wild geese, which soar overhead everywhere in Iceland, are a prized protein on the Icelandic table. Wild birds are coveted foods in the country, with the greatest reverence reserved for a breed of grouse called a ptarmigan, a bird primarily found in the eastern region whose feathers change from brown to white in winter as a form of camouflage. This makes it an extremely elusive target and accounts for the celebratory meal it prompts when a skilled hunter brings one home.

Smoked ptarmigan is a traditional part of many Christmas feasts in Iceland, but goose is frequently a stand-in when the grouse is not available. If goose is difficult to find where you live, substitute duck breasts and double the quantity. Gunnar serves goose at Dill in the fall and winter months. It is paired here with celery root and parsley and dill oil, making it a perfect dish to serve during the colder months of the year.

HERB OIL

1 ounce (30 g) flat-leaf parsley sprigs

1 ounce (30 g) dill sprigs

Scant 2 tablespoons rapeseed oil

CELERY ROOT PUREE

1^1/$_2$ cups (200 g) peeled and chopped celery root

^{1}/$_4$ cup (60 ml) milk

^{1}/$_4$ cup (60 ml) heavy cream, plus more as needed

^{1}/$_2$ teaspoon salt

1^1/$_2$ tablespoons unsalted butter

Beer Vinegar (page 30), for seasoning

FRIED CELERY ROOT

1 tablespoon unsalted butter, for frying

1 tablespoon rapeseed oil, for frying

1 large celery root, peeled and cut into bite-size pieces

1 tablespoon apple cider vinegar

^{1}/$_4$ cup (40 g) chopped shallots

^{1}/$_4$ cup burned butter (see page 119)

1 tablespoon chopped fresh chives

Salt

SAUCE

1 tablespoon unsalted butter

^{1}/$_4$ cup (40 g) chopped onion

2 tablespoons peeled and chopped carrot

1^1/$_2$ tablespoons peeled and chopped celery root

1 tablespoon chopped fennel bulb

2 whole cloves

2 juniper berries

1 star anise pod

1 sprig rosemary

Scant 3^1/$_2$ tablespoons sugar

^{1}/$_2$ cup (120 ml) cider vinegar

^{3}/$_4$ cup (180 ml) Chicken Stock, preferably homemade (page 89)

^{1}/$_2$ cup (120 ml) Veal Stock, preferably homemade (page 90)

Salt

Beer Vinegar (page 30), for seasoning

FRIED GOOSE BREAST

1 tablespoon unsalted butter

1 tablespoon rapeseed oil

^{1}/$_2$ bunch thyme

2 (1^1/$_3$ pounds/600 g each) goose breasts, trimmed of any excess fat and skin

Salt

To make the herb oil, combine the parsley, dill, and oil in a blender and process on high speed for 7 to 10 minutes, until steaming hot and the herbs are fully incorporated into the oil. Transfer to an airtight container and refrigerate for 12 hours. Strain through a fine-mesh sieve, then transfer to a squeeze bottle. The oil will keep in the refrigerator for up to 1 week.

To make the celery root puree, preheat an immersion circulator to 183°F (84°C). Place the celery root, milk, cream, and salt in a vacuum bag and seal on the lowest setting. Cook in the circulator for about 8 minutes, until tender. The timing will depend on how fine the cut. Test the doneness of the celery root by pinching it through the bag. If it is tender and breaks apart easily, it is ready. If not, cook for a few more minutes. Drain, reserving the celery root and cooking liquid separately. Transfer the celery root to the blender, add the butter, and process on high speed to a puree, adding a little of the cooking liquid if necessary to achieve a smooth consistency. Season with vinegar.

To make the fried celery root, melt the butter with the oil in a sauté pan over medium-high heat. Add the celery root and fry, turning every few minutes to ensure even cooking, for 8 to 10 minutes, until golden brown on the outside and creamy on the inside. Add the vinegar and cook until completely evaporated. Using a slotted spoon, transfer the celery root to paper towels to drain. Add the shallots to the same pan and sauté for about 7 minutes, until tender. Add the burned butter and chives and toss together with the celery root. Season with salt. Keep warm.

To make the sauce, melt the butter in a sauté pan over medium-high heat. Add the onion, carrot, celery root, fennel, cloves, juniper, star anise, and rosemary and sauté for about 9 minutes, until the vegetables are tender. Add the sugar and cook, stirring occasionally, until caramelized. Add the cider vinegar and cook until reduced by three-fourths. Add both stocks, cover, and simmer for about 30 minutes, until the sauce is glossy and coats the back of a wooden spoon. Strain through a fine-mesh sieve and season with salt and beer vinegar.

To make the fried goose breast, melt the butter with the oil in a large sauté pan over high heat. Add the thyme and sauté for 30 seconds. Season the breasts on both sides with salt and add to the pan, skin side down. Sear, turning once, for about 3 minutes on each side, until golden brown on both sides. Turn down the heat to medium-high and continue to cook for about 6 more minutes, until medium-rare, or to desired doneness. Transfer the breasts to paper towels and let rest for 7 minutes, flipping them once at the halfway point to distribute the internal juices evenly before serving. Thinly slice, dividing each breast into 2 servings.

To serve, spoon the celery root puree on a plate, top with goose breast slices, and arrange the fried celery root alongside. Drizzle everything with the sauce and the herb oil.

OPPOSITE: Fried Goose Breast, Celery Root Two Ways, and Parsley and Dill Oil (page 202)

ABOVE: Ástarpungar, Birch-Soaked Raisins, and Cream (page 206)

ÁSTARPUNGAR, BIRCH-SOAKED RAISINS, *and* CREAM

SERVES 6 TO 8 | PREPARATION TIME: ABOUT 2 HOURS (PLUS 12 HOURS TO DEHYDRATE THE BIRCH LEAVES) | PICTURED ON PAGE 205

Ástarpungar translates as "love balls" in Icelandic, and once you see their shape, you will realize it means exactly what you think it does. They are basically fried doughnut holes, and in some households in northern Iceland, they are still prepared weekly and typically served with rhubarb or crowberry jam. At Dill, Gunnar serves them with raisins that have been plumped in his birch schnapps and sprinkles them with birch sugar. Should you not have a bottle of birch schnapps on hand, dark rum is a good substitute. The one essential is a dollop of freshly whipped cream, and voilà, your love balls are ready to be served to the people in your life toward whom you feel the most affection. Gunnar's recipe is from an old Icelandic recipe book that belonged to his grandmother.

BIRCH-SOAKED RAISINS

1 cup (240 ml) Birkir schnapps or dark rum

1/2 cup (100 g) sugar

Scant 1 1/2 cups (200 g) black or golden raisins

BIRCH SUGAR

1 cup (3 g) dehydrated birch tree leaves (see note)

1 cup (200 g) sugar

CREAM

1/2 cup (120 ml) heavy cream

1/4 cup (50 g) crème fraîche

1 1/2 tablespoons sugar

LOVE BALLS

4 cups (500 g) all-purpose flour

1 1/2 tablespoons sugar

1 teaspoon salt

2 tablespoons baking powder

2 cups (480 ml) buttermilk

2 eggs

Birch-soaked raisins (at left)

Rapeseed oil, for deep-frying

NOTE

To dehydrate birch leaves, preheat a dehydrator to the lowest setting. Spread the leaves on a dehydrator tray and dehydrate for about 12 hours, until dry.

To make the birch-soaked raisins, combine the schnapps and sugar in a saucepan and bring to a simmer over medium heat, stirring until the sugar has dissolved. Remove from the heat and add the raisins. Let stand at room temperature for at least 1 hour.

To make the birch sugar, pulse the birch leaves in a spice grinder to a powder, then sift through a fine-mesh sieve to remove any large bits and stems. Transfer the ground leaves to a spice grinder, add the sugar, and pulse until a fine powder forms.

To make the cream, in a bowl, whip the cream to stiff peaks. Fold in the crème fraîche and sugar just until fully incorporated. Cover and refrigerate until chilled.

To make the love balls, combine the flour, sugar, salt, and baking powder in a bowl and stir to mix well. Make a well in the center of the flour mixture, add the buttermilk to the well, and then pull the flour into the well, mixing it with the liquid. Whisk until fully incorporated. The consistency should be thick but pourable. Do not worry about lumps; they make the balls better in the end. Whisk in the eggs one at a time, incorporating the first egg completely before adding the second. Finally, stir in half the birch-soaked raisins (reserve the other half for service), mixing well.

Pour oil to a depth of 3 to 4 inches (7.5 to 10 cm) into a deep, heavy pot and heat to 350°F (180°C). Line a large plate with paper towels. When the oil is hot, for each love ball, scoop up 2 to 3 tablespoons of the dough with an ice cream scoop or large spoon and carefully drop the ball into the oil. Do not make the balls any larger or they will be golden brown on the exterior but still raw in the center. Also, do not crowd them in the oil or they will not cook evenly and they will absorb the oil. Deep-fry the balls, turning them once, for about 3 minutes on each side, or until golden brown. Using a slotted spoon, transfer them to the paper towel–lined plate to drain. Repeat with the remaining batter.

To serve, sprinkle the warm balls with the birch sugar and drizzle them with the cream. Serve the reserved raisins on the side.

THE SHEEP FARMER

Mödrudal, Northern Iceland

∞

Smoked Lamb with Skyr and Nutmeg 216

Dried Trotters, Pickled Onions, and Hay-Smoked Mayonnaise 218

Lamb Sweetbreads, Caramelized Celery Root,
and Blood Sausage 221

Sautéed Lamb Fillet with Crowberries, Baked Lamb Fat,
and Sunchokes 224

Hay-Smoked Duck Breasts, Carrot Puree,
and Herb Emulsion 228

Roasted Lamb Shoulder, Braised Cabbage, Pickled Onions,
Leek Butter, and Chervil Syrup 230

Hay-Smoked Oil 233

In Iceland, after a long day of driving, you often yearn for a comfortable, safe refuge. Vast stretches of the country afford nothing but gas stations selling hot dogs and hamburgers, and although these are both better than most of their incarnations anywhere else in the world, sometimes the drive is so painfully long that a hot dog just won't satisfy you. A sliver of a dirt road in the north of the country conjures just such a desire for more than fast food, and at the moment that it strikes most intensely, nirvana in the form of turf houses and a restaurant with candlelit windows welcome the weary traveler for the night.

Fjalladyrd, which is surrounded by snowcapped volcanoes, is the highest settled farm in Iceland. Perched atop a broad, windy plateau known as The Highlands, it is a sheep farm owned by the same family for as long as anyone can remember. Elisabet Kristjánsdóttir married Viljálmur Vernhardsson, the present owner, before moving to this remote corner of Iceland, and now she and her husband raise sheep, run a restaurant and hotel, and look after their young daughter on one of the largest privately owned farms in the nation.

At their restaurant—which is the stuff of log-cabin dreams—they serve smoked lamb and freshly caught arctic char. For dessert, there are hot waffles drizzled with rhubarb jam and crowned with whipped cream. In the mornings, Elisabet offers hotel guests guided outdoor adventures in the surrounding countryside, and year-round, she helps tend the sheep.

The sheep wander in the fields throughout the spring and summer, before being rounded up each autumn from the remote corners of the property. Their wool is transformed into mittens, hats, socks, and sweaters, and their meat is dirt smoked (see page 43) to infuse it with the *terroir* of the region. It tastes of the arctic thyme, sorrel, and angelica that flourishes on the farm, reminding those who eat it of the welcoming refuge they discovered just when they were ready to settle for another hot dog.

A Conversation with Sheep Farmer
Elisabet Kristjánsdóttir

Q How long has this property been in your husband's family?

It has been in the family for many generations. We have a church on the property that my husband's grandfather built. He was an artist and a farmer. Over fifty people once lived on this land, but today only three people live here, my husband, our daughter, and me. I met my husband in 2004 and have lived here ever since. I had known him for only one month, and it was my birthday. For a gift he gave me a baby goat, and I knew he was the one.

Q Is it sometimes difficult to live in a place that is so isolated?

No, it really isn't. We have so many visitors who pass through here, and our daughter attends school for part of the year in Akureyri, which provides her with companions. I love living here, I love raising my daughter here, and I feel privileged to be a part of such a long tradition.

Q How many sheep do you have here?

We used to have over fifteen hundred. Today we have one hundred sheep and fifty goats. We would like to increase the number for both species a bit. We are trying to raise a specific breed of sheep that we feel has the best-tasting meat. In the early days, the sheep lived outside and their legs were very hearty from walking so much. We are trying to re-create that experience. The sheep house is open, and the sheep are allowed to roam wherever and whenever they want to. It's not a contained, isolated place. It's a house that is a shelter, but they have their freedom, too. Our sheep house can house two hundred sheep, so we are constantly working to increase our numbers. We produce the manure blocks in the traditional way, by letting the sheep compress the hay and manure as they pass back and forth, and then we use the blocks to smoke our meat.

Q Do you sell your meat?

Yes, we sell it directly from the farm. We are not allowed to slaughter our sheep here. They are slaughtered in the next town, because a license is required for every step. I don't believe any farm in Iceland slaughters at home, except for what the farmers consume themselves. So we send our sheep about forty miles away and then bring the meat back here, where we prepare it in our restaurant and also sell it to the public. We do run out of meat each year toward the end of the season, which is frustrating because we would like to serve and sell our own meat year-round. But we just can't keep up with the demand.

Q **What are some of your biggest challenges?**

The regulations imposed on us can be very frustrating, because so often they do not make sense and are in place only because of some bureaucratic system. I am not concerned about sheep farming in Iceland disappearing, because Icelanders appreciate what the sheep farmers do. But I am concerned that the regulations imposed on small family farms like ours will change the traditions that have been in place since the beginning.

Q **What do you enjoy most about living on the farm?**

People come to this area because it is so remote. What I like most of all is guiding our visitors in The Highlands. When I moved here, I discovered I did not always like being in the café. I don't like to be inside. I'm a true Icelander at heart. When I'm in the kitchen, I'm happy, but I am always yearning to be outside, too. I love showing people this beautiful region of Iceland, I love seeing Iceland through their eyes. It affirms for me again and again just how special this place is.

SMOKED LAMB *with* SKYR *and* NUTMEG

SERVES 4 TO 6 | PREPARATION TIME: ABOUT 30 MINUTES (PLUS A FEW HOURS TO FREEZE THE LAMB AND 12 TO 14 HOURS TO DEHYDRATE THE LAMB)

Lamb has been smoked in Iceland since the arrival of the first settlers. It's dirt smoked in the same manner as arctic char (see page 43) and is a beloved tradition at Fjalladyrd, in spite of the government regulations and expense that deter many farmers less determined than Elisabet Kristjánsdóttir to keep old practices alive.

Icelandic smoked lamb is available at some specialty food shops outside of the country, but if it is impossible to source where you live, prosciutto makes a respectable substitute. The natural earthiness of the skyr is treated to a tangy sweetness with the addition of sour cream, honey, and vinegar.

SMOKED LAMB

3¹/₂ ounces (100 g) boneless smoked lamb from leg

SKYR

¹/₄ cup (70 g) Skyr (page 162)

3 tablespoons sour cream

1¹/₂ teaspoons honey

Salt

Cider vinegar, for seasoning

Freshly grated nutmeg, for seasoning

NOTE

If you are substituting prosciutto for the lamb, it may take longer to dehydrate because of its higher fat content. The humidity level of where you live will also affect the dehydrating time.

To make the lamb, wrap it securely in plastic wrap and freeze it solid. Preheat a dehydrator to 147°F (64°C). Let the lamb sit for a few minutes at room temperature, then cut it into paper-thin slices on a mandoline (see notes, page 79) or a meat slicer.

Arrange the slices in a single layer on a dehydrator tray and dehydrate for 12 to 14 hours, until completely dry and crisp (see note). Store the slices between sheets of parchment paper in an airtight container in the refrigerator until ready to serve. The lamb will keep in the refrigerator for up to 2 weeks.

To make the skyr, whisk together the skyr, sour cream, and honey until well mixed. Season with salt, vinegar, and nutmeg. Cover and refrigerate until chilled.

To serve, arrange the smoked lamb chips in a bowl and accompany with the skyr for dipping.

DRIED TROTTERS, PICKLED ONIONS, *and* HAY-SMOKED MAYONNAISE

SERVES 4 | PREPARATION TIME: ABOUT 2½ HOURS (PLUS 24 HOURS TO REFRIGERATE AND DEHYDRATE THE LAMB AND TO PICKLE THE ONIONS)

In the United States, pig trotters are the most common source of "foot cheese," as Gunnar refers to the preparation here, but in Iceland, lamb trotters are more commonly used. Trotters are a chef's secret weapon, and you have likely enjoyed them tucked into other elements of a dish and marveled at their taste without even knowing what you were eating. Their tightly wound bits of sinew, meat, and fat, along with a healthy dose of gelatin, deliver deep, intense flavors that bring you back again and again for another bite.

For this recipe, Gunnar first cooks the trotters, bones them, weights the meat overnight in the refrigerator, and then dehydrates the meat. The result is a flavor-packed drier version of the standard trotter. The hay-smoked mayonnaise adds moisture and creaminess and connects the palate to the pasture in which the sheep once roamed, and the pickled onions deliver a nice acidic note.

DRIED TROTTERS

4 or 5 lamb trotters (see notes)

1 cup (240 ml) Veal Stock, preferably homemade (page 90), reduced to ½ cup (120 ml)

Salt

Beer Vinegar (page 30), for seasoning

PICKLED ONIONS

3 white pearl onions, halved lengthwise and petals separated

3 red pearl onions, halved lengthwise and petals separated

Scant 1 cup (200 ml) Beer Vinegar (page 30)

¼ cup (60 ml) water

½ cup (100 g) sugar

SMOKED MAYONNAISE

1 egg yolk

Scant 1 cup (200 ml) Hay-Smoked Oil (see page 233)

Salt

Beer Vinegar (page 30), for seasoning

Old man's pepper, for garnish (see notes, page 109)

NOTES

1. Your butcher will likely be so happy to supply you with an unusual request like lamb trotters, and he or she may also oblige your request to remove any residual hair on the skin.

2. The foot cheese can also be dehydrated for about 12 hours in an oven set to the lowest setting.

To make the dried trotters, torch any remaining hair on the trotters and scrape the hair away (see notes). Rinse well under cold running water and place in a large saucepan. Add water to cover by 1 inch (2.5 cm), place over low heat, and bring to a simmer. Cook for 1 to 1½ hours, until completely tender and the meat is falling from the bones. Drain the trotters, reserving the liquid. When the trotters are cool enough to handle, remove the skin and bones and discard. Shred the meat into small pieces.

In a bowl, mix together the meat, reduced stock, and ¼ cup (60 ml) of the reserved cooking liquid. Season with salt and vinegar. Wrap the meat mixture in a double layer of cheesecloth and secure with butcher's twine. Place the bundle on a baking sheet, or preferably a terrine mold, top with a second baking sheet (or terrine mold), and top with weights that provide considerable pressure (heavy cans work well). Refrigerate for 12 hours.

Preheat a dehydrator to 149°F (65°C). Unwrap the trotter mixture, or foot cheese, and, using a sharp knife, slice it thinly. Arrange the slices in a single layer on a dehydrator tray and dehydrate for 12 hours, until completely dry and golden brown (see notes).

To make the pickled onions, place the onions in a small heatproof glass jar. Combine the vinegar, water, and sugar in a saucepan and bring to a boil over medium heat, stirring until the sugar has dissolved. Pour the hot liquid over the onions, immersing them. Let cool to room temperature, then cover and refrigerate for 24 hours before using.

To make the smoked mayonnaise, in a bowl, whisk the egg yolk until blended. Then, whisking constantly, slowly add the smoked oil, drop by drop, until the mixture begins to thicken. Add the remaining oil in a slow, steady stream while whisking vigorously to form a mayonnaise. Season with salt and vinegar. Cover and refrigerate until serving.

To serve, place a spoonful of mayonnaise on a plate and sprinkle the trotter over the mayonnaise. Top with the pickled onions and garnish with old man's pepper.

LAMB SWEETBREADS, CARAMELIZED CELERY ROOT, *and* BLOOD SAUSAGE

SERVES 4 TO 6 | PREPARATION TIME: ABOUT 1¹/₂ HOURS (PLUS 14 HOURS IF THE SWEETBREADS ARE SOAKED IN MILK BEFORE COOKING)

Lamb sweetbreads, which are the thymus glands of the animal, are most easily sourced in spring, as they disappear as the lamb ages. They can be difficult to source in the United States, but veal sweetbreads, which are more commonly available, can be substituted here. The best way to prep sweetbreads for cooking is to soak them in milk in the refrigerator overnight to leach out some of their blood, and then carefully remove the tissue that surrounds them while they are still moist from the milk.

Blood sausage is also called for in this recipe, and while the thought may send some diners running for the door, others appreciate its heady flavor. In Iceland, it is called *slátur*, and it is prepared much as it is elsewhere in the world. The combination of sweetbreads and blood sausage packs an earthy punch that could prove overwhelming if it were not for the sweet caramelized celery root and heady dill puree that accompany them.

CARAMELIZED CELERY ROOT
AND SKYR

1¹/₂ cups (200 g) peeled and finely chopped celery root

4 teaspoons milk

4 teaspoons heavy cream

1¹/₂ tablespoons unsalted butter

Salt

¹/₃ cup (20 g) milk powder

¹/₃ cup (95 g) Skyr (page 62)

1 teaspoon cider vinegar

BLOOD SAUSAGE

1³/₄ ounces (50 g) blood sausage, casing discarded, coarsely chopped

Pinch of sugar

Unsalted butter, for frying

DILL PUREE

3¹/₂ ounces (100 g) fresh dill

4 teaspoons water, plus more as needed

Salt

0.5 g xanthan gum, plus more as needed (see note)

LAMB SWEETBREADS

1²/₃ cups (400 ml) light chicken stock, preferably homemade (page 89) as long as the bone roasting step is skipped

14 ounces (400 g) lamb sweetbreads

Rapeseed oil, for deep-frying

2 eggs

³/₄ cup (100 g) all-purpose flour

³/₄ cup (100 g) panko bread crumbs

Salt

To make the celery root and skyr, preheat an immersion circulator to 183°F (84°C). Place the celery root, milk, and cream in a vacuum bag and seal on the medium setting. Cook in the circulator for about 8 minutes, or until tender. The timing will depend on how fine the cut is. Remove the bag from the circulator and drain the celery root, reserving the celery root and liquid separately. Transfer the celery root to a blender, add the butter, and process on high speed to a puree, adding a little of the cooking liquid if necessary to achieve a smooth consistency. Season with salt.

Preheat the oven to 325°F (165°C). Spread the milk powder in an even layer on a baking sheet and bake, stirring frequently to prevent scorching, until light brown. Let cool to room temperature, then, in a small bowl, combine the toasted milk powder and skyr and mix well with the caramelized celery root. Season with salt and vinegar.

| *continued*

NOTE

Xanthan gum (see notes, page 34) will thicken the dill puree nicely, but if you cannot find it, the flavor of the puree will still complement the dish.

To make the blood sausage, in a small bowl, toss the sausage with the sugar. Melt a little butter in a small sauté pan over medium-high heat. Add the sausage and fry, stirring often, for about 5 to 7 minutes, until cooked through and crispy on the outside. Remove from the heat. Keep warm.

To make the dill puree, combine the dill and water in the blender and process on high speed to a puree, adding more water, if necessary, to achieve a smooth consistency. Strain through a fine-mesh sieve into a bowl, then season with salt. Add the xanthan gum and whisk until thickened (see note). It should have a glossy finish. Add additional xanthan gum if needed to achieve the desired consistency.

To make the lamb sweetbreads, pour the stock into a saucepan and bring to a low simmer. Add the sweetbreads and cook for about 15 minutes, until cooked through. Drain the sweetbreads with a slotted spoon and let cool just until they can be handled, then carefully peel off and discard the membrane surrounding them. Let cool to room temperature.

Pour oil to a depth of about 6 inches (15 cm) into a deep, heavy pot and heat to 325°F (165°C). Line a large plate with paper towels. While the oil is heating, crack the eggs into a shallow bowl and beat just until blended. Put the flour in a second shallow bowl, and then put the bread crumbs in a third shallow bowl. When the oil is hot, using one hand for the dry coatings, coat a sweetbread evenly with the flour, shaking off the excess. Switch hands and dip the sweetbread in the eggs, allowing the excess to drip off. Finally, switch back to the original hand and coat the sweetbread evenly with the bread crumbs, shaking off the excess. Add the sweetbread to the hot oil and fry for about 6 minutes, until golden brown. Using a slotted spoon, transfer to the paper towel–lined plate. Repeat with the remaining sweetbreads.

To serve, arrange the sweetbreads and the blood sausage on plates. Spoon some of the celery root and skyr and dill purees alongside.

HOT DOGS

No visit to Iceland is complete without trying a local hot dog. The country is mad for hot dogs, and they are served at virtually every roadside stop throughout the nation. Perhaps the most popular hot dog stand is directly across from the marina in Reykjavík. There, in the summer months, people line up by the dozens to purchase the classic combination of a bun, a hot dog, some mustard, and a tangle of crispy fried onions. Even Bill Clinton could not resist a hot dog from this famous stand during a visit to Iceland in the 1990s.

A hot dog might not sound that special, but Icelandic hot dogs are no ordinary dogs. They are made from the meat of free-range lambs stuffed in natural lamb casings that give each bite a pleasant snap. The bread is typically handmade and the perfect doughy counterpoint to the crispy onions and peppery mustard. But be warned, eating an Icelandic hot dog means your hot dogs back home will never taste as good.

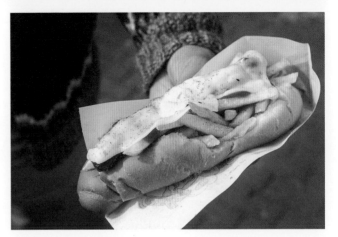

SAUTÉED LAMB FILLET *with* CROWBERRIES, BAKED LAMB FAT, *and* SUNCHOKES

SERVES 4 | PREPARATION TIME: ABOUT 1¹/₂ HOURS | PICTURED ON PAGE 226

Sunchokes, also known as Jerusalem artichokes, are a relatively new addition to the root vegetable repertoire of Iceland, and Gunnar celebrates their virtues in a variety of ways at Dill. They flourish in even relatively poor soil, which makes them well suited to Iceland's often unwelcoming planting conditions.

In this recipe, they are both pureed and fried to showcase them in two ways that pair well with lamb fillet and with a side of baked lamb fat. This latter element might leave some diners afraid to step on a scale, but a moderate sized slice baked to bubbling perfection is a rare and enticing treat.

Crowberries complement the other elements on the plate, but since they are difficult to source, blueberries are a good substitute, as are cranberries or cherries.

LAMB FILLET

1¹/₃ pounds (600 g) lamb fillet, fat trimmed away in large pieces and reserved

Salt

Unsalted butter, for sautéing

Rapeseed oil, for sautéing

Handful of crowberries or blueberries

BAKED LAMB FAT

3 ounces (75 g) reserved lamb fat (see above)

Sea salt

SUNCHOKE PUREE

7 ounces (200 g) sunchokes, peeled and chopped

¹/₄ cup (60 ml) milk, plus more if needed

¹/₄ cup (60 ml) heavy cream

¹/₂ teaspoon salt

1 teaspoon sugar

2 tablespoons unsalted butter

Beer Vinegar (page 30), for seasoning

FRIED SUNCHOKES

Unsalted butter, for frying

Rapeseed oil, for frying

8 small sunchokes (about 5 ounces/150 g), unpeeled, coarsely chopped

Salt

Beer Vinegar (page 30), for seasoning

To make the lamb fillet, preheat the oven to 325°F (165°C). Season the lamb on both sides with salt. Melt enough butter with oil in an ovenproof sauté pan over medium-high heat to coat the pan bottom lightly. Add the crowberries and then the lamb and sauté the lamb, turning once, for about 5 minutes on each side, until golden brown on both sides. Slip the pan in the oven and cook until an instant-read thermometer inserted into the center of the fillet registers 129°F (54°C), about 12 minutes. Let the fillet rest, flipping it at the halfway point to distribute the internal juices evenly, for 7 minutes before slicing to serve. Reserve the lamb and the berries separately.

To make the baked lamb fat, sprinkle the reserved fat with sea salt and let stand at room temperature for 30 minutes to leach out some of the internal liquids. Preheat the oven to 375°F (190°C). Place the fat in a small roasting pan and roast for 30 to 40 minutes, until brown and crispy. Remove from the oven, let the fat cool until it can be handled, then chop coarsely. Just before serving, fry the chopped fat and the reserved crowberries in a small sauté pan over medium heat for about 2 minutes, until the fat softens and is warmed through and coated in the berry juice.

To make the sunchoke puree, preheat an immersion circulator to 185°F (85°C). Place the sunchokes, milk, cream, salt, and sugar in a vacuum bag and seal on the lowest setting. Cook in the circulator for 18 minutes, until tender. Transfer the contents of the bag to a blender, add the butter, and begin processing on low speed to prevent the hot mixture from splattering. Once the elements are incorporated, increase the speed to high and continue to process until smooth, adding additional milk if necessary to achieve a smooth consistency. Season with salt and vinegar.

To make the fried sunchokes, melt enough butter with oil in a sauté pan over high heat to coat the pan bottom lightly. Add the sunchokes and fry, stirring often, for 4 to 5 minutes, until golden brown and crispy on the outside. Turn down the heat to medium and fry for about 8 minutes longer, until tender. Season with salt and vinegar.

To serve, arrange the lamb fillet and fat on a plate, spoon the sunchoke puree and fried sunchokes alongside, and drizzle the lamb fillet with the reserved crowberries.

ABOVE: Sautéed Lamb Fillet with Crowberries, Baked Lamb Fat, and Sunchokes (page 224)

OPPOSITE: Hay-Smoked Duck Breasts, Carrot Puree, and Herb Emulsion (page 228)

HAY-SMOKED DUCK BREASTS, CARROT PUREE, and HERB EMULSION

SERVES 4 | PREPARATION TIME: ABOUT 1½ HOURS | PICTURED ON PAGE 227

Gunnar originally created this dish with lamb in mind, but he had extra duck breasts on hand and substituted them for the lamb. The result, when served with a silky carrot puree and a vibrant herb emulsion, was a pleasing spring or summer dish with a whisper of the farm delivered by the hay smoking. If you do not use duck fat regularly, now is the time to add it to your list of essential pantry items. Here, it is toasted with semidried herbs to coax out its virtues.

DUCK BREASTS AND TOASTED DUCK FAT

4 duck breasts

Salt

Unsalted butter, for sautéing

Rapeseed oil, for sautéing

½ teaspoon dried angelica leaves

½ teaspoon semidried thyme leaves

CARROTS

Unsalted butter, for sautéing

Rapeseed oil, for sautéing

8 small carrots with stems intact, unpeeled, tops trimmed

Salt

HERB EMULSION

2½ teaspoons stone-ground mustard

2 teaspoons Beer Vinegar (page 30), plus more for seasoning

1 teaspoon chopped garlic

2 tablespoons chopped shallot

½ cup (30 g) chopped fresh dill

⅓ cup (20 g) chopped fresh flat-leaf parsley

¼ cup (60 ml) water, plus more as needed

1 cup (240 ml) rapeseed oil

Salt

4 handfuls hay, for smoking and garnish

CARROT PUREE

7 ounces (200 g) carrots, peeled and chopped

¼ cup (60 ml) water

2 tablespoons rapeseed oil, plus more if needed

Salt

Beer Vinegar (page 30), for seasoning

To make the duck breasts, score the fat on the breasts and season the breasts on both sides with salt. Line a large plate with paper towels. Melt enough butter with oil in a large sauté pan over medium-high heat to coat the pan bottom lightly. Turn down the heat to medium-low, add the breasts, skin side down, and sauté, turning once, for 7 to 8 minutes. Turn over, raise the heat to high and cook until medium-rare, about 2 minutes. Transfer the breasts to the paper towel–lined plate and let rest, flipping them once at the midway point to distribute the internal juices evenly, for 7 minutes. Season with more salt if needed.

To make the toasted duck fat, return the pan with the duck fat to medium heat. Add the angelica and thyme and heat for about 2 minutes, until aromatic. Reserve for serving.

To make the carrot puree, put the carrots and water in a pressure cooker (see page 50), lock the lid in place, bring to medium pressure, and cook for 15 minutes, until golden brown. Let the pressure release naturally. Remove the lid, drain the carrots, and transfer them to a blender. Add the oil and process with on high speed until smooth, adding more oil, if necessary, to form a smooth puree. Season with salt and vinegar.

To make the carrots, melt enough butter with oil in a large sauté pan over medium-high heat to coat the pan bottom lightly. Add the carrots and sauté for 8 to 10 minutes, until golden brown. Season with salt.

To make the herb emulsion, combine the mustard, vinegar, garlic, shallot, dill, parsley, and water in a blender and process on high speed to a puree, adding more water as necessary to form a smooth consistency. Add the oil in a slow, steady stream and continue to process until smooth. Season with salt and more vinegar, if desired.

To smoke the duck breasts, fill a deep hotel pan or similar vessel with hay. Arrange the duck breasts on a perforated hotel pan and place over high heat. Ignite the hay with a kitchen torch and let burn for about 5 minutes, until almost completely incinerated. Place the perforated pan on top and cover securely with aluminum foil (or a lid). Allow the smoke to smolder out completely, about 10 minutes, before removing the foil or lid. Remove the duck breasts. Crumble the residual ashes to use as a garnish.

To serve, slice the duck breasts and arrange the slices on plates. Arrange the carrots and carrot puree alongside. Dot duck and carrots with the herb emulsion and garnish with the ashes.

ROASTED LAMB SHOULDER, BRAISED CABBAGE, PICKLED ONIONS, LEEK BUTTER, *and* CHERVIL SYRUP

SERVES 6 TO 8 | PREPARATION TIME: ABOUT 2½ HOURS (PLUS 1 WEEK TO PICKLE THE CABBAGE AND ONIONS)

Like most chefs, Gunnar appreciates cuts of meat that prove a bit more of a challenge to cook than your standard tenderloin. The lamb shoulder in this recipe is a good example. It's a tougher cut of meat and requires a longer cooking time and a bit more culinary magic to roast it to its full potential. In this recipe, Gunnar pairs the lamb shoulder with cabbage, adds a generous amount of duck fat, sprinkles it with pickled onions, slathers leek butter over it, and drizzles it with chervil oil, resulting in a fall or wintertime dish your guests will want to tuck into and linger over for hours.

BRAISED CABBAGE

7 ounces (200 g) red cabbage, cored and thinly sliced

7 ounces (200 g) green cabbage, cored and thinly sliced

3 tablespoons cider vinegar

1 tablespoon salt

2 tablespoons sugar

½ cup (100 g) rendered duck fat, melted

LAMB SHOULDER

1 bone-in lamb shoulder, about 5 pounds (2.3 kg)

Salt

Leaves from ½ sprig thyme

LEEK BUTTER

2 teaspoons rapeseed oil

½ cup (110 g) unsalted butter, at room temperature

1¾ ounces (50 g) leek, white part only, finely chopped

2 tablespoons buttermilk

Salt

Beer Vinegar (page 30), for seasoning

CHERVIL SYRUP

1 tablespoon plus 2 teaspoons Beer Vinegar (page 30)

1 tablespoon unsalted butter

2 tablespoons sugar

¾ cup (180 ml) chervil oil (page 321)

PICKLED PEARL ONIONS

8 white pearl onions, halved lengthwise, and separated into petals

1 cup (240 ml) distilled white vinegar

¼ cup (60 ml) water

6½ tablespoons (80 g) sugar

To make the cabbage, place the cabbage, cider vinegar, salt, sugar, and duck fat in a vacuum bag and seal on the medium setting. Refrigerate for 1 week. Transfer the contents of the bag to a sauté pan over medium heat and sauté until warmed through.

To make the pickled onions, bring a saucepan of lightly salted water to a boil. Add the onions, blanch for 20 seconds, drain, and transfer to a small heatproof glass jar. Combine the vinegar, water, and sugar in a saucepan and bring to a boil over medium heat, stirring until the sugar has dissolved. Pour the hot liquid over the onions, immersing them. Let cool to room temperature, then cover and refrigerate for 1 week before using.

| *continued*

To make the lamb shoulder, using a paring knife, cut a crisscross pattern all over the exterior of the shoulder. Using a mortar and pestle or a spice grinder, combine the salt and thyme and grind together until finely crushed. Rub the mixture over the shoulder, then place the shoulder in a roasting pan. Set aside at room temperature for 30 minutes.

Preheat the oven to 325°F (165°C). Roast the shoulder for about 1^1/$_2$ hours, until tender. Remove from the oven and let rest, flipping the shoulder over once at the midway point to distribute the internal juices evenly, for about 30 minutes. Then, shred the meat.

To make the leek butter, heat the oil and 2 teaspoons of the butter over low heat. Add the leek and sauté for about 6 minutes, until tender but not golden brown. Transfer the leek and the cooking juices to a small bowl, cover, and refrigerate until chilled. In a stand mixer fitted with the whip attachment, beat the remaining butter on high speed until light and fluffy. Still on high speed, add the buttermilk in a slow, steady stream and beat until combined. Using a spatula or spoon, fold in the leeks and their cooking liquid until incorporated. Season with salt and vinegar.

Line a baking sheet with parchment paper. Spread the leek butter evenly in a thin layer on the parchment. Refrigerate until chilled.

To make the chervil syrup, combine the vinegar and butter in a small saucepan and bring to a simmer. Add the sugar and cook until the mixture is thick and syrupy. Remove from the heat and let cool to room temperature. Just before serving, stir together the chervil oil and one-fourth of the syrup for a sweet-and-sour flavor. Reserve the rest for another use.

To serve, arrange the shoulder, braised cabbage, and pickled onions on a plate. Drizzle with a generous amount of the chervil syrup.

Hay-Smoked Oil

MAKES 1 CUP (240 ML) | PREPARATION TIME: ABOUT 15 MINUTES

1 cup (240 ml) rapeseed oil
Hay for smoking (see page 93)

Pour the oil into a glass jar. Put the hay in a pot large enough to contain the jar easily, place over high heat, then ignite the hay with a kitchen torch. Once it has burned down to smoldering ashes (see notes, page 69), place the jar on the hay to extinguish any remaining flame and either cover the pot with a tight-fitting lid or with aluminum foil. Be sure the flame has completely subsided before smoking the oil or the oil will have an off flavor. Once the smoke has completely subsided, after about 10 minutes, remove the lid or foil, remove the jar, and repeat the process with fresh hay until the oil has the desired smokiness (see note). Let cool to room temperature, then transfer to a squeeze bottle. The oil will keep at room temperature for 1 month.

NOTE
The amount of smoking time required for the desired result will be shorter
if you use a bowl instead of a jar.

THE HARDFISKUR PRODUCER

Isafjördur, the Westfjords

∞

Tea-Crusted Catfish, Braised Root Vegetables, Barley,
and Lovage Oil 244

Sunchoke Ice Cream, Oatmeal Pudding,
and Oat Crumble 248

Dried Arctic Thyme 250

Dried Vegetable Peel 250

Pickled and Dried Angelica 251

Pickled and Dried Crowberries 251

Icelanders have always been resourceful. They have to be

in order to live in a climate that is unforgiving to the apathetic and punishes the uncreative with winters that they won't survive. The land of primarily porous lava stone affords little opportunity for farming, and the short spring and summer seasons ensure an empty pantry in the dead of winter, if foods are not preserved during the warmer months.

One of the country's oldest forms of preservation comes in the form of *hardfiskur*, a beloved snack coveted by many Icelanders who would happily trade in a loaf of warm bread for a fillet of ocean air–dried fish slathered in butter. Grain has little chance to flourish in Iceland, save for in a few remote regions, and *hardfiskur*, wolf fish that has been dried in the ocean air, is the healthy alternative.

Today, open-air wooden drying houses still dot the shores of the northern territories. But the practice of drying *hardfiskur* in the open air, which takes months, is rapidly being replaced by a far quicker method that relies on large, industrial dehydrating rooms, a trend that strips this time-honored food from its connection to the past. Among the stalwarts of traditional *hardfiskur* production are a father and his two sons who live in the remote Westfjords. Today, they must source their fish by buying it at auction, just as everyone is required to do, but little else has changed in the production method.

They fillet the fish themselves and dry the heads and bones on separate drying racks for sending to western Africa, where they are sold and used for making stews and sauces. The fillets are dipped in a brine, hung by hand on wooden sticks, and then piled into the back of a truck and transported to the massive drying house. Once there, the father hands the poles to one of his sons, who hangs them. Their cheeks are red and ruddy from the brisk ocean air, but their smiles are ready and their pride in preserving one of Iceland's most ancient traditions is palpable. The fish dries throughout the winter, and at the end of the season, what was once fresh from the sea is dehydrated to briny perfection. It's a tradition Icelanders still revere, and with one bite of *hardfiskur* spread with butter, it's easy to understand why.

An Interview with Hardfiskur Producer Finnbogi Jónasson

Q **How long has your family been in the *hardfiskur* business?**

My father started this business in 1985, and now my brother and I are co-owners. We sell our *hardfiskur* throughout Iceland and also to Norway. We own a fishing boat, but because we do not catch enough ourselves, we have to buy additional fish from the market to supplement our catch. We don't really own the fish we catch because of the quota system. All fish have to go to the market, so they are never really ours. You catch them and then you have to buy them back. It's very frustrating. We buy over 150 tons of fish per year. But the process itself has become easier in recent years, because instead of having to go to auctions held throughout the country, we can participate in them online. It has been a big time-saver for us. I watch the auction all day long and put in a bid when the fish reaches the price I am willing to pay. I do it almost every day.

From summer to fall, I work the line on the boat, and then in the fall, I begin processing the fish for *hardfiskur*. My brother and father also participate in this. Our boat is small, so we do only coastal fishing. You don't earn a lot of money for this fish. Some want the quota, some don't, and there are only certain days when you're allowed to fish. Because of overfishing, we're not allowed to fish halibut any longer. If you catch one, you have to throw it back. Slowly the quota system has created fewer and fewer jobs. In the early 1990s, the fishing industry started to decline. There used to be four trawlers here, now there are only two. The fish companies have merged, and nowadays it's becoming more difficult to be a family-owned business.

Q **How is *hardfiskur* produced?**

The fish are bigger in the winter, so we start filleting in September and then begin hanging the fillets in the drying sheds in October. We brine the fillets for four or five hours before we hang them, and then we hang from October through April. It's nice to get a good frost. But we don't like *skafrenningur* (when snow blows in from the side and builds up against the houses). This is bad for us. The snow comes into direct contact with the fish, which, of course, is something we don't want to happen.

Q **What is the history of *hardfiskur* in Iceland?**

We've been producing it for centuries. It started with the Vikings. In the past, the whole fish, including the head, would be hung.

Long ago, a type of cod called *skreith* was our main export. It is brined fish that is air-dried and then rehydrated for cooking. It's between *hardfiskur* and bacalao. It's not something we would ever use in Iceland. It was mainly used in Africa. We also start salting the fish to create bacalao. The Spanish and Portuguese wanted this salted cod, which is where it all began—and all of the cod went to them. This is why we started using wolffish for our own *hardfiskur*.

Q How has *hardfiskur* production changed over the years?

There are now modern ways of making *hardfiskur*: They use drying ovens instead of drying the fish in the open air. We are among the last ones to dry the fish the traditional way. My dad used to be a sailor, and he has always lived here. Our family's life is on the sea, and we do not want this tradition to disappear. There's a lot less work here now, and people are moving away because of it. The large freezing houses have closed down. When I was a child, there was much more business. From 1985 to 1990 was a golden age. It's slow now. Business is hard.

Q Has the increase in tourism in recent years helped?

Yes, but I don't think we will be able to survive on that. Tourists don't come in the winter because the roads are impassable. The authorities say winter tourism is increasing, but it's not affecting us. We see it a bit, but it won't help us survive the winter. Our fish is much more expensive because it takes much longer to dry in the traditional way. It is completely different from the machine-dried fish. When it's done this way, the *hardfiskur* contains the aromas and flavors of the ocean air that dries it.

Q How did the economic collapse affect you?

After the economic collapse, people from here moved south and also to Norway. We lost most of our quota at this time, too. The government is always interfering. We need jobs and we need quiet to conduct our business. The government is trying to control every-thing, and with the new taxation on businesses, many of them had to close their doors. So they destroyed jobs and the businesses, too.

Q Even with the challenges you face, do you find that people are still interested in traditionally produced *hardfiskur*?

Yes, demand is growing. There is hope.

TRAVEL IN THE WESTFJORDS

The Westfjords is one of the most remote regions of Iceland, and for a country at the top of the planet, that is quite a statement. It is not the distance from Reykjavík that makes the Westfjords remote, as its southern entrance point is only about a five-hour drive away. The fjords themselves are what can make driving along the coast feel endless—though always breathtaking.

The main town of Isafjördur, where *hardfiskur* producer Finnbogi Jónasson is located, is a quaint home base from which to explore the region. It boasts postcard-ready streets lined with boutiques and with restaurants serving some of the best fish stew in Iceland. Bird-watching opportunities abound in the Westfjords, and a roughly two-hour drive from Isafjördur is Dynjandi, home to one of the country's most breathtaking waterfalls.

A two-hour ferry ride from the town of Stykkishólmur on Snaefellsnes Peninsula is one way to access the Westfjords, but the drive along the southern roads from where it lands is painstakingly long. The town of Reykjanes in the northern fjords is the ideal entrance point if traveling by car. It's where the salt producer Saltverk is located (see page 250), and it is an easy drive from the town to the northern region. However you choose to get to the beautiful Westfjords region, it is likely you will agree that the extra effort you expended to get there was worth it.

TEA-CRUSTED CATFISH, BRAISED ROOT VEGETABLES, BARLEY, and LOVAGE OIL

SERVES 4 | PREPARATION TIME: ABOUT 1½ HOURS | PICTURED ON PAGE 246

Icelanders often refer to wolffish, the large, firm-textured white fish used primarily for making *hardfiskur*, as catfish. No one seems to know why, but one good guess would be because of the "whiskers" both fish share. Wolffish cannot be purchased outside of Iceland, so this recipe calls for catfish instead. However, any white fish with a firm texture, such as halibut or cod, would make a fine substitute. The fish is covered in powdered herbal tea, which delivers an unexpected flavor (Gunnar uses herbal tea from Sverrir). The barley used here is pearl barley, which provides a weighty counterpoint with an appealing chew to the seafood.

CATFISH

14 ounces (400 g) skinned catfish fillet, cut into 4 equal pieces

½ cup (65 g) powdered herbal tea

1 tablespoon rapeseed oil

1 tablespoon unsalted butter

Salt

BRAISED VEGETABLE PUREE

6½ tablespoons (50 g) peeled and chopped carrot

5 tablespoons (50 g) peeled and chopped celery root

5 tablespoons (50 g) peeled and chopped rutabaga

5 tablespoons (50 g) chopped white onion

¾ cup (180 ml) Chicken Stock, preferably homemade (page 89)

3 sprigs arctic thyme

3 bay leaves, incinerated (see note)

4 tablespoons (55 g) unsalted butter

Salt

Beer Vinegar (page 30), for seasoning

BARLEY

1 cup (200 g) pearl barley

1½ tablespoons unsalted butter

Salt

Beer Vinegar (page 30), for seasoning

SAUCE

Burned butter, oil, and tea from frying fish (above)

2 teaspoons stone-ground mustard

1 tablespoon unsalted butter

Fresh lovage leaves, for garnish

To make the catfish, cover the fish evenly with the tea to create a crust. Heat the oil and butter in a sauté pan over medium-high heat. Add the fish and panfry, turning once, for about 9 minutes, until cooked through. Remove from the heat, transfer the fish to a plate, and season with salt. Reserve the pan with the mixture of burned butter and oil and crust crumbs for making the sauce.

To make the vegetable puree, combine the carrot, celery root, rutabaga, onion, stock, thyme, bay leaves, and butter in a small saucepan, season with salt, and bring to a boil over

NOTE

To incinerate bay leaves, toast them in a small, dry frying pan over medium heat, turning them as needed, for about 7 to 9 minutes, until toasted and dry. Remove from the heat, let cool, then grind in a spice grinder to a powder.

medium-high heat. Reduce heat to low and cook at a gentle simmer for about 25 minutes, until the stock has evaporated and the vegetables have caramelized in the butter. Remove from the heat, transfer to a blender, and process at high speed until a smooth puree forms. Season with salt and vinegar.

To make the barley, combine the barley and water to cover by $1^{1}/2$ inches (4 cm) in a saucepan, salt lightly, and bring to a boil over high heat. Turn down the heat to a simmer and cook for 45 minutes to 1 hour, until tender. Remove from the heat and drain well.

Melt the butter in a sauté pan over medium heat and stir in the barley. Once the barley is glistening with butter, remove it from the heat and season it with salt and beer vinegar.

To make the sauce, place the pan in which you fried the fish over medium heat, add the mustard and a couple spoonfuls of water, and stir to deglaze the pan, dislodging any browned bits on the pan bottom. Add the butter and swirl the pan to melt the butter and emulsify the sauce.

To serve, arrange the catfish on plates with spoonfuls of the vegetable puree and barley alongside. Slick the fish with the sauce and garnish with the lovage.

ABOVE: Tea-Crusted Catfish, Braised Root Vegetables, Barley, and Lovage Oil (page 244)

OPPOSITE: Sunchoke Ice Cream, Oatmeal Pudding, and Oat Crumble (page 248)

SUNCHOKE ICE CREAM, OATMEAL PUDDING, and OAT CRUMBLE

SERVES 4 | PREPARATION TIME: ABOUT 1¹/₂ HOURS (PLUS 12 HOURS TO FREEZE THE ICE CREAM) | PICTURED ON PAGE 247

When we traveled to visit the *hardfiskur* producer in the Westfjords, we needed to carry provisions, as markets are few and far between in this remote area. Oatmeal is a good staple to pack: it will warm you up in the morning and can be drizzled with birch syrup and sprinkled with sea salt to conclude the evening.

This recipe illustrates Gunnar's commitment to showcasing vegetables in the dessert course, rather than restricting them to a savory course and finishing with a sugary concoction. If you are having difficulty locating sunchokes, parsnips or celery root are good substitutes. The oatmeal pudding and the oatmeal crumble provide a nice crunchy balance to the silky ice cream, but each element also makes a comforting breakfast item, together or separately. The ice cream is so good that it just might find its way to the breakfast table, too.

SUNCHOKE ICE CREAM

3¹/₄ cups (780 ml) milk

³/₄ cup (180 ml) heavy cream

14 ounces (400 g) sunchokes, peeled and cut into bite-size pieces

1¹/₄ cups (250 g) sugar

¹/₄ cup (50 g) liquid glucose (see notes, page 34)

³/₄ teaspoon salt

OATMEAL PUDDING

1 cup (150 g) steel-cut oats

1¹/₂ tablespoons sugar

1²/₃ cups (400 ml) milk, plus more as needed

1¹/₂ tablespoons chilled unsalted butter, cut into cubes

³/₄ teaspoon salt

OATMEAL CRUMBLE

6 tablespoons (85 g) unsalted butter

²/₃ cup (100 g) steel-cut oats

6¹/₂ tablespoons (50 g) all-purpose flour

¹/₄ cup (50 g) firmly packed light brown sugar

Salt

2 tablespoons fresh chervil leaves, chopped, for garnish

Raisins soaked in dark rum until plumped, for garnish

To make the ice cream, prepare an ice bath. Combine the milk, cream, and sunchokes in a saucepan and bring to a gentle simmer over medium-low heat. Cook for about 10 minutes, until the sunchokes are tender. Add the sugar and glucose and stir until dissolved. Remove from the heat, transfer to a blender, and begin processing on low speed to prevent the hot mixture from splattering. Once the elements are incorporated, increase the speed to high and continue to process until smooth. Season with salt, transfer to a bowl, and nest in the ice bath until chilled. Transfer to an ice cream maker and freeze according to the manufacturer's instructions. Scoop into an airtight container and place in the freezer for 12 hours, until solid.

To make the pudding, combine the oats, sugar, and milk in a saucepan and bring to a simmer over medium-low heat, stirring constantly. Remove from the heat and let stand at room temperature until the oats are tender and have absorbed much of the liquid. If the pudding is too thick, add some water or more milk to achieve the desired consistency. Add the butter, a cube at a time, stirring in each one until fully incorporated before adding the next cube. The texture should be that of a soft oatmeal cookie hot from the oven. Season with salt. Let stand at room temperature until ready to serve.

To make the crumble, preheat the oven to 350°F (180°C). Line a baking sheet with parchment paper. Melt the butter in a small pan over medium heat, then remove from the heat. In a bowl, stir together the oats, flour, and brown sugar. Pour the melted butter into the oat mixture and stir until the dry ingredients are evenly coated with the butter. Season with salt. Pour onto the prepared baking sheet and spread in an even layer. Bake, rotating the pan back to front at the midway point, for 8 to 10 minutes, until toasted and lightly browned. Let cool to room temperature. Transfer to a blender or food processor and pulse until coarsely ground.

To serve, spoon the ice cream and pudding onto a plate. Sprinkle with the crumble and raisins and garnish with the chervil.

DRIED ARCTIC THYME

YIELD DEPENDS ON AMOUNT DRIED | PREPARATION TIME: ABOUT 24 HOURS

Drying as a means of preservation is not used only for fish in Iceland. It is employed for countless raw ingredients as a way to afford a taste of them in even the darkest, coldest months of the year. Dried foods are not as flavorful as their fresh counterparts, but they do provide a fleeting memory of the summer when they were gathered.

Pick artic thyme sprigs with their blossoms intact or before their blossoms appear, as once the blossoms fall off, the thyme begins to taste slightly bitter. Dry the sprigs outdoors in the sun for about 24 hours (bringing them in at night to protect the thyme from the elements), until all of the moisture is gone. Carefully place the sprigs in an airtight container and store in a cool, dark place.

DRIED VEGETABLE PEEL

YIELD DEPENDS ON AMOUNT DRIED | PREPARATION TIME: VARIES DEPENDING ON HUMIDITY LEVEL AND THICKNESS OF PEEL

At Dill, Gunnar saves his vegetable peels, spreads them out on a tray, puts the tray in a moisture-free area, and leaves the peels to dry, taking no special effort to dehydrate them. There are many uses for dried vegetables peels, such as infusions and stocks, but Gunnar most often uses them for smoking. He sees them as just as good as wood chips, and they inevitably add a nice flavor.

Nearly any dried vegetable peel will prove useful. At Dill, onion, parsnip, and celery peels and odd bits of fennel are the most commonly dried. Store the dried peels in an airtight container at room temperature for up to 2 weeks.

PICKLED *and* DRIED ANGELICA

YIELD DEPENDS ON AMOUNT DEHYDRATED | PREPARATION TIME: ABOUT 3 HOURS

Use these bright-flavored angelica rings as a seasoning on vegetables. You can also grind them in a spice grinder to a powder and use the powder to season salads, soups, meat, or seafood.

Preheat a dehydrator to 120°F (48°C). Slice as many pickled angelica stalks (see page 137) as desired into thin rings. Arrange the rings in a single layer on a dehydrator tray and dehydrate for about 3 hours, until crispy. Do not overdry them or they will be flavorless. Store the angelica rings in an airtight container at room temperature for up to 2 weeks.

PICKLED *and* DRIED CROWBERRIES

MAKES ABOUT 2 CUPS (220 G) | PREPARATION TIME: ABOUT 1 MONTH (INCLUDES THE PICKLING TIME)

Crowberries are one of the most plentiful berry varieties in Iceland (see page 334) but are difficult to find elsewhere. Blueberries are a good substitute, though nearly any berry can be pickled and dried to give it a second life in its off-season. Use the berries on desserts or grind them to a powder in a spice grinder and use as a seasoning for game.

2 cups (300 g) crowberries

1 cup (240 ml) distilled white vinegar

1/2 cup (100 g) sugar

2 or 3 small crowberry bush branches

Put the berries in a heatproof glass jar. Combine the vinegar and sugar in a saucepan and bring to a boil over medium heat, stirring until the sugar has dissolved. Throw in a few crowberry branches and simmer for about 1 minute. Remove from the heat and let cool to 104°F (40°C). Discard the branches and strain the liquid through a fine-mesh sieve. Pour the liquid over the crowberries, immersing them. Let cool to room temperature, then cover and refrigerate for 1 month.

Preheat a dehydrator to 200°F (93°C). Drain the berries, reserving the berries and the liquid. Use the pickling juice on desserts and salads. Spread the berries in a single layer on a dehydrator tray and dehydrate the berries for about 12 hours, until crispy. Store the berries in an airtight container at room temperature for up to 1 month.

THE SALT MAKER

Reykjanes

∞

Sea Salt 258

Celery and Fennel Salad, Carrots,
and Faroe Island Scallops 260

Hay-Smoked Beets with Pine and Roses 264

Braised Wild Goose Leg, Red Beets, Blackberries,
and Pine Salt 266

Lamb Heart, Cabbage Two Ways, Raspberry Sauce,
and Heather and Moss Ash 270

Spiced Lamb Belly, Salt-Baked Celery Root,
and Pickled Celery Root 272

In the remote Westfjords, Saltverk offers hope that even if a tradition disappears, it is not necessarily gone forever. The owners were engineers before they stumbled on a long-forgotten era of Icelandic history and decided to give up their careers to revive a lost tradition. In the same spot where Saltverk now stands, the Danish, who once colonized Iceland, produced salt for the kingdom from the ocean water that laps at the edge of the production center and the geothermal heat billowing up from the earth.

The production is simple: The ocean water is pumped into large drying tanks that are heated geothermally. The water slowly evaporates, leaving behind large salt crystals that are transferred to drying racks, where they finish dehydrating. The anemic records left behind by the Danes offered little guidance to the new salt makers on how to create the ideal salt crystal, and discovering the perfect formula demanded trial and error. Being a salt maker in this remote area is a lonely business. Even the owners of Saltverk have sometimes wondered if they made the right decision. In spite of such doubts, they have persevered with their mission to revive a lost tradition, and today they have no regrets.

It seemed a fool's errand when Björn Stigursson and his business partner first decided to become salt makers with nothing more to work from than old records unearthed hundreds of years after the first salt producers left their shovels, seawater, and geothermal steam behind. The salt produced in the past and now is winter white and flaky, with a pristine flavor neutral enough to form the foundation of a dish and noble enough to finish it.

Today, white-and-blue boxes of Saltverk salt can be found in virtually every Icelandic pantry, and its owners struggle not with convincing people to buy their salt but with keeping up with demand. Gunnar likes Saltverk salt because of the refined finish it gives his dishes. But he also loves it for the story he can share with his guests about the engineers turned salt makers who revived a long-forgotten tradition.

An Interview with Salt Maker Björn Stigursson

Q **What makes your salt different from any other salt?**

Our salt is the first artisanally produced salt in the world that uses 100 percent geothermal energy to produce it. Nothing but pristine Icelandic seawater is pumped into our facility, which is just a few feet from the shoreline, and there the heat transforms the water into our salt. It's very clean, flaky salt—and we hope one of the best produced in the world.

Q **What is your history?**

I was a professional in Reykjavík before making the decision to found Saltverk with my business partner. We stumbled on some seventeenth-century documents recounting a salt-making business in the exact spot we are located today. Denmark once colonized Iceland, and the salt company was started by the Danish king to produce enough salt to meet the needs of the Icelandic bacalao business, as salted fish was an important export for the Danes. Salt making was established in the town of Reykjanes in the Westfjords because of its proximity to the ocean and to the geothermal heat needed to produce it. The Danish empire sent the salt makers, tools, and calcium from Norway needed to produce over eighty tons of salt per year. Eventually, the Danes stopped making salt here, but the Icelanders continued to do so until the nineteenth century. I wanted to do something new, and when I discovered this long-forgotten tradition, reviving it seemed like a fulfilling challenge.

Q **Why has there always been a lack of salt in Iceland?**

You would assume, because Iceland is surrounded by an ocean, that salt would be plentiful. But you need heat to make salt, and that usually means either wood to make fires or strong, steady sunlight. Iceland has a shortage of wood and a lack of sun, which means it was nearly impossible to make salt before this innovative geyser-heat method was discovered.

Q **How do you produce your salt?**

We pump the 97°C [206°F] geyser water in from the Reykjanes hot springs and use it to preheat, boil, and dry our salt. It is incorporated from the beginning to the end of the process. This means that our carbon emissions are zero, something we are very proud of.

Q What was the initial reaction to your salt?

At first, it was a bit of a challenge to convince Icelanders to try something new. But soon they came around and seemed to appreciate that we had revived a tradition that had once been so important to our heritage. Now our salt can be found in almost every supermarket in the country, and it is gratifying to know that Icelanders have so fully embraced it.

Q What are some of the challenges you currently face?

One of the biggest challenges right now is keeping up with demand. We supply many of the restaurants and markets in both Iceland and Copenhagen, and it is hard to find the balance between saying yes to orders and knowing how you will fulfill them. We now produce our original salt, a lava salt, an arctic thyme salt, a licorice salt, and a birch-smoked salt. At first, it was lonely making salt in the remote Westfjords, and we wondered how well it would be received. We now have the opposite problem and find ourselves worrying about how we can produce more salt while still maintaining our commitment to quality. But I am not complaining. It is not a bad problem to have.

SEA SALT

MAKES 1½ CUPS (340 G) ⎸ PREPARATION TIME: ABOUT 24 HOURS, DEPENDING ON HUMIDITY

Gunnar is obsessed with making his own sea salt and is a firm believer that where it is sourced defines how it will taste. He has collected salt from virtually every corner of Iceland and is committed to a few areas where he feels the ocean is the purest and the filtration is the most robust. It's a lesson for what criteria to look for should you decide to make your own salt at home, and although you might not have water as pristine as what laps the shores of Iceland, it's likely you will discover a source close to home if you live near the sea.

Once you've collected your seawater, producing salt is surprisingly easy, and it makes a unique gift. Flavor it with ingredients in the same way the owners of Saltverk do. Everything from dried herbs to dried flower petals to smoked and powdered tree leaves will work. The other bonus to making your own salt is that once the ocean water is at a vigorous boil, your home will smell of the coastline from which the seawater was sourced.

7 quarts (7 L) seawater from a pure source

To make the salt, line a fine-mesh sieve with a coffee filter, place it over a large pot, then pour the water through the filter to remove any silt and sediment. Bring the pot of water to a boil over high heat and boil for about 30 minutes to encourage the reduction process to begin. Turn down the heat to a lazy simmer, maintaining the water temperature between 189°F and 194°F (87°C and 90°C). Continue to reduce for about 5 hours, until the water is 1 to 1½ inches (2.5 to 4 cm) deep and a salt skin has formed on the surface. Your house will smell briny and you will swear you're spending the day at the beach.

Lower the heat to its lowest setting to prevent scorching and continue to reduce the liquid until the salt begins to crystallize on the bottom of the pot and resembles wet sand. Depending on the humidity, this can take an additional 1½ to 2½ hours.

Transfer both the liquid and solids to an unlined rimmed baking sheet or tray and place it in a warm place, such as next to the stove or on top of an unused burner until the remaining liquid has evaporated. The amount of time required depends on the humidity and warmth of the kitchen.

Transfer the salt to an opaque container with a tight-fitting cap and store in a dry, dark environment. The salt will keep indefinitely.

A HISTORY WITH DENMARK

The Danes colonized Iceland for centuries, and as a result many benchmark Icelandic dishes are actually interpretations of Danish recipes. Everything from soups and breads to roasted meats and vegetable dishes have ties to the Danish kitchen. Most Icelandic pastries are directly linked to Denmark, and some people in Iceland insist that Icelandic bakers now make better Danish pastries than the Danes themselves. Many Icelanders speak fluent Danish and many also work in Denmark for at least a few years during their careers, including Gunnar, who cooked in Copenhagen for several years. The two countries are necessary allies and, also, both fiercely independent.

A contemporary example of Denmark and Iceland collaborating to improve the conditions of both nations is the Manifesto for a New Nordic Kitchen, which was spearheaded by Danish chefs Claus Meyer and René Redzepi and was signed by chefs throughout the region. It declares a commitment to sourcing ingredients as locally as possible and to celebrating the virtues of the region's many culinary resources.

Gunnar was the first chef to introduce the tenents of the manifesto to Iceland, and at first he faced resistance from a population that preferred to continue to import expensive foods and ignore its own resources. But with the economic collapse of 2009, less expensive Icelandic products became more appealing, which ushered in a newfound appreciation for Gunnar's mission.

CELERY *and* FENNEL SALAD, CARROTS, *and* FAROE ISLAND SCALLOPS

SERVES 6 | PREPARATION TIME: ABOUT 2 HOURS (PLUS 12 HOURS TO DEHYDRATE THE SCALLOP TRIMMINGS) | PICTURED ON PAGE 262

Iceland has a long history with the Faroe Islands, which lie about 450 miles to the southeast. Today, one of the most valuable resources this tiny archipelago of eighteen islands provides its bigger neighbor is scallops. They grow large and winter white in the brisk Faroe waters, and are showcased in this recipe two ways: marinated and dried. The dried and powdered scallops also make an excellent seasoning for salads, vegetables, and fish.

The anise flavor of the fennel pairs wonderfully with the brininess of the scallops, and the bright orange carrots offer a stunning contrast to the snowy white shellfish.This recipe calls for baking carrots in a canning jar, which sounds dangerous but is no different than roasting foods in a ceramic container. The cooking process marries the carrots with the seasonings, infusing them with flavor in the same intense way that immersion cooking does but without using an expensive piece of equipment. Gunnar garnishes this dish with flakes of Saltverk just before service, its crunch reminding guests with every bite that this recipe was born of the sea.

MARINATED SCALLOPS

24 small scallops

Salt

Rapeseed oil, for seasoning

DRIED SCALLOPS

1³/4 ounces (50 g) reserved scallop trimmings (above)

CELERY AND FENNEL SALAD

2 celery stalks, peeled

1 fennel bulb, cored

Salt

Rapeseed oil, for seasoning

CARROT SALAD

3 carrots, peeled

1 small sprig rosemary

4 whole cloves

1 cinnamon stick

Rapeseed oil, to cover

CARROT PUREE

4 carrots, peeled and finely chopped

Salt

¹/3 cup (80 ml) rapeseed oil

Beer Vinegar (page 30), for seasoning

Fresh dill sprigs, for garnish

Crème fraîche, for garnish

Sea salt, for garnish

To make the marinated scallops, preheat a dehydrator to 150°F (66°C). Trim the scallops, removing the muscle from each one, and reserve the trimmings for dehydrating; you should have 1³/4 ounces (50 g). If any scallop is particularly small or doesn't look good, add it to the trimmings as well. Slice the whole scallops in half horizontally and season with salt and oil. Refrigerate until ready to use.

To make the dried scallops, arrange the scallop trimmings in a single layer on a dehydrator tray and dehydrate for 12 hours, until crispy. Transfer to a spice grinder and grind to a powder. The powder will keep in an airtight container at room temperature for up to 2 days.

To make the celery and fennel salad, prepare an ice bath. Thinly slice the celery and fennel lengthwise on a mandoline (see notes, page 73). Transfer the slices to the ice bath, immersing them, and leave for about 20 minutes, until chilled and crisp. Drain and pat dry with paper towels. Transfer the slices to a bowl, season with salt, and then toss with just enough oil to make them glisten. Cover and refrigerate until ready to use.

To make the carrot salad, preheat the oven to 250°F (120°C). Trim the carrots until just long enough to fit inside a canning jar. Stand the carrots in the jar and add the rosemary, cloves, and cinnamon. Fill the jar with oil, secure the lid in place, and bake for about 1 hour, until the carrots are cooked through but just tender. Drain the carrots immediately, being careful not to let the hot oil splatter; you may discard the oil or save it for another use. Once the carrots are cool enough to handle, slice them in half lengthwise. Keep warm.

To make the carrot puree, preheat an immersion circulator to 183°F (84°C). Season the carrots with salt, place the carrots and oil in a vacuum bag, and seal on the medium-high setting. Cook in the circulator for 45 minutes to 1 hour, until tender. To test for doneness, pinch a carrot through the bag. If it is tender and you are able to easily pinch through it, the carrots are ready. Remove the bag from the circulator, and when cool enough to handle, transfer the contents to a blender. Begin processing on low speed to prevent the hot mixture from splattering. Once the elements are incorporated, increase the speed to high and continue to process until smooth. Season with vinegar until the flavor is bright.

To serve, arrange the scallops and celery and fennel salad on plates and spoon the carrot puree alongside. Place a small spoonful of the carrot salad next to the puree and garnish the plate with dill and crème fraîche. Season everything with the powdered scallops and sprinkle with sea salt.

OPPOSITE: Celery and Fennel Salad, Carrots, and Faroe Island Scallops (page 260)

ABOVE: Hay-Smoked Beets with Pine and Roses (page 264)

HAY-SMOKED BEETS
with PINE *and* ROSES

SERVES 4 TO 6 | PREPARATION TIME: ABOUT 1 HOUR (PLUS 24 HOURS TO PICKLE THE BEETS) | PICTURED ON PAGE 263

The combination of beets, pine, and roses might leave some cooks scratching their heads, but the trio proves congenial for this vibrantly colored, explosively flavored recipe. The red of the beets and the addition of roses make this an ideal dish for a romantic evening when the standard romance recipes seem overdone. There are several ways to hay smoke beets (see photos at right and page 93); however, for this dish the beets are baked under a cap of dough that ensures they will retain their juices as they cook and will marry with the fragrance of pine. They are a perfect pairing for a white fish such as halibut or cod, and lovely on their own, too.

Generous 1 pound (500 g) medium red beets, trimmed, scrubbed, and dried

Hay, for smoking (see page 93)

7 (6-inch) pine tree twigs, rinsed well under ice-cold water to remove residue and sap

Scant 1 cup (250 g) plus 4 teaspoons salt

2 cups (250 g) all-purpose flour, plus more for dusting

2/3 cup (150 ml) water

1 cup (240 ml) cider vinegar

1/3 cup (75 g) sugar

Petals from 3 chemical-free rose heads

NOTE
Depending on the size of the roasting pan, you may need to increase the ingredients for the dough cap proportionately. It is important that the dough sheet extend 2 inches (5 cm) beyond the rim of the pan on all sides to ensure a proper seal.

To make the beets, preheat the oven to 425°F (220°C). Cover the bottom of a small, deep roasting pan with hay about 2 inches (5 cm) deep. Distribute 6 of the pine twigs evenly over the hay. Arrange the beets on top.

In a bowl, stir together the scant 1 cup (250 g) of salt, the flour, and the water to form a dry dough. Dust a work surface with flour and transfer the dough to it. Roll out the dough 1/4 inch (6 mm) thick and wide and long enough to extend beyond the rim of the roasting pan by 2 inches (5 cm) on all sides (see note).

Carefully transfer the dough sheet to the pan, covering the top and then pinching the edges of the dough to the rim of the pan to seal securely. Bake for 10 minutes, then turn down the heat to 350°F (180°C) and continue to bake for 20 to 30 minutes longer, until the dough sheet is baked through but not golden brown. The sheet's surface will harden and begin to develop thin cracks once it is cooked through. At this stage the beets should be barely cooked through. Remove from the oven, let cool to room temperature, and then remove and discard the dough sheet. Wearing plastic gloves to prevent staining your hands with beet juice, peel the beets, cut them into bite-size pieces, and transfer them to a large glass jar with an airtight lid.

In a saucepan over medium heat, whisk together the vinegar and sugar until the sugar dissolves. Add the remaining pine twig and bring the liquid to a boil over medium-high heat. Remove from the heat, add the rose petals and the remaining 4 teaspoons of salt, and stir gently until the salt has dissolved. Let cool to room temperature. Pour the cooled mixture over the beets, immersing them. Cover tightly and refrigerate for 24 hours before using. The beets will keep in the refrigerator for up to 1 month.

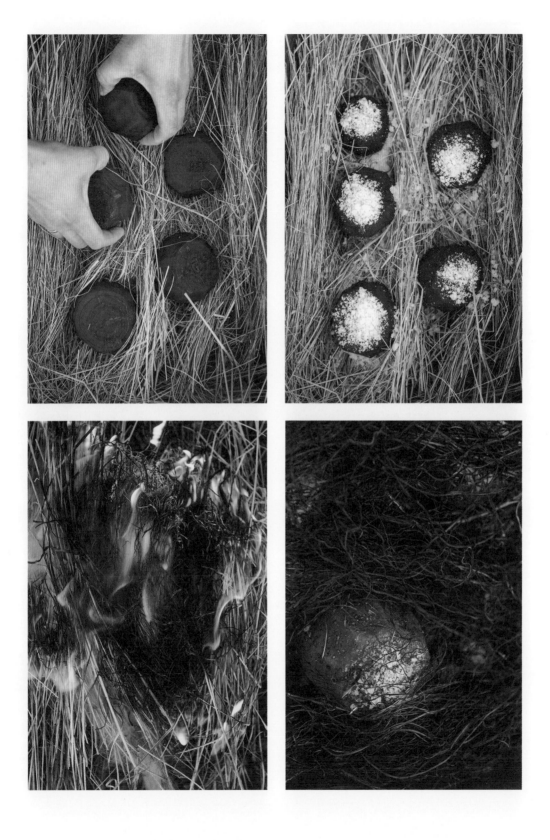

BRAISED WILD GOOSE LEG, RED BEETS, BLACKBERRIES, *and* PINE SALT

SERVES 4 | PREPARATION TIME: ABOUT 1 HOUR (PLUS 16 HOURS TO COOK THE GOOSE LEGS, 12 HOURS TO REFRIGERATE THE PINE TREE OIL, AND 1 WEEK TO PICKLE THE BEETS) | PICTURED ON PAGE 268

This recipe is the ideal composition for a holiday feast or for any other festive cold-weather occasion. Here, Gunnar creates his version of a Nordic spring roll, with the goose tucked inside a pickled beet casing for an appetizer guests won't soon forget. Blackberries and raspberries are called brambleberries in Iceland and either berry would work for this recipe. They do not grow wild in the Icelandic countryside but do flourish in its greenhouses (see page 146).

If you have trouble sourcing goose, four duck legs make a good substitute. Any fruit vinegar with a dominant flavor, such as pomegranate or blackcurrant, makes a good stand-in for the cherry vinegar. The pine element appears several times in this recipe, driving home the jubilant tone this dish strikes.

PICKLED BEETS

1 large red beet, peeled and cut into 8 thin slices

1/2 cup (120 ml) cherry vinegar

1/4 cup (50 g) sugar

1 tablespoon plus 2 teaspoons water

1 (6-inch/15-cm) pine tree twig, rinsed well under ice-cold water to remove residue and sap

BEER-BRAISED LEG OF GOOSE

Unsalted butter, for frying

Rapeseed oil, for frying

2 goose legs, trimmed of excess fat

1 tablespoon plus 2 teaspoons salt

2 1/2 tablespoons sugar

2 cups (480 ml) water

1 cinnamon stick

3 juniper berries

2 whole cloves

1 small pine tree twig, rinsed well under ice-cold water to remove residue and sap

1/2 cup (120 ml) Chicken Stock, preferably homemade (page 89)

2 tablespoons burned butter (see page 119)

2 shallots chopped

Beer Vinegar (page 30), for seasoning

PINE TREE OIL

1 cup (240 ml) rapeseed oil

Needles from 4 (6-inch) pine tree twigs, rinsed well under ice-cold water to remove residue and sap, and dried

BLACKBERRIES

2 1/2 teaspoons sugar

1 tablespoon water

Scant 1/3 cup (50 g) blackberries

RED BEET JUICE

1 cup (240 ml) red beet juice

2 1/2 tablespoons honey

1 small pine tree twig, rinsed well under ice-cold water to remove residue and sap

Cherry vinegar

Salt

RAW RED BEETS

32 thin circles red beet

PINE SALT

Needles from 2 (6-inch) pine tree twigs, rinsed well under ice-cold water to remove residue and sap

1/4 cup (70 g) salt

Arctic thyme sprigs, for garnish

To make the pickled beets, bring a saucepan of salted water to a boil. Add the beet slices, blanch for a few seconds, and, using a slotted spoon, transfer to a small heatproof glass jar. Combine the cherry vinegar, sugar, water, and pine twig in a saucepan and bring to a boil over medium heat, stirring until the sugar has dissolved. Pour the hot liquid over the beets, immersing them. Let cool to room temperature, then cap tightly and refrigerate for 1 week. Drain and discard the pickling liquid just before serving.

To make the goose, melt enough butter with oil in a large sauté pan over medium heat to coat the pan bottom lightly. Season the goose legs with salt, add to the hot pan, and fry, turning once, until just golden on both sides. Preheat an immersion circulator to 172°F (78°C). Place the salt, sugar, water, cinnamon stick, juniper, cloves, pine twig, stock, and goose legs in a vacuum bag and seal at the lowest setting. Cook in the circulator for 16 hours. Remove the bag from the circulator, then remove the legs from the bag and discard the remaining contents. When the legs are cool enough to handle, bone them, discarding the bones and skin, and finely shred the meat.

Heat the burned butter in a sauté pan over medium heat. Add the shallots and sauté for about 7 minutes, until caramelized. Add the goose meat and stir to combine. Season with salt and beer vinegar.

To make the pine tree oil, combine the oil and pine needles in a blender and process on high speed for 10 minutes, until steaming hot and completely blended. Transfer to an airtight container and refrigerate for 12 hours. Line a fine-mesh sieve with cheesecloth and strain the oil through it. Transfer to a squeeze bottle and refrigerate until ready to use.

To make the blackberries, whisk together the sugar and water until the sugar has dissolved. Place the berries in a bowl, pour the sugar syrup over the top, and let stand at room temperature for 1 hour, then drain.

To make the red beet juice, combine the beet juice, honey, pine twig, and cherry vinegar in a saucepan and bring to a simmer over medium heat. Cook for 15 to 17 minutes, until thick enough to coat the back of a wooden spoon. Remove from the heat, season with salt, and keep warm.

To make the raw beets, prepare an ice bath. Using a cutter 1 inch (2.5 cm) in diameter, punch out 1 disk from each beet slice. Transfer the disks to the ice bath until ready to serve.

To make the pine salt, heat a small, dry frying pan over medium-high heat, add the pine needles, and sauté until blackened. Let cool, transfer to a spice grinder, add the salt, and grind to a powder. (If your spice grinder is small, you will need to grind the salt in batches.) The salt will keep in an airtight container for up to 1 month at room temperature.

To serve, roll up the goose meat in the pickled red beet slices, as you would roll a spring roll. Arrange 2 rolls on a plate with the raw beets and blackberries alongside. Drizzle with the pine tree oil and beet juice, sprinkle everything with a light dusting of pine salt, and garnish with arctic thyme.

ABOVE: Braised Wild Goose Leg, Red Beets, Blackberries, and Pine Salt (page 266)

OPPOSITE: Lamb Heart, Cabbage Two Ways, Raspberry Sauce, and Heather and Moss Ash (page 270)

LAMB HEART, CABBAGE TWO WAYS, RASPBERRY SAUCE, *and* HEATHER *and* MOSS ASH

SERVES 4 | PREPARATION TIME: ABOUT 2 HOURS (PLUS 3 MONTHS TO SALT THE CABBAGE) | PICTURED ON PAGE 269

Gunnar likes using the offcuts of animals that many other chefs discard. For him, the most symbolic of these is the heart, with its pronounced notes of iron and its rich, dark meat. Because of the cultural significance of the heart, many people shy away from eating it. But if you try it just once, you will discover just how tasty it is. The good news is that the heart is a fairly lean cut. The bad news is that its interior contains bits of sinew and connective tissue that you need to remove before cooking.

You will need to plan ahead to make the salted cabbage, as it must sit for a few months. You can substitute sauerkraut in its place, draining it well and seasoning it with rapeseed oil. Icelandic moss and heather (*mosi og lyng* in Icelandic) are also called for in this recipe. The moss isn't really a moss at all (see page 334), but a lichen that has sustained Icelanders through many cold winters. It can be difficult to source outside of Iceland but is available online. No good substitute exists, so if you cannot find it, you can simply omit it. Heather grows in some parts of Iceland and should be fairly easy to find elsewhere in the world. It can be ordered online, as well, and is a beautiful garnish for savory dishes and desserts alike.

SALTED CABBAGE

14 ounces (400 g) green cabbage, cored and chopped

1 tablespoon salt

Rapeseed oil, for seasoning

LAMB HEART

4 lamb hearts

1¹/₂ tablespoons burned butter (see page 119)

3 tablespoons pomegranate seeds

Salt

CARAMELIZED CABBAGE PUREE

1¹/₂ tablespoons unsalted butter

7 ounces (200 g) green cabbage, cored and chopped

1 teaspoon chopped garlic

1¹/₂ tablespoons chopped shallot

¹/₂ teaspoon baking soda

Salt

Beer Vinegar (page 30), for seasoning

RASPBERRY SAUCE

¹/₄ cup (50 g) sugar

¹/₂ cup (120 ml) cherry vinegar, plus more for seasoning

Scant 1 cup (100 g) raspberries

2¹/₂ teaspoons burned butter (see page 119)

Salt

Heather and moss ash (see note), for garnish

Arctic thyme, for garnish

To make the salted cabbage, in a large bowl, toss the cabbage with the salt until evenly coated, then transfer to a crock, small bucket, or other container. Select a heavy plate or similar weight that is the same diameter as the container and place it on the cabbage. Let stand at room temperature for 5 hours.

Remove the plate, cover the crock with a cotton cloth or a double layer of cheesecloth, and store in a cool, dark place for 3 months, occasionally skimming off any scum that collects on the surface beneath the cheesecloth, and replacing the cheesecloth once every 2 weeks. It should not need any additional liquid since the cabbage will release liquid on its own, but should it become dry, add a saltwater solution with a ratio of eight parts water to one part salt until the liquid covers the cabbage completely. Drain the cabbage before seasoning it with oil. It will keep in the refrigerator for up to 2 months. Before serving, season with more oil if needed.

To make the lamb heart, using a paring knife, trim the exterior of each heart of any excess fat or connective tissue, then cut each heart in half lengthwise. Cut away any additional fat, tough tissue, and knobby bits, working as deeply as possible with breaking apart any ventricles. Preheat an immersion circulator to 136°F (58°C). Place the hearts, burned butter, pomegranate seeds, and $1/2$ teaspoon of salt in a vacuum bag and seal on medium. Cook in the circulator for $1^1/2$ hours. Remove the bag from the circulator, and when cool enough to handle, remove the hearts from the bag and discard the remaining contents. Slice the hearts into $1/4$-inch (6-mm) strips and season with salt.

To make the cabbage puree, melt the butter in a pressure cooker (see page 50). Add the cabbage, garlic, shallot, baking soda, and a little salt, lock the lid in place, bring to medium pressure, and cook for 10 minutes, until the vegetables are caramelized and tender. Let the pressure release naturally, then remove the lid and drain the contents well, reserving the solids and liquid separately. Transfer the solids to a blender and process on high speed to a puree, adding a little of the cooking liquid if necessary to achieve a smooth consistency. Season with salt and beer vinegar.

To make the raspberry sauce, put the sugar in a small, heavy saucepan, place over low heat, and heat, swirling the pan, until caramelized. Do not stir the sugar to prevent scorching. When the sugar is a good amber, slowly and carefully add the cherry vinegar while stirring constantly. Simmer over low heat until syrupy, then add the berries and stir until well coated. Stir in the burned butter and season with salt and with more vinegar, if needed.

To serve, arrange the salted cabbage on plates and spoon the cabbage puree alongside. Place the lamb heart slices on top of the salted cabbage and drizzle everything with the raspberry sauce. Garnish with a sprinkle of heather and moss ash and a little arctic thyme.

SPICED LAMB BELLY, SALT-BAKED CELERY ROOT, *and* PICKLED CELERY ROOT

SERVES 6 TO 8 | PREPARATION TIME: ABOUT 7 HOURS (PLUS 1 WEEK TO PICKLE THE CELERY ROOT AND 12 HOURS TO BRINE THE LAMB BELLY)

Gunnar uses his own homemade salt (page 258) or, if he does not have enough on hand, kosher salt, to bake the celery root in this dish. The salt is added to a simple flour-and-water dough that he uses to cover the celery root as it slowly caramelizes in the oven to a juicy-sweet conclusion. Rutabaga or parsnip can be substituted for the celery root. Other flavors in this recipe include pickled celery root for brightness and a spiced glaze that lacquers the lamb belly in a cloak of birch and thyme. This recipe is worthy of dinner guests, and when it is brought to the table garnished with birch sprigs, the conversation is sure to begin.

PICKLED CELERY ROOT

7 ounces (200 g) celery root, peeled and cut into slices 1/4 inch (6 mm) thick

1/2 cup (120 ml) cider vinegar

2 tablespoons water

2 1/2 tablespoons sugar

Ground fennel, for seasoning

Salt

LAMB BELLY

Generous 1 pound (500 g) lamb belly

3/4 cup (70 g) finely chopped fresh thyme and birch tree leaves, in equal amounts

2 tablespoons plus 3/4 teaspoon salt

2 1/2 tablespoons granulated sugar

2 cups (480 ml) water

1/4 cup (60 ml) rapeseed oil

1 tablespoon unsalted butter

1/4 cup (50 g) firmly packed light brown sugar

SAUCE

1/4 cup (50 g) sugar

1/2 cup (120 ml) Beer Vinegar (page 30)

1/2 cup (120 ml) Birkir schnapps (see page 174) or dark rum

1/2 cup (120 ml) Chicken Stock, preferably homemade (page 89)

1/2 cup (120 ml) beef stock

1 bay leaf

1 sprig thyme

1 birch tree twig

1 1/2 tablespoons unsalted butter

Salt

Cider vinegar, for seasoning

SALT-BAKED CELERY ROOT

1 celery root, peeled, and cut into slices 1/4 inch (6 mm) thick

Scant 1 cup (250 g) salt

2 cups (250 g) all-purpose flour

2/3 cup (150 g) water

1/2 teaspoon ground fennel

Rapeseed oil, for seasoning

Cider vinegar, for seasoning

To make the pickled celery root, bring a saucepan of lightly salted water to a boil. Add the celery root, blanch for 1 minute, and drain. Transfer the celery root to a small heatproof glass jar. Combine the cider vinegar, water, and sugar in a small saucepan and bring to a boil over medium heat, stirring until the sugar has dissolved. Pour the hot liquid over the celery root, immersing it. Let cool to room temperature, then cap tightly and refrigerate for 1 week before using. Just before serving, drain, cut into bite-size pieces, and sprinkle with the fennel and salt.

NOTES

1. The belly and liquid can instead be refrigerated in a ziplock bag, with all of the air pressed out before sealing.

2. The sugar will seize when the liquid is added. This is normal and you should not be alarmed. Just continue to whisk and it will eventually dissolve and become syrupy.

To make the lamb belly, trim the belly until it is about 1/2 inch (12 mm) thick. Lay the belly flat on a work surface and sprinkle evenly with the thyme and birch. Roll up the belly tightly. Lay the rolled belly, seam side down, atop 4 evenly spaced lengths of butcher's twine long enough to tie around the rolled belly. Securely tie each length of twine around the roll, then snip off any loose ends.

To make the brine for the belly, combine the salt, granulated sugar, and water in a saucepan and bring to a simmer. Remove from the heat and let cool to room temperature. Place the belly and the brine in a vacuum bag and seal on the highest setting to ensure that the belly is completely covered with brine (see notes). Refrigerate for 12 hours.

Remove the belly from the refrigerator, then remove the belly from the bag and discard the brine. Pat the belly dry with paper towels. Preheat the oven to 300°F (150°C). Rub the belly with the oil, place in a roasting pan, and roast for 4 hours.

Melt the butter in a small saucepan over medium heat, add the brown sugar, and cook until the sugar has dissolved (the sugar may still be slightly granulated even after it has dissolved). Brush with about half of the butter-sugar glaze over the lamb belly and continue to roast for another 2 hours. Brush with the remaining glaze (it might have to be reheated to melt the butter), turn up the oven heat to 400°F (200°C), and roast for 5 more minutes. Let the belly rest for 10 minutes before removing the twine and thinly slicing for serving.

To make the sauce, put the sugar in a small, heavy saucepan, place over medium heat, and heat, swirling the pan, until an amber syrup forms. Add the beer vinegar and cook until reduced by three-fourths (see notes). Remove the pan from the heat and add the schnapps. Return the pan to the heat and add the stocks, bay leaf, thyme, and birch twig and cook until reduced by half. You should have just over 1/2 cup (120 ml) of liquid. Stir in the butter until incorporated, strain through a fine-mesh sieve, and let cool to room temperature. Season with salt and cider vinegar. Reheat just before serving.

To make the baked celery root, preheat the oven to 400°F (200°C). Arrange the celery root in a single layer on a baking sheet or in a roasting pan. In a bowl, stir together the salt, flour, and water to form a dry dough. Dust a work surface with flour and transfer the dough to it. Roll out the dough 1/4 inch (6 mm) thick and wide and long enough to extend beyond the rim of the pan by 2 inches (5 cm) on all sides (see note, page 264).

Carefully transfer the dough sheet to the pan, covering the top and then pinching the edges of the dough to the rim of the pan to seal securely. Bake for 10 minutes, then turn down the heat to 350°F (180°C) and continue to bake for 20 to 30 minutes, until the dough sheet is cooked through but not golden. Remove from the oven and let cool until you can safely remove the dough sheet, then remove the dough and discard. Using a cutter of choice, cut the celery root slices into the size desired. Season with fennel, salt, oil, and cider vinegar.

To serve, arrange thin slices of the lamb belly on plates. Arrange the pickled celery root and salt-baked celery root alongside. Drizzle the sauce in between the elements on the plate.

THE HÁKARL TRADITION

When people hear that you're writing a cookbook about Icelandic food, one of the first questions they often ask is if it includes a recipe for rotten shark. Iceland's notorious preserved shark tradition trumps nearly everything else people know about Icelandic food, and they usually assume that Icelanders eat the strong-smelling fish every day. It couldn't be further from the truth.

Although opaque ivory cubes of *hákarl* are sold in most supermarkets, this specialty is primarily appreciated by the older generations, who recall a time when eating in Iceland meant trying to survive the long winters and regular vegetable shortages.

The process of making *hákarl* is not a pleasant one. It calls for catching the shark, hacking up its white flesh into large rectangles, fermenting the flesh in a lye solution, and then hanging it to dry in an open-air wooden house on the edge of the ocean. It dries there for several months, and in the process, it rots.

The flesh of the Greenland shark contains unusually high levels of urea and of trimethylamine oxide, which turns into toxic trimethylamine (TMA) in our digestive process. The flesh of a shark cannot be eaten raw due to this TMA; the only way to make it edible is to allow it to decay, eliminating the toxicity. The process results in an odor that smells like the dirtiest cat litter box imaginable. The mildest *hákarl* tastes like an extra-strong Stilton cheese, but this is only if you brainwash yourself into believing that before you try it. It is unappetizing to most palates and noses, but for some, it is a reminder of when food meant survival, and survival meant being clever with the few resources available.

Iceland's earliest settlers did not find the country's fierce winds and large stretches of unfarmable terrain a welcoming environment. The conditions forced them to be inventive with how they prepared their foods, which include pickled lamb testicles; fermented seal blubber; whale blubber preserved in whey; lamb heart wrapped in lamb intestines and covered in suet, then eaten raw; liver sausage either smoked or preserved in whey; sheep's head cut in half and either eaten raw or preserved in whey; and blood pudding.

Younger generations rarely eat these foods today, but for the older generations, they remain symbols of perseverance in difficult times. Today, at the festival of Thorrablot, traditional foods—meats, fish, and pickled vegetables—are washed down with the caraway-spiked schnapps known as *brennivín* (see page 290).

Thorrablot is a relatively new tradition, thought to have been started by a Reykjavík-based restaurateur who wanted to give tourists a taste of the foods of the past. The idea took off, and Thorrablot celebrations are now held in nearly every town and village in Iceland during late February. They pay tribute to the older generations who were resilient and tenacious enough to survive and pass on to their descendants an easier life.

A few *hákarl* producers are still working in Iceland today. One of the most revered is Hildibrandur Bjarnason, a seventy-year-old-plus gentleman with a white shock of hair, a ready smile, smooth skin that he attributes to shark oil, and a gleam in his eye that illustrates how much pleasure he derives from keeping an ancient Icelandic tradition alive.

He dries his shark on a windy peninsula in the moss-covered lava fields of the Snaefellsnes Peninsula, just as his family has done for decades. There is a shark museum on the property filled with relics that date to when Hildibrandur's grandfather and father hunted the massive Greenland shark from a wooden boat not much longer than the fish they were catching.

Today, Hildibrandur doesn't fish for the shark himself. He instead relies on fishing trawlers that accidentally catch a shark in their nets to drop one off occasionally. Due to the introduction of new regulations, the fishermen are no longer allowed to sell *hákarl* producers their bycatch. They must dump them back into the sea, even though they are dead. It is an unfortunate policy that has caused a shortage in *hákarl* and is one more step toward the tradition disappearing forever. Hildibrandur must now source closer to home, but as interest in the *hákarl* tradition wanes, so too does the availability of Greenland shark, since fewer people are fishing for them.

A Conversation with Hákarl Maker Hildibrandur Bjarnason

Q **How do you source your shark?**

The boats don't go out to fish shark specifically. When the larger German boats were fishing for other things, they would sometimes catch shark in their nets near Greenland, but now due to a conflict between Greenland and Germany, the shark they used to save for me is thrown back into the sea, already dead. The shark is a very clean animal and catches very few diseases, so it is a waste to be throwing it away when it could be used instead to make *hákarl*.

Q **Did your family ever hunt for shark themselves?**

Yes, when my father hunted shark, the best time to fish for them was in January or February, when the sharks, who usually hunt in the deepest parts of the ocean, would come up closer to the surface because of the extreme cold and darkness of the season. My father would hunt for them in the wooden boat you can see in my shark museum. It was a cold and dangerous job, but it is our tradition and the only thing we know. My father and grandfather were both *hákarl* producers. At the age of twelve, I started fishing with my father, but every time I went out, I got seasick. I eventually got over it, but it was a difficult time for me.

I came here to the Snaefellsnes Peninsula from northern Iceland. My parents had a farm there, but they started fishing more than farming. One day the fish stopped coming, so we moved to a place where we could find them again, and along with this move came the shark. My father was getting old, and he wanted to move to an easier place to live. I am the oldest of ten siblings, five boys and five girls, and we all moved here together. I was the only one in my family left here. The others relocated abroad to receive an education, but they all eventually returned.

Q **Are there any health benefits to eating *hákarl*?**

I grew up eating *hákarl* every day and I still do. Sometimes I eat it in a rye bread sandwich with butter. When we were sitting down for dinner as children, each of us would be given a piece of it. We often ate it spread with skyr. Sometimes we also ate sour blood pudding with it.

Whenever I'm cutting it down after drying, I taste a sample from each portion to make sure it is good to eat. We compress the shark in a cooler for about six weeks before hanging it, and this compression can sometimes cause the shark to go bad. Shark is very nutritious and good for you, and I attribute my strong health to it. The oil from the shark is very good for arthritis, but that's not all. It's also good for bronchitis and for your skin. I believe shark is good for whatever ails you.

Q Is there a growing interest in the *hákarl* tradition?

Yes, tourists do seem to be more interested. Icelanders are still purchasing *hákarl*, although it is mostly the older generation. It will take the younger generation to keep the tradition alive. But I believe in them and know they will not let it disappear. I just hope that once I am gone, there will be someone here to continue making it.

THE GOAT
FARMER

Háafell, Western Iceland

∞

Celery Root, Herb Cream, Goat Cheese,
and Arctic Char Roe 284

Dry-Aged Beef, Smoked Bone Marrow, Pickled Angelica,
and Vegetable Strings 288

Preserved Duck 291

Beer Mustard 292

Almond and Hazelnut Praline, Caramel Nut Parfait,
and Brown Butter Cake 294

Red Beet and Rosemary Sorbet, Almond Cake,
and Sugared Almonds 298

Whey Caramel, Buttermilk, and Horseradish 300

Johanna Thorvaldsdóttir was studying to be a nurse in Reykjavík until she heard that Iceland's goat population, a unique species on the planet, had fallen to fewer than seventy animals. Virtually overnight, Johanna made the decision to sacrifice the future she had planned for herself to nearly single-handedly save the Icelandic goat population from extinction.

Iceland's goats now number over one thousand, and their products—milk, cheese, meat— are finding their way back into the marketplace. In the past, goat meat and dairy products were popular with Icelanders. Gunnar remembers his grandmother waxing fondly about the rich goat's milk that once graced her table, but until a few years ago, he had never tasted Icelandic goat's milk himself.

It is only because of pioneers like Johanna that the Icelanders are once again able to taste the products enjoyed by their ancestors. During a visit with Johanna, she gave Gunnar two quarts of goat's milk in old-fashioned glass bottles. Back at Dill, he transformed the milk into an impossibly silky ice cream. With his first bite, he began to cry. The ice cream was certainly good, but not enough to elicit tears, and the other chefs in the kitchen wondered what inspired such emotion, until they realized it was the first time Gunnar had ever tasted goat's milk, which caused the memories of his grandmother's stories to come flooding back.

Gunnar served Johanna's ice cream that night at Dill, the waiters explaining to guests its significance on the menu. As they took their first bite, the same wave of joy that washed over Gunnar's face earlier in the day washed over theirs. It illustrated how important Gunnar's cuisine is to his nation. It is not simply about serving resplendent food in a radiant setting. It is also about preserving a way of life. By connecting modern diners to producers like Johanna at the tables of Dill, he helps Johanna continue her work and pass on the tradition to the next generation.

A Conversation with Goat Farmer Johanna Thorvaldsdóttir

Q **Have you always been a goat farmer?**

No, I was studying to be a nurse in Reykjavík before I decided to take over the farm. My father never wanted me to raise goats, but I've loved them ever since I was a child.

Q **How many goats did you have when you began farming?**

I started out with three goats, and then in 1999, I bought a group of fifty. I now have over three hundred goats. It's important to raise a large number to prevent inbreeding. Today, many of Iceland's goats are owned by hobby farmers who keep them as pets, which makes it difficult to encourage diversity.

Q **What is the history of goats in Iceland?**

When the first settlers arrived in the ninth century, they brought a lot of goats with them. They were easy to carry, provided a lot of milk, and required very little food. During the seventeenth century, the climate turned colder and volcanic eruptions disturbed the air quality. I believe that during this time, many of the goats perished, and the people turned to sheep for wool and food. Goats could not provide the fatty meat that was needed during the harsh winters. People started to lose their interest in goats, and only poorer citizens kept them. Goats gained a reputation for being the animals of the destitute.

After World War II, people became more affluent and started to grow their own gardens, which the goats, of course, loved. That prompted laws against keeping goats in smaller communities because they were eating the gardens. The newfound wealth also meant that Icelanders turned to expensive imports from other parts of the world.

It seemed that only older women continued to believe in the nutritional benefits of goat's milk, and they were often the primary goat keepers. There are old tales of elderly women with perfect teeth because of their preference for goat's milk. But the younger generations soon lost their taste for the milk. Goats nearly went extinct in Iceland during the last century, which is why I decided to take up their cause. If I didn't do it, I'm not sure if anyone would have, and they might have disappeared forever.

Q **What products do you produce from your goats?**

Goats are not able to grow fat on the outside, but they don't have the ability to get rid of their fat, or tallow, on the inside. I use the tallow along with a variety of herbs and flowers from my gardens to make soaps and creams. I believe in the health benefits of these products. I also sell goatskins. I try to collect their cashmere—that is, the under layer of their coats—but it's difficult because it requires extensive brushing, and I do not have the time or help I need to do it. I am working with a dairy in the area to produce goat's milk and also to produce sausages and ice cream. Once my goats are slaughtered, I try to use each and every part of them. It would be a disgrace not to.

Q Where do you find information about caring for your goats and making your products?

It's difficult, as there is so little written information about goats in Iceland. Because they almost disappeared, this knowledge was lost through neglect and disinterest. Even my veterinarian has had a hard time learning how to care for my goats, which are a unique species, and some aspects of other goat species differ from Icelandic goats. I have visited goat farms in Italy to learn, and I have trained in Norway to make cheese. I have been told by the organizers of Slow Food in Italy that if I am able to make cheese from unpasteurized milk, my cheese will be designated a slow food. But in Iceland, I will never be allowed to do this.

Q Why not?

It's the same as in the United States; authorities believe drinking raw milk is dangerous. All dairy here must be pasteurized. It amazes me that people think they will die if they drink a healthful thing like raw milk, yet they are fine with feeding their children food loaded with preservatives and other chemicals. People who visit the farm sometimes ask to buy raw milk, and I do sell it to some families who have children with allergies. There is a protein missing in goat's milk that enables these children to process the milk, unlike cow's milk. It is a shame not to be able to sell my raw milk and produce unpasteurized cheese. But it is the nature of our industrialized society that prevents it.

Q Do you receive any funding from the government?

Very little. I have gone to the minister of agriculture and begged for help, but because goats are considered hobby animals in Iceland, the government provides only a small subsidy for up to twenty animals. That's not very helpful when you have over three hundred. The government has yet to see the importance of protecting a species unique to the world. Since the economic crisis, the interest rates on loans have soared as a means of paying back the national debt. It has put an additional burden on small family farms like mine. I do have renewed hope, though. In recent years, the number of visitors to the farm has skyrocketed. There is much more interest in Icelandic goats than there was just a few years ago. Many of my visitors come from around the world, but what makes me happiest is welcoming the large number of Icelanders who come to Háafell. They have begun to realize the value and beauty of this nation's goats, and I am hoping that this will help my family and, in turn, help our goats. I have given up a lot for them, but I believe in them, and it lightens my burden a little to see Icelanders are beginning to believe in them again, too.

CELERY ROOT, HERB CREAM, GOAT CHEESE, *and* ARCTIC CHAR ROE

SERVES 4 | PREPARATION TIME: ABOUT 1 HOUR | PICTURED ON PAGE 286

This beautifully constructed appetizer, with its vibrant colors and carefully assembled elements, was one of the first dishes Gunnar served when he opened Dill, and it has appeared often on the menu ever since. Gunnar changes his menu frequently based on available ingredients, but this recipe is a mainstay, for it is a true celebration of all that Iceland has to offer. The celery root, used three ways, illustrates the creativity Gunnar employs when creating his dishes and pays homage to a humble root vegetable by showcasing it. The incorporation of goat farmer Johanna Thorvaldsdóttir's goat cheese pays homage to a producer whom Gunnar deeply respects.

CELERY ROOT

1 large celery root, peeled

Salt

HERB CREAM

1 egg

2 shallots, coarsely chopped

1 clove garlic

6 sprigs dill

6 sprigs flat-leaf parsley

1 cup (240 ml) rapeseed oil

Salt

Cider vinegar, for seasoning

GOAT CHEESE FOAM

1 cup (240 ml) milk

1³/₄ ounces (50 g) fresh goat cheese

Salt

Freshly squeezed lemon juice, for seasoning

1 g soy lecithin (see notes, page 27)

2 ounces (50 g) fresh goat cheese, crumbled into small pieces

1 tablespoon arctic char or salmon roe

Crispy rye bread (page 72)

Garden cress, for garnish

To make the celery root, using a mandoline (see notes, page 73) or knife, cut 4 slices of celery root, each ¹/₈ inch (3 mm) thick. Using a 2-inch (5-cm) round cutter, punch out 8 disks from the slices. Chop the remaining celery root (including the leftover bits from the slices) into ¹/₄-inch (6-mm) pieces.

Bring a saucepan of salted water to a boil. Add the celery root disks, blanch for a few seconds, drain, and pat dry with paper towels. Repeat the process with the chopped celery root. Cover and refrigerate all of the celery root until chilled.

To make the herb cream, prepare an ice bath. Bring a saucepan of water to a vigorous boil. Using a slotted spoon, lower the egg into the water and cook at a vigorous boil for 3¹/₂ minutes. Transfer the egg to the ice bath until well chilled. Remove the egg from the ice bath and immediately crack it lightly on all sides on a flat surface. Peel the egg, put it in a blender, and add the shallots, garlic, dill, and parsley. Process on high speed for about 3 minutes, until smooth. Add the oil in a slow, steady stream and process for about 1 minute longer, until the consistency of thick mayonnaise. Fold in the chopped celery root, season with salt and vinegar, cover, and refrigerate until chilled.

To make the goat cheese foam, combine the milk and cheese in a saucepan over medium heat and heat, stirring frequently to prevent scorching, until the cheese melts. Season with salt and lemon juice and whisk in the soy lecithin. Process with an immersion blender until foamy.

To serve, in a bowl, toss together the goat cheese, roe, and crispy rye bread. Place the 2-inch (5-cm) round cutter on a plate, and put one of the celery root disks inside the cutter. Top with a mound of the herb cream about 1 inch (2.5 cm) tall, and then top with a second disk. Carefully lift off the cutter, top the second disk with a spoonful of the roe mixture, and garnish with cress. Process the foam a second time, if necessary, and spoon it over the cress.

ABOVE: Celery Root, Herb Cream, Goat Cheese, and Arctic Char Roe (page 284)

OPPOSITE: Dry-Aged Beef, Smoked Bone Marrow, Pickled Angelica, and Vegetable Strings (page 288)

DRY-AGED BEEF, SMOKED BONE MARROW, PICKLED ANGELICA, *and* VEGETABLE STRINGS

Angelica flourishes in the pastures surrounding Johanna Thorvaldsdóttir's goat farm in Háafell. In this recipe, Gunnar pickles it and serves it with dry-aged beef that is gently seared a golden brown but not completely cooked through, in order to showcase the virtues of the beef. Dry-aged beef is meat that has been hung and slowly aged. It speaks to Gunnar's love for preservation and is a new twist on the Icelandic smoked lamb he admires.

Dry-aged beef has become a popular item in restaurants outside of Iceland, and if you have trouble sourcing it locally, it is widely available online. Gunnar pairs the beef with smoked bone marrow, which enhances it with a smokiness that complements its tenderness. He uses several ingredients to garnish the dish, including *maríustakkur*, an Icelandic version of lemon balm that is nearly impossible to find outside of Iceland.

VEGETABLE STRINGS

¹/₄ cup (25 g) peeled and julienned carrots

¹/₄ cup (25 g) peeled and julienned celery root

¹/₄ cup (25 g) peeled and julienned rutabaga

1 cup (250 ml) apple cider vinegar

1 cup (250 ml) water

1 tablespoon salt

DRY-AGED BEEF

Unsalted butter, for frying

Rapeseed oil, for frying

16 ounces (450 g) dry-aged beef tenderloin

2 bay leaves

1 sprig thyme

1 sprig rosemary

Salt

SMOKED BONE MARROW

3¹/₂ ounces (100 g) bone marrow (see notes)

Wood chips or dried onion peels (see page 250), for smoking

Salt

Maríustakkur or lemon balm leaves, for garnish

Powdered incinerated leeks and onions, for garnish (see notes, page 141)

Pickled angelica stalks (page 137), for garnish

Pickled Angelica Butter (page 137), for garnish

Herb oil (page 202), for garnish

NOTE

Removing uncooked marrow from a beef bone often results in a globular mess of marrow and blood. The trick is to soak the bones in lightly salted water in the refrigerator for 12 to 24 hours. This causes the marrow to seize up, which makes it easier to pop it out of the bone. The long soak also helps to leach out much of the blood.

To make the vegetable strings, put the carrot, celery root, and rutabaga each in its own small heatproof glass jar. Combine the vinegar, water, and salt in a saucepan over medium heat and bring to a simmer. Pour the hot liquid over the vegetables, dividing it evenly and immersing them. Let cool to room temperature, then cap tightly and refrigerate for 24 hours. Drain when ready to serve.

To make the aged beef, preheat the oven to 200°F (95°C). Melt enough butter with some oil in an ovenproof sauté pan over low heat to generously coat the bottom of the pan. Once it is hot, add the beef and herbs and fry gently, turning once and basting with the oil and butter the entire time, just until the beef begins to turn golden brown on both sides. Let rest for about 7 minutes, turning once as it rests to evenly distribute the juices.

Discard the herbs, transfer the pan to the oven, and cook the beef until an instant-read thermometer inserted into the center registers 131°F (55°C). Let the beef rest at room temperature for 20 minutes, keeping the oven on. Return the beef to the oven for 1 minute, then return the beef to the stove top and sauté the beef in the butter and oil, turning once, until caramelized. Season with salt and slice when ready to serve.

To smoke the bone marrow, arrange wood chips or dried onion peels on the bottom of a deep hotel pan lined with foil. Place the bone marrow directly in a perforated hotel pan that fits inside the first pan and place over high heat. Ignite the chips or peels with a kitchen torch and place the pan over low heat. When the flame is nearly extinguished, place the perforated pan on top and seal the entire set-up securely with aluminum foil. Allow the smoke to smolder out completely, about 20 minutes, before removing the foil. Season with salt.

To serve, arrange the beef slices and marrow on a plate, top with the vegetable strings, garnish with the lemon balm and angelica stalks, and sprinkle with the leek and onion ash. Place a spoonful of angelica butter alongside the beef and drizzle everything with the herb oil.

VIKING STOCK

The earliest Norse settlers in Iceland carried animals on board their long ships to sustain them through the long, dark winters when the sun doesn't rise for weeks and the only lights visible are the glassy, streaking purple, green, and red ribbons of the northern lights. They brought with them goats, cows, horses, chickens, pigs, geese, and sheep that they slaughtered in the fall, smoking their meat or fermenting it in whey to eat through the winter.

In Iceland, strict laws prohibit any animal that leaves the nation from returning, in order to prevent cross-breeding and the introduction of diseases. New breeds are not allowed into Iceland, save for the recent arrival of new pig and chicken breeds because of the scarcity of the original breeds. This has resulted in pure breeds with lineages that can be traced back to the Vikings and that have changed little, if at all, over the centuries.

It seems appropriate then to refer to these breeds as "Viking stock," and Icelanders take great pride in the unique species of animals that roam their countryside. There have been a few disasters over the centuries, such as when the pig was allowed to go extinct in the sixteenth century (see page 166) and the recent near-extinction of the Icelandic goat. But thanks to pioneers like goat farmer Johanna Thorvaldsdóttir, it is nearly assured that the unique Icelandic goat species will survive.

DISTILLED SPIRITS OF ICELAND

Distilled spirits such as schnapps and vodka have long been consumed in Iceland. One of the best-known of these alcoholic beverages is *brennivín*, a clear caraway-spiked schnapps sold in a green bottle with a black label that was designed to discourage people from purchasing it, to no avail. Also known as "black death," *brennivín* packs quite a wallop and is usually served ice-cold with *hákarl* and other fermented foods whose flavors are complemented by a swig of the peppery schnapps.

Today, Icelanders are experimenting with local harvests to create artisanal spirits, such as rhubarb and crowberry vodkas and Gunnar's own line of libations celebrating the birch tree, Birkir schnapps and Björk liqueur. His products are sold throughout Iceland and include a birch twig inside each bottle, to remind consumers of the spirit's connection to one of Iceland's most important native plants. Gunnar uses his schnapps and liqueur in his cooking in a variety of ways, including reduced and drizzled over ice cream, for caramelizing vegetables, and for adding to sauces.

PRESERVED DUCK

MAKES 2 DRIED DUCK BREASTS | PREPARATION TIME: ABOUT 1 YEAR

Icelandic ducks flourish in the region around the goat farm of Háafell, since it offers both abundant stretches of empty land and easy access to open water. Gunnar often serves the ducks fresh, but this recipe is far from fresh. Don't let that put you off, however. The recipe is also a little daunting because it has the longest preparation time in this book—and probably longer than for any recipe in most cookbooks.

Once the breasts are aged, Gunnar grinds them and uses the powder as a seasoning that exceeds the flavor complexity of nearly any other seasoning. He commonly adds it to duck and vegetable dishes to finish. If you have the patience to wait the year for the breasts to cure properly, this recipe will be your secret flavoring weapon. It will also inevitably lead to questions from your dinner guests about how you made it, to which you will respond, "Have you got a year? Then let me tell you."

2 wild duck breasts, boned

^{1}/$_3$ cup (5 g) birch tree leaves, finely chopped

1 teaspoon finely chopped fresh thyme

3 tablespoons finely chopped crowberries or blueberries

1 tablespoon sugar

2^1/$_2$ teaspoons salt

2 g pink curing salt No. 1

Line a baking sheet with a cotton kitchen towel or other cotton cloth. Trim the duck breasts well, remove the skin, and put the breasts on the prepared baking sheet. In a small bowl, stir together the birch leaves, thyme, crowberries, sugar, salt, and curing salt, mixing well. Sprinkle the curing mix over the duck breasts, coating them evenly and completely on both sides. Cover the breasts with a second towel or cloth and refrigerate for 1 week.

Rinse the curing mix off of the breasts under cold running water, then dry the breasts with paper towels and wrap them in a clean, dry cotton cloth. Secure the cloth with a rope, so it doesn't unroll, and hang the "packet" for 1 year in a dark, cool space such as a cellar or basement. Once the duck breasts are dried, they can be kept in the cloth for up to 1 year.

To use the dried breasts, grind whatever you would like to use into a powder in a spice grinder and save the rest of the breast for later use.

BEER MUSTARD

MAKES ABOUT 1¹/₂ CUPS (275 G) | PREPARATION TIME: 3 WEEKS

Gunnar is an ardent fan of both beer and mustard in his dishes, and this recipe showcases both ingredients.

1¹/₄ cups (300 ml) arctic thyme beer or other pale ale

1 tablespoon dry yellow mustard

3 tablespoons black mustard seeds

3 tablespoons yellow mustard seeds

¹/₂ cup (120 ml) cider vinegar

6 juniper berries

6 whole allspice

3 tablespoons dried arctic thyme

1¹/₂ tablespoons light brown sugar

2 tablespoons sea salt

In a bowl, stir together the beer, dry mustard, and mustard seeds, mixing well. Cover and refrigerate for 12 hours.

Combine the vinegar, juniper, allspice, and thyme in a saucepan and bring to a boil. Add the sugar and salt and stir until dissolved. Remove from the heat, add the mustard seed base, and mix well. Transfer to a heatproof glass jar and let cool to room temperature. Cap tightly and refrigerate for 3 weeks before using.

ALMOND *and* HAZELNUT PRALINE, CARAMEL NUT PARFAIT, *and* BROWN BUTTER CAKE

SERVES 4 | PREPARATION TIME: ABOUT 2 HOURS (PLUS 12 HOURS TO FREEZE THE PARFAIT AND 4 HOURS TO REFRIGERATE THE FOAM) | PICTURED ON PAGE 294

Berries grow in abundance on Johanna Thorvaldsdóttir's goat farm. Wild bushes flourish there, but Johanna also cultivates berries in the meticulously groomed and curated rose and vegetable garden just beyond her front door. How she has time to care for the vast array of plants is a marvel, as she seems to tend her goats nonstop from the moment she opens her eyes each morning. Johanna also incorporates the botanicals into healthful creams and lotions. A bench stands in the center of the garden, which overlooks the river just beyond her property. She sometimes says, "My dream is to one day find the time to sit down on that bench with my husband, take a deep breath, and relax."

When she does find the time to relax in her garden, she will hopefully be enjoying this dessert from Gunnar. It's an addictive combination of comforting flavors brightened by freeze-dried berries (a handy technique Gunnar uses to preserve his berries for the winter) and sweetened with honey. Each of the elements would be a star in its own right, but when combined on the plate, they prove irresistible.

PRALINE

¹/2 cup (100 g) sugar

Scant ³/4 cup (100 g) blanched almonds, toasted

About ²/3 cup (100 g) blanched hazelnuts, toasted (see notes)

CARAMEL NUT PARFAIT
(*see* NOTES)

3 egg yolks

¹/3 cup (75 g) sugar

³/4 cup (180 ml) heavy cream

3 tablespoons ground praline (above)

¹/4 teaspoon salt

FRUIT AND NUT GRANOLA

¹/2 recipe praline (above)

³/4 cup (25 g) freeze-dried blueberries (see notes)

³/4 cup (25 g) freeze-dried raspberries (see notes)

2 tablespoons coarsely ground roasted coffee beans

1 tablespoon finely chopped dehydrated parsnip

Pinch of ground cinnamon

Scant ¹/2 teaspoon sea salt

BROWN BUTTER CAKE
(*see* NOTES)

1 cup (240 ml) egg whites

2¹/2 cups (250 g) sifted confectioners' sugar

²/3 cup (75 g) all-purpose flour

1¹/2 teaspoons baking powder

1 cup (95 g) ground almonds

1 cup (240 ml) burned butter (see page 119), at room temperature

HONEY FOAM (*see* NOTES)

¹/2 cup (120 ml) water

Scant ²/3 cup (200 g) honey

¹/2 teaspoon salt

1 sheet gelatin, soaked in cold water to cover until softened, then squeezed to remove excess water

Dehydrated parsley, for garnish (see Dried Arctic Thyme, page 250)

To make the praline, line a baking sheet with parchment paper. Put the sugar in a small, heavy saucepan, place over medium heat, and heat, swirling the pan, until caramelized. Stir in the nuts and toss carefully until coated with the caramel. The nuts and sugar will seize and stick together. This is not a problem, however, as the praline will be ground. Pour the hot nut mixture onto the prepared baking sheet and spread in an even layer. Let cool to room temperature. Once cooled, reserve half for the fruit and nut granola, and grind the

NOTES

1. Hazelnuts are much less expensive with their skins intact, and it is easy to remove the skins. Toast the nuts in a 350°F (175°C) oven for about 7 to 8 minutes, until they are fragrant and have taken on color, then wrap the still-hot nuts in a kitchen towel and rub them vigorously between your palms to remove the skins.

2. Look for a wide array of freeze-dried fruits, including grapes, cherries, strawberries, and blueberries, in specialty food markets or online.

3. The parfait ingredients make more parfaits than you need for serving. If your silicone mold will not hold all of the excess mixture, freeze it in ice-cube trays. The frozen parfaits are nice to have on hand whenever a sweet bite is desired.

4. Once the honey foam has been charged, it must be refrigerated for at least 4 hours before dispensing or it will not hold up well. If you do not have a siphon, whisk the mixture as vigorously as possible just before serving. It will not be as light and airy as with the siphon method, but it will still be tasty.

remaining half in a food processor to a fine powder. (You will need only 3 tablespoons of the ground praline; reserve the remainder for another use.)

To make the caramel nut parfait, prepare an ice bath. In the bowl of a stand mixer fitted with the whip attachment, combine the egg yolks and sugar and beat on high speed until well blended and thickened. In a saucepan, combine the cream, praline, and salt over medium heat and heat gently while whisking constantly. When the mixture is steaming hot, remove from the heat and pour one-third of it into the yolk mixture while whisking constantly. Slowly pour in the remaining cream mixture while continuing to whisk. Return the mixture to the saucepan, place over medium-low heat, and heat, whisking constantly, to 158°F (70°C). Strain through a fine-mesh sieve placed over a bowl, then nest the bowl in the ice bath and let stand until completely cooled.

Spoon the cooled parfait mixture into a silicone mold with 1-inch (2.5-cm) half-spheres (see notes). Freeze until solid, about 12 hours. Just before serving, unmold the parfaits. It will be easier to unmold them if you let them stand at room temperature for five minutes beforehand.

To make the granola, coarsely chop the reserved praline, transfer to a food processor, and pulse a few times to break it up a little more. Add the berries, coffee beans, parsnip, cinnamon, and salt and process until finely crumbled.

To make the cake, preheat the oven to 350°F (180°C). In the bowl of a stand mixer fitted with the whip attachment, whip the egg whites on high speed until stiff peaks form. Sift together the confectioners' sugar, flour, and baking powder into a bowl. Fold the sifted mixture into the egg whites just until combined. Then fold in the almonds and butter just until evenly incorporated.

Spoon the cake batter into a silicone mold with 2-inch (5-cm) half-spheres (see notes). Bake for 10 to 15 minutes, until golden brown and a cake tester inserted into the center of a cake comes out clean. Let cool to room temperature on a wire rack before unmolding. Note that this batter yields more than 4 cakes.

To make the honey foam, prepare an ice bath. Combine the water, honey, and salt in a saucepan over medium-high heat and bring to a boil. Remove from the heat, add the gelatin, and stir until completely dissolved. Nest the pan in the ice bath and let the contents cool to room temperature. Transfer the honey mixure to a siphon and charge the siphon with 2 nitrous oxide (NO_2) chargers according to the manufacturer's instructions. Shake the siphon vigorously and refrigerate for at least 4 hours, until chilled (see notes).

To serve, place a cake on a plate and position a parfait alongside it. Sprinkle the granola over the praline parfait, dispense some honey foam alongside the cake, and garnish with dehydrated parsley.

OPPOSITE: Almond and Hazelnut Praline, Caramel Nut Parfait, and Brown Butter Cake (page 294)

ABOVE: Red Beet and Rosemary Sorbet, Almond Cake, and Sugared Almonds (page 298)

RED BEET *and* ROSEMARY SORBET, ALMOND CAKE, *and* SUGARED ALMONDS

SERVES 6 TO 8 | PREPARATION TIME: ABOUT 2 HOURS (PLUS 24 HOURS TO PICKLE THE BEETS AND 8 TO 12 HOURS TO FREEZE THE SORBET) | PICTURED ON PAGE 295

Red beets are cultivated in abundance in the region where Johanna Thorvaldsdóttir's farm is located. In this recipe, Gunnar transforms them into a refreshing sorbet that, because of the addition of rosemary, hovers on the line between savory and sweet, a balancing act that Gunnar often employs in his desserts. The sorbet is paired with sugared nuts and a mildly sweet almond cake that rounds out an array of wonderful textures.

PICKLED RED BEETS

3 (2-inch/5 cm) red beets, peeled, and sliced as thinly as possible on a mandoline (see page 73)

3/4 cup (180 ml) water

1/3 cup (80 ml) distilled white vinegar

3 1/2 tablespoons sugar

1 sprig rosemary

Scant 1 1/2 teaspoons salt

RED BEET AND ROSEMARY SORBET

2 cups (480 ml) freshly squeezed red beet juice (see note)

3/4 cup (150 g) sugar

1 tablespoon liquid glucose (see notes, page 34)

2 sprigs rosemary

4 teaspoons raspberry vinegar

ROASTED RED BEETS

2 red beets, peeled and each cut into 6 wedges

2 sprigs rosemary

Scant 1/3 cup (100 g) honey

7 tablespoons (100 g) unsalted butter, melted

3/4 teaspoon salt

3/4 cup (180 ml) water

SUGARED ALMONDS

1 cup (140 g) almonds

1/2 cup (100 g) sugar

1 1/2 teaspoons salt

ALMOND CAKE

2/3 cup (150 g) unsalted butter, at room temperature

3/4 cup (150 g) sugar

6 eggs

3/4 cup (105 g) ground almonds

2/3 cup (80 g) all-purpose flour

To make the pickled beets, place the beet slices in a heatproof glass jar. Combine the water, vinegar, sugar, rosemary, and salt in a saucepan and bring to a simmer over medium heat, stirring until the sugar has dissolved. Pour the hot liquid over the beets, immersing them. Let cool to room temperature, then cap tightly and refrigerate for 24 hours before using.

To make the red beet and rosemary sorbet, combine the beet juice and sugar in a saucepan and bring to a lazy simmer over medium-low heat. Add the glucose and rosemary and stir until combined. Remove from the heat and let stand at room temperature for 20 minutes. Strain through a fine-mesh sieve into a clean vessel, add the vinegar, and stir to combine. Freeze in an ice cream maker according to the manufacturer's instructions, then transfer to an airtight container, place in the freezer, and freeze for 8 to 12 hours, until frozen solid.

NOTE

Juice the beets just before you begin making the sorbet. The juice will darken if held in the refrigerator. Be sure to wear kitchen gloves during this step, to avoid having hands that match your sorbet.

To make the roasted beets, preheat the oven to 350°F (180°C). In a bowl, toss together all of the ingredients until the beets glisten. Transfer to a roasting pan, cover with aluminum foil, and bake for 30 minutes. Remove the foil, turn down the heat to 300°F (150°C), and continue to bake, flipping the beets over a few times as they roast to prevent burning, for 2 hours longer, until tender. Cool to room temperature and cut into wedges.

To make the sugared almonds, line a baking sheet with parchment paper. Toast the almonds in a sauté pan over low heat, shaking the pan often, for about 8 minutes, until golden brown. Slowly add the sugar while stirring constantly. Continue to cook, stirring frequently, for about 10 minutes, until the sugar is golden brown. Be attentive during this step to prevent burning. Season with the salt, transfer to the prepared baking sheet, spread in a single layer, and let cool to room temperature.

To make the almond cake, preheat the oven to 350°F (180°C). Butter a 9 by 5-inch (23 by 12-cm) loaf pan. In the bowl of a stand mixer fitted with the paddle attachment, combine the butter and sugar and beat on medium-high speed until light and fluffy. Add the eggs, one at a time, incorporating each egg completely before adding the next egg. In a separate bowl, stir together the almonds and flour. Add the egg mixture to the flour mixture and stir until combined.

Transfer the batter to the prepared loaf pan and bake for about 30 minutes, until golden brown and a cake tester inserted into the center of the cake comes out clean. Let cool in the pan on a wire rack to room temperature, then turn out of the pan, and let cool on a rack at room temperature.

To serve, place a slice of the cake on a plate and place a quenelle of the sorbet alongside, sprinkling sugared almonds over top. Arrange the pickled beet slices and roasted beet wedges around the plate.

WHEY CARAMEL, BUTTERMILK, *and* HORSERADISH

SERVES 4 TO 6 | PREPARATION TIME: ABOUT 1 HOUR

Goat farmer Johanna Thorvaldsdóttir is not allowed to sell her raw goat's milk, but Gunnar dreams that one day his government will relax its strict dairy regulations and he will be able to transform her goat's milk into the buttermilk used in this recipe. Until then, cow's milk will have to suffice. It does double duty in this recipe, in the form of buttermilk and whey. Gunnar's dessert recipes are rarely very sweet, and the pairing of sweet caramel with pungent horseradish and tangy buttermilk here ensures that he is staying the course. He serves the buttermilk in the form of a foam, but it is just as good drizzled in a tangy, viscous ribbon over the caramel.

BUTTERMILK FOAM

2 1/2 tablespoons sugar

1/4 cup (60 ml) heavy cream

1 sheet gelatin, soaked in cold water to cover until softened, then squeezed to remove excess water

1 1/4 cups (300 ml) buttermilk

WHEY CARAMEL

2 cups (480 ml) skyr whey (see page 162)

1/4 cup (50 g) sugar

1/2 teaspoon freshly grated horseradish, for garnish

3/4 cup (30 g) watercress leaves, for garnish

To make the buttermilk foam, combine the sugar and cream in a saucepan and bring to a simmer over medium-high heat, stirring until the sugar has dissolved. Remove from the heat, add the gelatin, and stir until fully dissolved. Add the buttermilk in a slow, steady stream, stirring to incorporate. Transfer the mixure to a siphon and charge the siphon with 2 nitrous oxide (NO_2) chargers according to the manufacturer's instructions. Shake the siphon vigorously and refrigerate until chilled.

To make the whey caramel, combine the whey and sugar in a saucepan over low heat and heat, stirring until the sugar has dissolved. Then continue to cook until a syrupy consistency forms. It can take up to 1 hour for the syrup to form. At the end of the process, you will be left with about one-tenth of the volume that you started with. Remove from the heat and let cool for 1 minute. Line a baking sheet with a nonstick baking mat. Pour the caramel onto the mat. Once it has cooled to room temperature it will be thicker but still pourable.

To serve, drizzle the caramel on a plate and dispense the buttermilk foam on top. Garnish with the horseradish and watercress.

THE BLUE MUSSEL AND DULSE HARVESTER

Stykkishólmur, Western Iceland

∞

Seaweed Butter 308

Dulse-Spiced, Sea-Salted Potato Chips with
Dandelion Cottage Cheese 310

Blue Mussel Soup, Dry-Aged Beef, Celery Root Salad,
and Mushroom Aioli 314

Shrimp Ceviche, Whey Gelatin, Buttermilk Espuma,
and Chervil Oil 321

Salted Cod, Shoestring Beer Crisps,
and Pickled Kelp 324

Apples, Apple Cake, Porter Fudge Caramel,
and Hazelnut Granola 326

Red Beet Stones 330

Blue mussels are one of the most prized ingredients on restaurant menus in Iceland today. But just a few short years ago, no one was eating them. It wasn't because there was something wrong with them. They were in fact flourishing in the pristine waters of Iceland, just as they had been for centuries. No one ate blue mussels in Iceland because no one had ever eaten blue mussels in Iceland. Sometimes starting a new tradition can be just as difficult as preserving an old one. It took Gunnar and his insatiable appetite for local ingredients to change the opinion of his countrymen. Once they sat down to a dish of blue mussels that had been freshly plucked from the ocean, they understood how good they could be.

To serve those mussels, Gunnar had to join forces with Simon Sturluson, arguably Iceland's most successful blue mussel farmer. Simon says that at first Gunnar was the only chef who was calling with orders, and he would sometimes venture out into the calm blue waters surrounding his idyllic village of Stykkishólmur just to fill an order of a couple of kilograms from Gunnar. Those days are past, and now Simon can barely keep up with demand. He has hired a crew and bought an additional boat to fulfill orders that pour in from every region of the country. He also farms dulse, a type of red seaweed, which he sells in Iceland and also ships to customers in Europe, including to Copenhagen's famed Noma restaurant. He grows the dulse and kelp on his mussel lines, harvesting it throughout the year.

It took Gunnar and Simon working in harmony—even if in the early days the harmony was sometimes fraught with pressure—to convince Icelanders that their blue mussels were a treasure to celebrate at the table. Icelanders are still generally leery of cooking them at home, but just like the tourists who can't get enough mussels, locals regularly order them now in restaurants. Because of the efforts of a chef like Gunnar, who was intent on introducing a new food to Icelanders, and of a producer like Simon, who was willing to fulfill even the most humble order, it is quite likely that eating blue mussels will be an old tradition in the future.

A Conversation with Blue Mussel and Dulse Harvester Simon Sturluson

Q Have you lived in Stykkishólmur your entire life?

No, I've lived here for thirty years. I came from the south, but I met a lady who lived here and now it is history. I was working for the electrical company and traveled all around Iceland, but when I met her, she convinced me to stay, and I'm glad I did. She's not my wife any longer, but I'm grateful to her for talking me into moving here, because I really enjoy my life.

Q How long have you been collecting blue mussels and dulse?

I have been working with mussels since 2007, but I had to wait for three years for them to mature. We harvest once a week to supply the restaurants. I also harvest dulse, and I prefer this because I can export it, unlike the mussels, which are very cheap throughout Europe. I can sell the mussels only in Iceland. At first, Gunnar was the only chef asking for my mussels, and sometimes in the beginning, I would collect a kilogram or two just for him and that would be my only order. So much has changed since those first days of struggle.

Even though now there is demand for my mussels throughout the country, I will always be grateful to Gunnar, because he was one of the first to take an interest in them and other chefs followed his lead. The company is getting bigger and bigger every day. One hope is that the government will provide me with more help, as this is one of the few companies harvesting mussels in Iceland. I hope the government begins to see the importance of the work we do here.

Gunnar was also the only chef to begin using my dulse. Iceland had an ancient dulse tradition, but it was lost over the years. Gunnar brought it back into the kitchen, and people are now interested in it again, thanks to him. When interest started picking up, we would harvest about four tons of mussels and two tons of seaweed. It grew to fourteen tons of mussels quite quickly, but the seaweed has held fairly steady, because we don't have enough time for it. We are struggling to keep up with demand, though we are working on it.

Q **What are some of the challenges you face when you harvest your dulse and mussels?**

Dulse is best to harvest in September, but kelp is best to pick in May and June and it can be tricky to keep it all in balance. I have a drying house nearby, and dulse only takes about twenty-four hours to dry. I sell my dulse to customers in Sweden and also to Noma in Copenhagen. They buy it because it's healthful and because the Icelandic ocean salt that permeates it, which comes from clean, cold waters, is some of the best in the world. One of the biggest challenges I face is convincing Icelanders to try their own dulse. Ducks are one of the biggest challenges with regard to harvesting mussels. They love mussels, and they eat a few tons every year, so they are a big headache. But in the end, I suppose there is enough to go around.

Q **Where did you learn to farm mussels and seaweed?**

Older people taught me some of the things I needed to learn, but I also learned a lot by trial and error; that is, I learned from my mistakes. Because these traditions are relatively new in Iceland, there is not a great deal of documentation. A man from Canada was helpful too. I have had to look to other countries for guidance, since Icelanders have not done this before.

Q **What is the history of blue mussels in Iceland?**

It is strange, but Icelanders don't have a tradition of eating blue mussels. At first, they were just served in the restaurants in Reykjavík, and it was mainly tourists ordering them. Since then, Icelanders have slowly gained an interest in them, but they will still primarily only eat them when they are eating out. It is hard to change traditions in Iceland. Even though Icelandic mussels are delicious, it takes a lot of effort to convince people to think in a new way. But year by year, this is changing. Hopefully, blue mussels will be a common ingredient in Icelandic homes one day.

SEAWEED BUTTER

MAKES 1¹/₂ CUPS (340 G) | PREPARATION TIME: ABOUT 1 HOUR

Gunnar pays special attention to his butter service at Dill (see page 137), and this butter turns up often at the restaurant. It's ideal for drizzling onto fish and shellfish dishes, as it carries both richness and the taste of the sea. If you have trouble sourcing Icelandic dulse or another seaweed variety, nori is a good substitute.

1 cup plus 1¹/₂ tablespoons (250 g) unsalted butter, at room temperature

¹/₂ cup (120 ml) buttermilk

4 teaspoons seaweed vinegar (see note)

2 teaspoons powdered seaweed (see notes, page 310)

NOTE

To make the seaweed vinegar, steep 1 cup (25 g) of dried seaweed in 2 cups (480 ml) of distilled white vinegar for 1 hour, then drain. Store in a tightly capped bottled in a cool cupboard. It will keep indefinitely. It is also a good seasoning for seafood.

In a stand mixer fitted with the whip attachment, whip the butter on high speed for about 5 minutes, until white and fluffy. In a small bowl, whisk together the buttermilk and vinegar. On medium speed, add the buttermilk mixture in a slow, steady stream until incorporated. Be sure to add it slowly or the butter will seize. Add the seaweed powder and continue to whip on low speed until incorporated. Cover and refrigerate until chilled before serving.

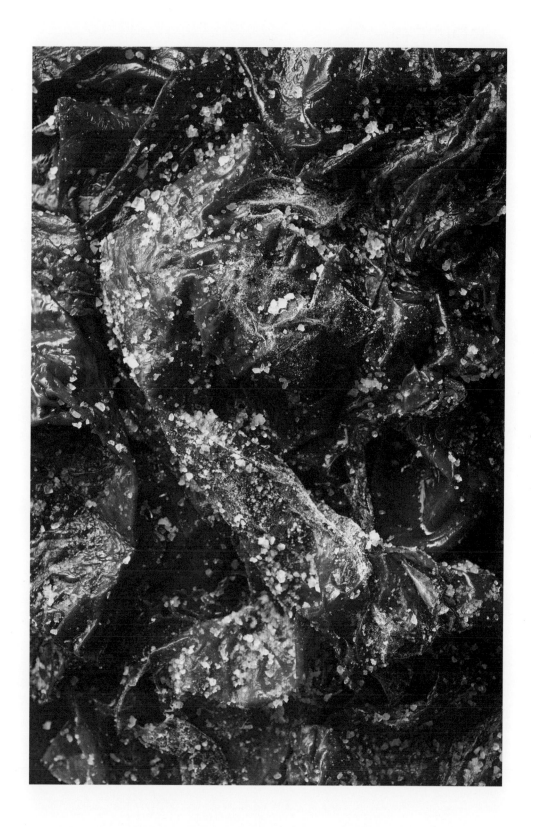

DULSE-SPICED, SEA-SALTED POTATO CHIPS *with* DANDELION COTTAGE CHEESE

SERVES 6 TO 8 | PREPARATION TIME: ABOUT 1¹/₂ HOURS (PLUS 4 TO 6 HOURS TO DEHYDRATE THE SEAWEED) | PICTURED ON PAGE 312

Dandelions flourish throughout Iceland and are transformed into everything from wine to syrup. Gunnar garnishes this dish with dandelion petals that can be easily foraged from your own backyard, but the roots may be challenging to source. A good alternative is to purchase dandelion root vitamin supplements at a health food store and break open the capsules. The chips are very light, and the roasted dandelion root powder gives them depth and richness. Be sure to roast your roots for at least 10 minutes in or they will impart a bitter flavor to the dish.

Gunnar uses seawater for his sea-salted potato chips, but if you do not have access to pristine ocean water near where you live, heavily salted tap water will suffice. He uses a potato called Gunaugh in Iceland, and the closest match is Yukon gold.

ROASTED DANDELION ROOT POWDER	SEA-SALTED POTATO CHIPS	DANDELION COTTAGE CHEESE	Salt
Dandelion root from 10 vitamin capsules	4¹/₄ cups (1 L) clean seawater	¹/₃ cup (70 g) small-curd cottage cheese	Cider vinegar, for seasoning
	2 Yukon gold potatoes, peeled	2¹/₄ teaspoons dandelion syrup (see notes)	Dandelion petals, for seasoning and garnish
	Rapeseed oil, for deep-frying		
	1 tablespoon powdered seaweed (see notes)		

NOTES

1. Nori is a good and easily sourced ingredient for the powdered seaweed, but if you can find dried dulse from Iceland, it is better. To dehydrate either seaweed enough to grind it, spread it on a baking sheet and place in an oven set to the lowest setting for 4 to 6 hours. It must be brittle enough to grind or it will gum up in the blades. Grind in a spice grinder.

To roast the dandelion root powder, preheat the oven to 350°F (180°C). Sprinkle the dandelion root powder onto a parchment-lined baking sheet and roast until aromatic, about 10 minutes. Keep a close eye on it during the roasting process to prevent burning. Cool to room temperature. Stored in an airtight container at room temperature, the roasted dandelion root powder will keep for up to 1 week.

To make the sea-salted potatoes, bring the seawater to a boil and boil until reduced by two-thirds. Turn down the heat to a gentle simmer, then prepare an ice bath. Slice the potatoes as thinly as possible on a mandoline (see notes, page 73). Add them to the seawater, blanch for 2 seconds, then, using a slotted spoon, transfer the slices to the ice bath, immersing them. Let stand until chilled. Drain and pat dry with paper towels.

NOTES, continued

2. Dandelion syrup takes a little time to make, but it is a versatile ingredient that you can drizzle over a variety of foods, from vegetables and ice cream to fish and cheese. It is an ideal way to use the dandelions that flourish in the summer, and it makes a wonderful gift. To make the syrup, combine ¹/2 cup (100 g) of sugar, 1 cup (240 ml) of water, the petals from 20 dandelions, and a squeeze of lemon juice in a saucepan and bring to a simmer over medium-high heat, stirring until the sugar has dissolved. Cook, stirring frequently to prevent the petals from scorching, for about 30 minutes, until a syrupy consistency forms. Strain through a fine-mesh sieve into a heatproof container. Let cool to room temperature, then cover tightly and refrigerate. The syrup will keep in the refrigerator for up to 1 month.

Pour oil to a depth of 4 inches (10 cm) into a heavy, deep pot and heat to 320°F (160°C). Line a large plate with paper towels. Add half of the potato slices to the hot oil and fry for about 7 minutes, until light golden brown. Using a slotted spoon, transfer the chips to the paper towel–lined plate and season with half of the seaweed. Repeat with the remaining potato slices and seaweed. The cooled chips will keep in an airtight container at room temperature for up to 3 days.

To make the cottage cheese, combine the cottage cheese and syrup in a small bowl and mix well. Season with salt and vinegar. Fold in some dandelion petals and 2 teaspoons of the roasted root powder, reserving a bit of each for garnish.

To serve, place the potato chips in a bowl. Sprinkle the cottage cheese with the reserved dandelion petals and root powder and serve alongside for dipping.

OPPOSITE: Dulse-Spiced, Sea-Salted Potato Chips with Dandelion Cottage Cheese (page 310)

ABOVE: Blue Mussel Soup, Dry-Aged Beef, Celery Root Salad, and Mushroom Aioli (page 314)

BLUE MUSSEL SOUP, DRY-AGED BEEF, CELERY ROOT SALAD, *and* MUSHROOM AIOLI

SERVES 4 | PREPARATION TIME: ABOUT 1½ HOURS | PICTURED ON PAGE 313

Gunnar's blue mussel soup is something everyone should try at least once in his or her lifetime. It's just that good, and it seems to capture the essence of the blue mussel in a way that not even a simple bowl of steamed mussels does. The flavors are intense, and when paired with the complex notes of dry-aged beef and the umami quality of the mushrooms, it makes for a standout dish worthy of making again and again.

DRY-AGED BEEF

1 (3-ounce/85 g) piece dry-aged beef tenderloin

Salt

Rapeseed oil, for seasoning

MUSHROOM MAYONNAISE

3½ ounces (100 g) dried larch or chanterelle mushrooms

1 cup (240 ml) rapeseed oil

1 egg yolk

Salt

Beer Vinegar (page 30), for seasoning

CELERY ROOT SALAD

1 small celery root, peeled and grated on the large holes of a box grater

Mushroom mayonnaise (at left)

Salt

Beer Vinegar (page 30), for seasoning

MUSSEL SOUP

1 tablespoon rapeseed oil

1 carrot, peeled and coarsely chopped

1 celery stalk, coarsely chopped

1 small yellow onion, coarsely chopped

1½ pounds (680 g) blue mussels, scrubbed and debearded

¾ cup (180 ml) dry white wine

¾ cup (180 ml) heavy cream

4 tablespoons (55 g) unsalted butter

Salt

Beer Vinegar (page 30), for seasoning

0.5 to 1 g xanthan gum (see notes, page 34)

Sweet-and-sour dill oil (page 32)

Fresh dill leaves, for garnish

Sea salt

To make the dry-aged beef, using a sharp knife, slice the loin against the grain as thinly as possible. Beat each slice on both sides with a meat pounder or the bottom of a metal bowl until each slice is very thin and tender. Season the slices with salt and oil and refrigerate until chilled.

To make the mushroom mayonnaise, combine the mushrooms and oil in a blender and process at high speed for 7 to 10 minutes, until completely smooth. Transfer to a small saucepan, place over low heat, and heat to 172°F (78°C). Remove from the heat, strain through a fine-mesh sieve into a pitcher, and let cool to room temperature. In a bowl, whisk the egg yolk until blended. Then, whisking constantly, slowly add the mushroom oil, drop by drop, until the mixture begins to thicken. Add the remaining oil in a slow, steady stream while whisking vigorously to form a mayonnaise. Season with salt and vinegar. The mayonnaise will keep in an airtight container in the refrigerator for up to 1 week.

To make the celery root salad, in a bowl, fold together the celery root with enough mushroom mayonnaise to coat generously. Season with salt and vinegar. Cover and refrigerate until serving.

To make the mussel soup, heat the oil in a pot over medium-high heat. Add the carrot, celery, and onion and sauté for about 8 minutes, until caramelized. Discard any mussels that do not close to the touch, reduce heat to medium, then add the mussels and wine to the pot, cover, and simmer over low heat for 10 to 15 minutes, until the mussels have opened. Remove from the heat and strain through a fine-mesh sieve, reserving the solids and the stock separately. Discard the vegetables and reserve the mussels for another use, discarding any mussels that failed to open. Return the stock to the pot, place over medium heat, and simmer until reduced by half. Add the cream and continue to simmer, stirring frequently to prevent scorching, until reduced by one-fourth. Add the butter, season with salt and vinegar, and stir until the butter melts. Add 0.5 g of the xanthan gum and stir for 1 minute. The soup should be thick but still smooth and pourable. If it is does not thicken enough, add the remaining 0.5 g xanthan gum and stir for 1 minute, until thickened.

To serve, bring the beef to room temperature. Ladle the soup into a bowl and dot with the dill oil. Spoon the salad on one side of the soup and top the salad with the aged beef to conceal it. Garnish with dill and sprinkle with sea salt.

ICELANDIC DULSE

Dulse, the iron-red seaweed that flourishes in the cold
waters along the Icelandic shoreline, is a staple of the
Icelandic diet and has been since the earliest times.
One of its biggest contemporary proponents is Eyjólfur
Fridgeirsson, an eighty-four-year-old Icelandic Buddhist
biologist who several years ago founded a company, Íslensk
Hollusta, to promote Iceland's dulse, herbs, and moss.
Today, his successful company sells its products to home
cooks and restaurant chefs in Iceland and abroad. His
dulse is used by Copenhagen's Noma restaurant and by
Gunnar, who shares a deep and abiding friendship with
his friend, a kindred spirit who appreciates Iceland's local
ingredients as much as he does.

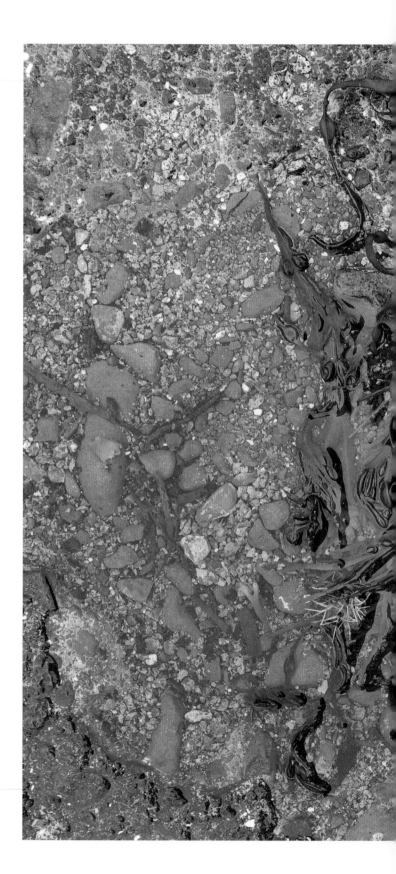

A Conversation with Dulse Harvester Eyjólfur Fridgeirsson

Q When did you decide to become a Buddhist?

I've been practicing Zen for decades. I first grew to appreciate it during a visit to a Buddhist monastery in San Francisco. If you practice Zen Buddhism, it clears your mind and it's easy to implement an idea. I always wanted to improve myself. Something inside of me was calling for more balance and I found it in Buddhism. It's good for the mind and body and helped me find simplicity in my life. Many people have noise in their heads and it drowns out their ideas, but it's easy to have a successful business if you are floating in your environment with a clear mind.

Q How do you implement your beliefs into your business?

One of the principles of Buddhism is to cause no harm, and I try to convey this philosophy in my business by using native resources rather than sourcing from other places in the world. I keep it local and as pure as I can by creating products such as teas, lotions, and vitamins that are derived naturally and are extremely good for you. I am a biologist by training and was always interested in Icelandic nature.

I sell Icelandic moss that, once hydrated, is similar in texture to Japanese kombu. I sell to some Japanese companies who like to use it as something different in their food preparations. I use a lot of Icelandic berries for jams, I have chutneys, and I have herbal teas. Last year I bought eight metric tons of berries to use in my products. One example of how I incorporated Buddhism into the creation of my tea was that I started with moss, birch, and angelica. At first I thought that I needed to add more, because everything you see in the market is always so packed with different ingredients. But then I told myself to stop. You need only these three things to produce a perfect tea. I sell my blueberry juice and my tea to China, which seems strange to me. Sending tea to China seems like sending sun to the Sahara.

Q What is the history of dulse in Iceland?

The knowledge of using dulse came from the Vikings, who brought it with them from Ireland, which they passed through to collect slaves on the way to Iceland. These Celtic people cooked for the Vikings and used dulse and other seaweed in their recipes. Today, we use dulse in breads and soups, and we use a northern seaweed called *fjorurgos* as a thickener. At one point, Icelanders were using up to twelve varieties of seaweed, with dulse the primary one. During times of famine, it was a necessity to survive, and for a while it gained the reputation of being food for the poor. People used it only in secret, but everyone was using it. Today it is considered a delicacy.

Dulse has had a long history of coming into and going out of fashion, and the debate as to whether or not it is a legitimate form of sustenance rages on. In the sagas, there is the story of a Viking who lost his son. In his despair, he decided to kill himself through starvation. His daughter told him that she would then starve herself, too, but she continued to eat dulse. He asked if it was food and she said no, so he decided to eat it, too. The salt made him thirsty, and she told him to drink milk to wash away the saltiness. The combination of dulse and milk kept him alive, and by the time he was through with grieving, he realized his daughter had fooled him. But he was not angry with her. He was grateful that the dulse saw him through his dark time.

Q How do you collaborate with Gunnar?

Gunnar has inspired me over the years. I have known him for a long time, since before he was a chef, and he is like family to me. We have similar philosophies. We both love Icelandic raw materials and want to make something healthful and beautiful from them. I always call Gunnar to ask for his opinion about things, and I really value the suggestions he gives me.

Q What does your family think of your business?

My wife is always telling me to slow down, but I can't. I feel I am on a mission to inspire people to use Iceland's raw ingredients. She supports me in the end, as do my two sons and my daughter. My oldest son is married to a Roman Catholic from Portugal, the other one is married to a Greek Orthodox woman, my granddaughter is an atheist, my wife is Catholic, and I am a Buddhist. We all come together on Christmas Eve with all of our differences. But the differences do not matter, because we are family and at our table there is peace. This is how life should be.

SHRIMP CEVICHE, WHEY GELATIN, BUTTERMILK ESPUMA, *and* CHERVIL OIL

SERVES 4 | PREPARATION TIME: ABOUT 30 MINUTES (PLUS 2 TO 4 HOURS TO DRAIN THE BUTTERMILK AND TO SET THE WHEY GELATIN)

This beautiful recipe combines the delicate flavor of small shrimp with the tanginess of buttermilk and whey for a light spring or summer dish that you will turn to again and again for dinner parties. It's relatively simple to construct, with most of the time being inactive hours during which the buttermilk drains and the whey gelatin sets. These elements, along with the chervil oil, the ceviche, and the toasted bread, can be completed in advance, making this recipe an easy one to assemble once guests arrive. It is best to use small shrimp, as they are essentially prepared as a ceviche and will "cook" more quickly in the vinegar than larger shrimp.

BUTTERMILK ESPUMA

2 cups (480 ml) buttermilk

WHEY GELATIN

Scant $1/2$ cup (120 ml) whey from buttermilk espuma (above)

1 gelatin sheet, soaked in cold water to cover until softened, then squeezed to remove excess water

CHERVIL OIL

Leaves from 1 bunch ($1^2/3$ ounces/50 g) wild chervil, parsley, or tarragon

$1/2$ cup (120 ml) rapeseed oil

SHRIMP CEVICHE

9 ounces (250 g) small shrimp, peeled, deveined, and tail segments removed

2 tablespoons rapeseed oil

1 teaspoon cider vinegar

Salt

TOASTED BREAD

1 tablespoon butter

$5^1/2$ ounces (155 g) rye bread, coarsely chopped

Salt

Arctic char or salmon roe, for garnish

Fresh wild chervil, parsley, or tarragon leaves, for garnish

NOTE

A double layer of cheesecloth can be used in place of the coffee filter. If you do not have a siphon, just before serving, froth the buttermilk espuma with an immersion blender or whisk it vigorously. It will not be enough to form a true espuma (a thick foam or froth), but it will be enough to lighten and aerate the thickened buttermilk.

To make the espuma, line a colander with a coffee filter and place over a bowl. Pour the buttermilk into the colander and let drain at room temperature for 2 to 4 hours, until it resembles a thickened crème anglaise. If it is too thick, whisk in some of the whey captured in the bowl. Reserve the whey for making the gelatin. Transfer the thickened buttermilk to a siphon and charge the siphon with 2 nitrous oxide (NO_2) chargers according to the manufacturer's instructions. Shake the siphon vigorously and refrigerate until chilled (see note).

To make the whey gelatin, in a saucepan over medium heat, bring the whey to a simmer. Remove from the heat, add the gelatin, and stir until fully dissolved. Pour onto a small, shallow plate or other container, creating a layer $1/4$ inch (6 mm) thick. Refrigerate for about 2 hours, until chilled and set. Cut into $1/4$-inch (6-mm) squares and refrigerate until ready to use.

| continued

| Shrimp Ceviche, Whey Gelatin, Buttermilk Espuma, and Chervil Oil, *continued*

To make the chervil oil, combine the chervil and oil in a blender and process on high speed for 5 to 8 minutes, until steaming hot and the chervil is completely incorporated into the oil. Line a fine-mesh sieve with cheesecloth and strain the oil through it. Transfer to a squeeze bottle. The oil will keep in the refrigerator for up to 1 week.

To make the shrimp ceviche, combine the shrimp, oil, and vinegar in a bowl and toss together until the shrimp glisten evenly. Season with salt, cover, and refrigerate until chilled. As the shrimp cool, the acid in the vinegar will tenderize them and they will appear cooked on the outside but still rare inside.

To make the toasted bread, melt the butter in a sauté pan over medium heat. Add the bread and fry, stirring often, for several minutes, until evenly toasted. Transfer to paper towels to drain. Season with salt.

To serve, dispense the buttermilk espuma onto the center of a plate and surround the espuma with the shrimp. Sprinkle the espuma with the bread, dot with the chervil oil, and garnish with the whey gelatin, roe, and chervil.

VISITING SNAEFELLSNES PENINSULA

In spite of the difficulty in pronouncing its name, Snaefellsnes Peninsula is one of the easiest locations to access from Reykjavík for those looking beyond the touristy Golden Circle (see page 146). About a two-hour drive from the capital, the peninsula offers spectacular views of its glacier along a shoreline dotted with inviting villages. Hotel Budir, one of Iceland's best country hotels, is located on the southern shore, and nearly everything on the peninsula is accessible from it, should you decide to make it your base for visiting the area. Nearby is the road to access the Snaefellsnes Glacier, one of the west's few remaining glaciers, and if weather cooperates and your vehicle can handle a steep incline on a dirt road, it's worth a visit.

A few miles west is the tiny village of Hellnar, where the warm and inviting Hellnar Café serves some of the best fish stew and waffles (with rhubarb jam and whipped cream) in Iceland. The café is located at the beginning of one of the country's most beautiful cliffside hikes, which should not be missed if the day is sunny.

Farther west is Dritvik, a beach of round black rocks that Gunnar sometimes sources to serve his butter on at Dill. The rocks are lined with the rusty vestiges of an old shipwreck, a series of stones of different weights that sailors once used to measure their strength as a means of designating their position on a ship, and crimson seaweed that Gunnar collects and dehydrates to use as serving vessels. In the northwest corner of the peninsula is Bjarnarhöfn, where *hákarl* producer Hildibrandur Bjarnason lives on the edge of a craggy bed of mossy lava fields (see page 276). This is also where the village of Stykkishólmur is located. Its enticing restaurants beckon with blue mussels harvested by producer Simon Sturluson (see page 306) in the cold waters surrounding the town.

SALTED COD, SHOESTRING BEER CRISPS, *and* PICKLED KELP

SERVES 4 | PREPARATION TIME: 1 HOUR (PLUS 12 HOURS TO PICKLE THE KELP)

Here is Gunnar's version of a healthy Icelandic fish and chips dish, only the fish are not fried and healthful kelp is a stand-in for the chips. When the fish is paired with pickled kelp, it is elevated to a sophisticated yet fun recipe perfect for a casual weekend lunch with friends. Any firm white fish can be substituted for the cod, and the kelp can be omitted if it proves too difficult to source. That said, Gunnar encourages you to spend a little time trying to find it, as it does impart the true spirit of Iceland to the dish.

PICKLED KELP

1³/₄ ounces (50 g) dried, salted kombu (see notes)

¹/₂ cup (120 ml) distilled white vinegar

2 tablespoons water

¹/₄ cup (50 g) sugar

COD

1¹/₂ pounds (680 g) skinned cod or halibut fillet

1¹/₂ tablespoons rapeseed oil

SOUR CREAM

Scant ¹/₂ cup (60 g) sour cream

Beer Vinegar (page 30), for seasoning

Salt

CARROTS

4 carrots, peeled and cut into uniform pieces about 1 inch (2.5 cm) long

1¹/₂ tablespoons rapeseed oil

2 star anise pods

Salt

SHOESTRING BEER CRISPS

Rapeseed oil, for deep-frying

6¹/₂ tablespoons (50 g) all-purpose flour

³/₄ teaspoon baking powder

¹/₄ cup (60 ml) brown ale

1 teaspoon salt

Powdered kelp (see notes), for seasoning

Sea salt

To make the pickled kelp, rinse the dried, salted kombu under cold, running water for at least 10 minutes to remove as much salt as possible (as an alternative, soak the kombu in cold water for 20 minutes, refreshing the water twice during the process), then place in a heatproof glass jar. Combine the white vinegar, water, and sugar in a saucepan and bring to a boil over medium heat, stirring until the sugar has dissolved. Pour the hot liquid over the kombu, immersing it. Let cool to room temperature, cap tightly, and refrigerate for at least 12 hours. The kombu will keep in the refrigerator for up to 1 month.

To make the cod, preheat an immersion circulator to 149°F (65°C). Place the cod and oil in a vacuum bag and seal on the lowest setting. Cook in the circulator for about 13 minutes, depending on the size of the cod. Check for doneness by pinching the cod through the bag. If it's tender and you are able to pinch through its flesh, it's ready. If not, continue to cook it for 1 to 2 minutes more. Remove the bag from the circulator and the cod from the bag, discarding the oil. Cut the cod into 4 equal pieces and keep warm.

NOTES

1. Dried, salted kombu, a variety of kelp, is sometimes available from resourceful fishmongers or can be special ordered through them. It can also be ordered online and is sold at some specialty food markets. The trick is to rehydrate it in cold water, changing the water at least once to remove as much salt as possible.

2. To make powdered kelp, arrange long, flat, rehydrated strips of kombu on a baking sheet and dry in an oven on the lowest setting for 6 to 8 hours. Grind the dried kombu in a spice grinder to a powder, then store in an airtight container in a cool, dark place for up to 1 week. Use the powder to season vegetables, seafood, and salads.

To make the sour cream, in a bowl, whisk the sour cream until fluffy. Season with salt and beer vinegar.

To make the carrots, preheat the oven to 350°F (180°C). Preheat the immersion circulator to 167°F (75°C). Place the carrots, oil, and star anise in a vacuum bag and seal on the lowest setting. Cook in the circulator for 13 minutes, until the carrots are tender. (If the carrots are particularly thick, they may take a few minutes longer.) Remove the bag from the circulator and, when cool enough to handle, drain the carrots, reserving the carrots and cooking liquid separately. Heat $1^1/2$ tablespoons of the cooking liquid in an ovenproof sauté pan or frying pan over medium heat. Add the carrots, stir until evenly coated with the liquid, and transfer the pan to the oven. Roast for about 12 minutes, until caramelized. Season with salt.

To make the shoestring beer crisps, pour oil to a depth of 6 inches into a deep, heavy pot and heat to 356°F (180°C). Line a large plate with paper towels. While the oil is heating, sift together the flour and baking powder into a bowl. Whisk in the ale and salt until incorporated. Transfer to a piping bag fitted with a $1/8$-inch (3-mm) plain tip. (Alternatively, transfer to a heavy-duty plastic bag and snip off the corner of the bag.)

When the oil is ready, squeeze the batter in thin strings about $1/4$ inch (5 mm) wide and about 8 inches (20 cm) long into the hot oil, being careful not to crowd the pan. Fry for about 2 to 3 minutes, until puffed and golden brown. Using a slotted spoon, carefully transfer the strings to the paper towel–lined plate to drain. Season with kelp and sea salt. Repeat until all of the batter is used.

To serve, place a portion of the cod on a plate and arrange the carrots and a generous handful of the beer crisps alongside. Dot the plate with the sour cream. Tear a portion of the pickled kelp into bite-size pieces and use it as a garnish.

APPLES, APPLE CAKE, PORTER FUDGE CARAMEL, *and* HAZELNUT GRANOLA

SERVES 6 TO 8 (PLUS LEFTOVER CAKE, ICE CREAM, AND GRANOLA FOR OTHER USES) | PREPARATION TIME: ABOUT 4 HOURS | PICTURED ON PAGE 328

In the town of Stykkishólmur where Simon Sturluson harvests his blue mussels and dulse, there is a cozy restaurant that serves a beer called Black Death, which features a skull and crossbones on its label. The beer dates back to only 2011, but it was inspired by the story of a family that lived on a small island just off the coast from Stykkishólmur in the early twentieth century. They brewed a dark beer to trade with sailors who passed by the island for items they had collected on their journeys through Europe. This is why the contemporary version is nicknamed the "sailor's beer" and has a flavor profile that recalls roasted coffee and chocolate. Gunnar uses the beer in this recipe, but any good-quality porter will work. This elaborate dessert of porter-infused apples, cake, and fudge is decadent and delicious, but any of the elements would provide plenty of enjoyment on its own.

PORTER-INFUSED APPLES

1^1/$_3$ cups (315 ml) porter

^{1}/$_2$ cup (100 g) sugar

^{1}/$_4$ cup (60 ml) cider vinegar

Scant ^{3}/$_4$ teaspoon salt

2 green apples (such as Granny Smith), peeled and cored, then flesh scooped with a melon baller (reserve scraps for apple puree, below)

APPLE PUREE

4 tablespoons (55 g) unsalted butter

^{1}/$_4$ cup (50 g) sugar

Scraps from apples (above)

^{1}/$_4$ teaspoon salt

APPLE CAKE

4 eggs

1 cup (220 g) firmly packed light brown sugar

1^1/$_3$ cups (300 g) unsalted butter, melted

2^1/$_3$ cups (300 g) all-purpose flour

Scant ^{3}/$_4$ teaspoon baking soda

2^1/$_2$ teaspoons baking powder

Scant ^{3}/$_4$ teaspoon salt

1^1/$_2$ teaspoons ground cinnamon

1^1/$_2$ teaspoons ground cardamom

1^1/$_2$ teaspoons ground cloves

Rounded 1^1/$_2$ teaspoons ground ginger

Rounded 1 teaspoon freshly grated nutmeg

^{1}/$_2$ cup (100 g) apple puree (above), at room temperature

PORTER FUDGE CARAMEL

Scant ^{1}/$_2$ cup (95 g) sugar

^{1}/$_3$ cup (70 g) liquid glucose (see notes, page 34)

^{1}/$_2$ cup (120 ml) porter

^{3}/$_4$ teaspoon salt

^{1}/$_3$ cup (75 g) unsalted butter

^{1}/$_2$ cup (120 ml) heavy cream

GRANOLA

^{2}/$_3$ cup (100 g) steel-cut oats

^{2}/$_3$ cup (100 g) barley flour (see notes)

^{1}/$_3$ cup (50 g) whole wheat flour

Scant ^{1}/$_2$ cup (100 g) firmly packed light brown sugar

Scant 1^3/$_4$ teaspoons salt

^{1}/$_2$ cup (115 g) unsalted butter, melted

Scant ^{1}/$_2$ cup (50 g) toasted and chopped hazelnuts

2 tablespoons puffed barley (see notes)

Milk Ice Cream (page 32)

To make the porter-infused apples, combine the porter and sugar in a small saucepan and bring to a simmer over medium heat, stirring until the sugar has dissolved. Stir in the vinegar and salt, remove from the heat, and let cool to room temperature. Combine the porter mixture and the apples in a vacuum bag and seal on the highest setting until the apples are

(see notes)

NOTES

1. Brown rice flour is easier to source than barley flour and can be substituted. The one caveat is that it will not bind as well as barley flour.

2. Puffed barley is available in some specialty food stores, but it is also easy to make at home. To make it, preheat the oven to the lowest setting. Spread hulled barley on a baking sheet and dehydrate in the oven for 12 hours, until golden brown. Pour rapeseed oil to a depth of 2 inches (5 cm) into a heavy, deep pot and heat to 365°F (185°C). Add the dehydrated barley to the hot oil and fry for 3 to 4 minutes, until puffed and golden brown. Using a wire skimmer, transfer to paper towels to drain. Let cool to room temperature before using.

3. The mixture of porter and apples can instead be refrigerated in a large ziplock bag, with all of the air pressed out before sealing.

as compressed as possible in order to infuse them with the liquid. Refrigerate for at least 1 hour, then reserve the liquid and solids together (see notes).

To make the apple puree, melt the butter in a saucepan over medium heat. Add the sugar and apple scraps and cook, stirring, for about 20 minutes, until the apples are mushy and nearly caramelized. Season with the salt. Transfer to a blender and process at high speed until a puree forms, adding a little water if necessary to achieve a smooth consistency.

To make the apple cake, preheat the oven to 350°F (180°C). Butter two 4^{1}/$_{2}$ by 2^{1}/$_{2}$-inch (11 by 6-cm) loaf pans. In the bowl of a stand mixer fitted with the whip attachment, beat the eggs on medium speed until fluffy. Add the brown sugar and butter and whisk by hand until dissolved. In a bowl, combine the flour, baking soda, baking powder, salt, cinnamon, cardamom, cloves, ginger, and nutmeg and stir to mix well. Add the flour mixture and the apple puree to the egg mixture and stir until incorporated.

Transfer the batter to the prepared loaf pans, dividing it evenly. Bake for about 30 minutes, until golden brown and a cake tester inserted into the center comes out dry. Let cool in the pans on a wire rack to room temperature, then turn out of the pans.

To make the caramel, prepare an ice bath. Combine the sugar, glucose, porter, salt, and butter in a small, heavy saucepan and bring to a boil over medium-high heat, stirring constantly until it registers 356°F (180°C) on a candy thermometer. This is a finicky step in this recipe and the temperature should be monitored extremely closely to prevent burning. The glucose will help to prevent it but attentive eyes help too. While whisking constantly, add the cream in a slow, steady stream, remove from the heat, then continue to heat to 234°F (112°C). Nest the pan in the ice bath, then let the caramel cool to room temperature, stirring frequently so that it remains smooth. It will have a fudgelike consistency. Transfer to a container, cover, and refrigerate until ready to use.

To make the granola, preheat the oven to 350°F (180°C). Line a baking sheet with parchment paper. In a bowl, combine the oats, flours, brown sugar, and salt and stir to mix well. Add the butter and stir until all of the ingredients are evenly coated.

Transfer the mixture to the prepared baking sheet and spread it in an even layer about 1 inch (2^{1}/$_{2}$ cm) thick. Bake for 10 to 12 minutes, until golden brown. Let cool to room temperature, then break into bite-size pieces. Add the hazelnuts and puffed barley and toss and stir to combine. Transfer to an airtight container and store at room temperature until ready to use. It will keep for up to 3 days.

To serve, place a scoop of the ice cream on a plate and arrange a slice of the cake, a spoonful of the porter-infused apples, and a bite-size piece of the caramel alongside. Garnish the plate with the granola.

OPPOSITE: Apples, Apple Cake, Porter Fudge Caramel, and Hazelnut Granola (page 326)

ABOVE: Red Beet Stones (page 330)

RED BEET STONES

MAKES ABOUT 50 STONES | PREPARATION TIME: ABOUT 1 HOUR (PLUS 3 HOURS TO
CHILL THE STONES) | PICTURED ON PAGE 329

Gunnar likes to serve sweets after dinner, and this unique presentation is a favorite at Dill.
The shape of the stones mirrors the stones on a black rock beach near where Gunnar gets
his blue mussels and dulse. He sometimes serves the rocks on a bed of dehydrated seaweed
to showcase the inspiration behind them. The black food coloring and dusting of confectioners' sugar makes them look like stones, but the beet-red interior is the real fun. They
are fairly simple to make and such a joy to eat. They are also a great way to slip a few beets
into a child's diet, for no one, young or old, can resist the flavor of Gunnar's beet stones.

1¼ cups (300 ml) red beet
juice

2½ tablespoons granulated
sugar

1 sprig rosemary

6½ tablespoons (100 ml)
heavy cream

21 ounces (600 g) white
chocolate

Salt

1½ cups (180 g)
confectioners' sugar

2 g powdered black food
coloring (see note, page 56)

Combine the beet juice, granulated sugar, and rosemary in a saucepan over medium-high
heat and bring to a vigorous simmer. Cook until reduced to ¼ cup (60 ml). Meanwhile,
put the cream in a small saucepan over medium heat, bring to a simmer, and cook until
reduced to ¼ cup (60 ml). Remove both pans from the heat.

Add the cream to the beet juice mixture and whisk until incorporated. Place 10½ ounces
(300 g) of the white chocolate in the top pan of a double boiler over barely simmering
water and heat, whisking as needed to prevent scorching, until melted. Do not let the
chocolate exceed 100°F (38°C). Whisk in the cream mixture until emulsified, season with
salt, and remove from the heat. Let cool to room temperature. The mixture will become
firm as it cools.

When the mixture has firmed up but is still pliable, mold it into stonelike shapes, using
1 to 1½ tablespoons of the mixture for each stone. As the stones are shaped, place them on
a baking sheet. When all of the stones have been shaped, cover and refrigerate them until
chilled.

In a blender, combine the confectioners' sugar and 1 g of the food coloring and process on
medium speed until stone gray. Transfer to a bowl large enough to dredge the stones. Melt
the remaining 10½ ounces (300 g) of the chocolate in the same manner as you melted the
first half. Whisk the remaining 1 g of food coloring into the chocolate.

Line a baking sheet with parchment paper. While the melted chocolate is still fluid and
warm, dredge the chilled stones, one at a time, in the chocolate, coating each stone completely and then placing it on the prepared baking sheet. Once the stones have cooled
slightly, dredge the stones in the confectioners' sugar, coating evenly and shaking off
the excess. Arrange on a large plate or baking sheet, cover, and refrigerate until chilled
before serving.

To store the stones, layer them between sheets of parchment in an airtight container.
They will keep in the refrigerator for up to 1 week.

INGREDIENTS FOR AN
ICELANDIC PANTRY

ANGELICA: Found in colder climates as remote as Greenland and Lapland, angelica is a tall, hearty plant with a cap of greenish white blossoms. Gunnar uses every part of the angelica—stems, leaves, flowers, and seeds—in both fresh and pickled preparations. Its flavor is similar to that of celery, and in some parts of the world it is known as wild celery. Good alternatives for angelica are either tarragon or lovage.

ARCTIC CHAR: Arctic char has been fished in Iceland since the arrival of the earliest settlers. It is a slow-growing fish with deep coral flesh, similar to that of salmon. Numerous char varieties exist, with some living part of their life at sea and finding their way back to Iceland's pristine rivers where they were born and others spending their entire life in rivers. The arctic char is similar to trout in its firm structure and flavor. In Icelandic, both trout and arctic char are called *silunger*.

ARCTIC THYME: You will find arctic thyme growing nearly everywhere in Iceland. In spite of its abundance, it wasn't until recently that it started showing up as both a cooking ingredient and a garnish in Icelandic kitchens. Today, it is a favorite with the nation's restaurant chefs and home cooks alike, who are delighted that it often flourishes just outside their kitchen door. Arctic thyme is available in some specialty food markets outside of Iceland. It perfumes a dish with subtle florals, and its cheerful violet flowers prove an attractive garnish. A good substitute for arctic thyme is regular thyme.

BACALAO: Cod that has been salted and dried in the traditional way for several months is a staple in Iceland. It is also popular in Spain and Portugal, which import much of Iceland's salted cod production. But Icelanders make sure to keep enough of the firm, briny fish for their dinner tables. Portuguese, Spanish, Italian, and Greek specialty markets will most likely stock bacalao on their shelves.

BIRCH: It is only recently that Icelandic cooks have begun to look to their native trees for cooking ingredients. Contemporary Icelandic chefs are smoking and infusing oils with birch leaves, as well as grinding the dried leaves to a powder to use as a seasoning. Bay leaves are a comparable flavoring, though taking the time to source birch leaves will add an appealing woodsy flavor to recipes.

BLUE MUSSELS: Although blue mussels have long been in the clean, clear waters off Iceland, they are only now being eaten by locals. Large and sweet with flesh the color of apricots, blue mussels derive their name from their shells, which gleam an electric blue in the sunlight. They are available in most fish markets.

CROWBERRIES: Dark, tart crowberries are one of the few berries that grow in Iceland. Similar in flavor and color to blueberries (which can be substituted), they are abundant in most areas of the country and are a favorite pairing with skyr and a sprinkling of sugar.

DULSE: One of the foods eaten by Iceland's earliest inhabitants, dulse, a deep red seaweed, has a leathery texture when fresh and is therefore typically dried before using. It is eaten as a snack and also used to flavor soups and breads, imparting a salty flavor that hints of the sea. Dulse is typically available dried, and sometimes it is salted and dried. Many Asian and Nordic specialty markets will carry it, but a good substitute is kombu.

HARDFISKUR: The volcanic terrain of much of Iceland has meant that agricultural land is in short supply, and as a result, grains for making bread are an expensive proposition. Icelanders have devised a clever and healthful way to replace bread at the table with ocean-dried fish known as *hardfiskur*. It is made from wolffish, which is dried for several months in open-air houses perched just steps from the sea. Wind and salt blow through the fish as it dries, resulting in a briny flavor that pairs perfectly with sweet Icelandic butter.

ICELANDIC MOSS: Despite the name, Icelandic moss is actually a lichen, and since the earliest times, it has been prized for both its health benefits and its flavoring properties. It is available dried in markets, and in the past, it provided—and continues to do so in some households—much-needed nutrients for vegetable-deprived Icelanders. It grows in nearly every region of the country and has the texture of dried shiitake mushrooms before rehydration. Once it is rehydrated, it becomes soft and gelatinous, making it an ideal ingredient for soups, breads, and sausages. Unfortunately, there is no substitute for Icelandic moss and should you not have it and a recipe calls for it, the best thing to do is omit it.

LOVAGE: A hearty, tall-growing plant, lovage has a robust celerylike flavor, smooth green leaves, and small yellow flowers. It stands up to cooking in such preparations as soups, stews, and even sautés, and in early spring, when its flavor is less intense, it also makes a good salad ingredient. Tender celery leaves are a good substitute.

LUMPFISH: Also known as lumpsuckers, stocky, short lumpfish thrive in the cold waters of Iceland, where they are a vital part of the fishing industry. Their roe is valued in Scandinavian cooking as an inexpensive alternative to sturgeon caviar and is used extensively throughout Iceland as a briny garnish. Salmon roe or whitefish roe are good substitutes.

RAPESEED OIL: The neutral flavor of rapeseed oil makes it an ideal cooking oil. It also contains half the amount of saturated fat as olive oil and higher amounts of omega-3, omega-6, and omega-9 fatty acids than any other vegetable oil. Canola oil is the same thing as rapeseed oil. The name was changed by a Canadian company that did not think the word "rapeseed" would appeal to American and Canadian consumers. In Iceland, it's always referred to as rapeseed.

RUGBRAUD: Also known as geyser bread, this sweet rye bread has been baked for centuries using geothermal heat naturally pumped into ovens dug in the ground. Its dense texture and hearty composition make it an ideal companion to a slick of softened butter.

SORREL: Frequently used as an herb in salads, sorrel grows wild throughout much of Iceland. It has a bright, zesty flavor and is also enjoyed plucked straight from the bush. Wherever he finds himself in Iceland, Gunnar knows the herb composition of the land beneath his feet, and you'll often find him nibbling on wild sorrel as he explores the countryside. A good alternative to sorrel is a robust green such as spinach or arugula sprinkled with lemon juice.

SKYR: Although skyr is technically a cheese, it is often compared to thick Greek yogurt in texture and flavor. Icelanders are crazy for skyr, and it is sold in virtually every market, both plain and in such flavored varieties as melon, almond, and banana. Skyr was originally a by-product of the lacto-fermentation technique used to ferment lamb by soaking it in milk. Icelanders soon developed a taste for the residual thickened milk that formed on the interior barrel walls. They eventually began to make a vegetarian version of skyr, and today it is hard to imagine an Icelandic refrigerator without skyr in it. Skyr is available at many large grocery store chains. A suitable alternative is Greek yogurt.

WHEY: A by-product of skyr making in Iceland, whey is the liquid that remains when the curds have separated. It is used in marinades to add a vibrant tanginess to meats and is a nice addition to bread and pastry recipes. It can be used to preserve and ferment such items as lamb and fish. In Iceland, it has been traditionally used to make mysuostur, a caramelized brown cheese spread beloved throughout the country.

INDEX

Copyright © 2014 by Gunnar Karl Gíslason and Jody Eddy
Foreword copyright © 2014 by René Redzepi
Photographs copyright © 2014 by Evan Sung

All rights reserved.
Published in the United States by Ten Speed Press,
an imprint of the Crown Publishing Group,
a division of Random House LLC,
a Penguin Random House Company, New York.
www.crownpublishing.com
www.tenspeed.com

Ten Speed Press and the Ten Speed Press colophon
are registered trademarks of Random House LLC

Library of Congress Cataloging-in-Publication Data
Gíslason, Gunnar Karl.
  North : the new Nordic cuisine of Iceland / Gunnar Karl
Gíslason and Jody Eddy. — First edition.
       pages cm
  1. Cooking, Icelandic. I. Eddy, Jody. II. Title.
  TX723.5.I2G57 2014
  641.594912—dc23
                        2014003525

Hardcover ISBN: 978-1-60774-498-6
eBook ISBN: 978-1-60774-499-3

Printed in China

Design by Toni Tajima
Original cover design by Emma Campion

10 9 8 7 6 5 4 3 2 1

First Edition